Celebration of TRUTH
with the letters of light.

A child of light.

ISBN: 978-1-961879-20-1 (sc)
978-1-961879-21-8 (e)

Publishing rev. date: 11/16/2023

AUTHOR CABIN
THE PLACE FOR YOUR STORY

Celebrating Our Creator's Truth *of* Love, Life, and Light

Memory of the twenty-two letters of Light

Written by

A child of light.

CONTENTS

CHAPTER 1

ALEPH

ת ש ר ק צ פ ע ס נ מ ל כ י ט ח ז ו ה ד ג ב א

The twenty-two letters of light are arranged going from right to left:
Aleph, Bet, Gimel, Dalet, Hay, Vav, Zayin, Chet, Tet, Yod, Kaf,
Lamed, Mem, Nun, Samech, Ayin, Pay, Tzadi, Kuf, Resh, Shin, and Tav.

The Bible, called <u>The Scriptures,</u> is used as the reference Bible
in all twenty-two letters. Other bibles were used to compare
passages of translation to receive a better understanding of the
wisdom presented. The Strong's concordance used for Hebrew and
Greek research of the Aleph—bet was published in 1986.

The "first day" using letters of light is called Yom Rishon. It is called Sunday on the Gregorian calendar. It is written like this with the Aleph-Tav: יום ראשון

Rishon written with letters of light are achad, aw-khad or echad, ekh-awd—means united—that is, one, altogether, alone, and to unify. Letters of light are Aleph, Chet and Dalet, meaning given to the writer—**our Creator's breath of life is the doorway to physical existence here on the earth.**

Aleph has the Gematria (number value) of 1. In the English language, it is the letter A.

Aleph is **the difference between exile or confinement and freedom or expansion**.

King David wrote eight affirmations to each aleph-bet (Aleph to Tav) found in Psalm 119. This is called acrostic writing—seeking the answers to truth questions both practical and theological. When we search the meaning of each light letter, each letter manifests the truth and shows characteristics of human nature, such as jealously.

We know our Creator who made the heavens and earth is ALL in ALL and has no specific name. Our Creator is love, life, and light with perfect perfection. Only religious institutions give a name to their god and not necessarily are they talking about the true Creator of the heavens and the earth. These religions, with their own names for their god, caused division and confusion to truth. To name the only Creator is to put Perfect Presence into a box, which goes against pure truth. The Hebrew scribes did exactly what the other nations did—by naming their god for their people. There is only one Creator who created everything and everyone. Why is there so much resistance to this beautiful wisdom? Our Creator is not a god or a man!

The Aleph-Tav is said to be the letters that created the Hebrew language and that language was used to write the Bible, the Old Testament, or the Tanak. At times of rest, man was given the opportunity to write down information, facts, history about how they viewed their god and his dealings with man. By understanding the light letters, we gain insight and discernment into their scriptures. To search, meditate, and study, is necessary to gain wisdom of love, life, and light. To just read the words as a story in the scripture will not give you the mature understanding of the Aleph-Tav, but the stories do give a history of the Hebrew past and how the scribes understood their god, in their time. Each dispensation of time has allowed more advancing light to shine on all people that search, meditate, and study with the desire for truth. Long ago man understood our true Creator without religion's interference. Today, all can know truth and live by true love and true light. Go outside and see for yourself. Just observe what happens in a day and you will see our Creator in miraculous action. True love cast out fear!

You can feel the breath of love penetrating our world system! Hallelujah!

By making word connections from Hebrew to English, this will enhance truth already known and uncover wisdom that was known from the beginning of creation but forgotten because of fear, religious traditions and man-made lies for gain and power. **Wisdom is not knowledge or information but present time discernment of light.**

Little truth is found in holidays, fashions, traditions, and recreation. However, they do gather families and people together for reunion and continual support of each other. These distractions will have you continue doing the same thing year after year with no maturity or eternal progress. What you will have is the aging of the body and earthly experiences with the progression of time. What you do during these holidays will show if you are still connected to them, the world, or have moved on with the awakening light of our Creator. Plant a tree or flowers, or make a garden, pick up the garbage on the side of a road, cut the grass, and beautify your yard or bring the children to a park. Read to your children the truth about each animal and their habitat. Then, have the children watch, if they can, the live animal in action.

The word *recreation* even has the word *creation* in it. Be mindful and still as you read these words of wisdom so that your inner being can confirm to you that the words are true. "Do your upmost to present yourself approved of love, a worker who does not need to be ashamed [the word *ashamed* first appears in Genesis after Adam and Eve made an unhealthy choice in the garden], because he or she knows how to rightly handle the word of truth." What does "rightly handle the word of truth mean in the Bible?" The true answer is discernment! **Let's see what has been written in the Bible.**

> Study to shew thyself approved unto Yehovah, a workman that needeth not to be ashamed, rightly dividing the **word of truth**. (2 Timothy 2:15)

BIBLE SEARCH RESULT

1. Genesis 42:16

    Send one **of** you, and let him fetch your brother, and ye shall be kept in prison, that your **word**s may be proved, whether there be any **truth** in you: or else by the life **of** Pharaoh surely ye are spies.

2. 1 Kings 2:4

    That Yehovah may continue his **word** which he spake concerning me, saying, If thy children take heed to their way, to walk before me in **truth** with all their heart and with all their soul, there shall not fail thee (said he) a man on the throne **of** Israel.

3. 1 Kings 17:24

    And the woman said to Elijah, now by this I know that thou art a man **of** Yehovah, and that the **word of** Yehovah in thy mouth is **truth**.

4. 2 Kings 20:19

    Then said Hezekiah unto Isaiah, Beautiful is the **word of** Yehovah which thou hast spoken. And he said, is it not perfect, if peace and **truth** be in my days?

5. Esther 9:30

And he sent the letters unto all the Jews, to the hundred twenty and seven provinces **of** the kingdom **of** Ahasuerus, with **word**s **of** peace and **truth**.

6. Psalm 33:4

For the **word of** Yehovah is right; and all his works are done in **truth**.

7. Psalm 119:43

And take not the **word of truth** utterly out **of** my mouth; for I have hoped in thy judgments.

8. Proverbs 22:21

That I might make thee know the certainty **of** the **word**s **of truth**; that thou mightest answer the **word**s **of truth** to them that send unto thee?

9. Ecclesiastes 12:10

The preacher sought to find out acceptable **word**s: and that which was written was upright, even **word**s **of truth**.

10. Isaiah 39:8

Then said Hezekiah to Isaiah, beautiful is the **word of** Yehovah which thou hast spoken. He said moreover, For there shall be peace and **truth** in my days.

11. Jeremiah 26:15

But know ye for certain, that if ye put me to death, ye shall surely bring innocent blood upon yourselves, and upon this city, and upon the inhabitants thereof: for **of** a **truth** Yehovah hath sent me unto you to speak all these **word**s in your ears.

12. Hosea 4:1

Hear the **word of** Yehovah, ye children **of** Israel: for Yehovah hath a controversy with the inhabitants **of** the land, because there is no **truth**, nor mercy, nor wisdom **of** Him in the land.

13. John 1:14

And the **Word** was made flesh, and dwelt among us (and we beheld his glory, the glory as **of** the only begotten **of** the Father), full **of** grace and **truth**.

2 Corinthians 4:2

But have renounced the hidden things **of** dishonesty, not walking in craftiness, nor handling the **word of** Yehovah deceitfully; but by manifestation **of** the **truth** commending ourselves to every man's conscience in the sight **of** Yehovah.

14. 2 Corinthians 6:7

By the **word of truth**, by the power **of** Yehovah, by the armour **of** righteousness on the right hand and on the left.

15. Ephesians 1:13

In whom ye also trusted, after that ye heard the **word of truth**, the gospel **of** your salvation: in whom also after that ye believed, ye were sealed with that Holy Spirit **of** promise.

16. Colossians 1:5

For the hope which is laid up for you in heaven, whereof ye heard before in the **word of** the **truth of** the gospel.

17. 1 Thessalonians 2:13

For this cause also thank we Yehovah without ceasing, because, when ye received the **word of** Yehovah which ye heard **from** us, ye received it not as the **word of** men, but as it is in **truth**, the **word of** Yehovah, which effectually worketh also in you that believe.

18. 2 Timothy 2:15

Study to shew thyself approved unto Yehovah, a workman that needeth not to be ashamed, rightly dividing the **word of truth**.

19. James 1:18

Of His own will begat He us with the **word of truth**, that we should be a kind **of** first fruits **of** His creatures.

The profound sense of truth's presence led to a deep desire to honor the Creator, resulting in the composition of eight affirmations following each letter of Light. If King David had a heart for his god, Yehovah, and wrote eight affirmations, then to write eight affirmations about the true Creator who created love, life, and light, hallelujah, to anyone else with that same HEART. By this, may you be led to the full word of truth.

"Children, leave those empty idols and follow love and kindness so that you may live out your life in truth and peace."

You do not bring love, life, and light to naught, for wisdom does not leave the one without their own consequences (disease and pain) who brings our Creator's perfect presence to naught! Somehow, in your daily routine, speak of our Creator out loud to someone or simply eat from the table of creation. If all you can do is speak beauty of creation to your children, it is accepted, but to go a day and not give thanks to truth is bringing our Creator's omnipotence to naught. We live as a daily offering (the act of giving up selfish desires that are valued by the world for the sake of truth) to the egos wants/pride, so sing praises to our Creator of all.

Do not hurry though these letters. You will want truth and peace written in your heart and mind. Pay attention and please do not go past a sentence or word that is unclear to you. Look up the word in the concordance and find the Hebrew or Greek **root** so that you will have a **mature** understanding for daily discernment.

It is written in the Bible that the commandments were written with the finger of god. This is allegorical. What is the deeper meaning?

First, allegorical means an expression of truths or generalizations about human existence by means of symbolic fictional figures and their actions.

What is the letters of light for <u>finger</u>? Ets-bah. Spelled Alef, Tzaddik, Bet, and Ayin. Finger means to dip, grasping, something to seize with. Now the understanding of the Bible's second commandment when it says, "He is a jealous Elohim, visiting the crookedness of the fathers on the children to third and fourth generations of those that hate me, but showing loving commitment to thousands, to those who love me and keep my commands."

The understanding given to the writer for the word finger and the above commandment. **Our Creator's presence dwells in all bodies; however, more truth and light are given to those that discern with wisdom how to rightly divide the word of truth.**

Man is jealous and fearful. Our Creator is love, life, and light!

May you be granted our Creator's truth, so that you eternally eat from the tree of life, wisdom, and use your fingers to expand the light of truth and freedom where you are planted.

Aleph is pronounced "ah-lef" and is silent, no sound of its own but usually has a vowel associated with it. Note: it is more powerful to remain quiet thereby proving to oneself, Born from within," possessing self-control (settle down, quietness).

The design of the Aleph is actually made up of three different letters: the letter YUD or DOT above; a YUD or DOT below; and a diagonal VAV, or line suspended in between. The YUD above represents our Creator's presence who is love, life, and light.

The YUD below represents us—we are children of light, learning how to have harmony, peace, and joy.

The way that we awaken to our Creator's wisdom, to the extent that a person is capable, is by being HUMBLE **(mature discernment)**. This word *humble* is in every letter of light. Please take time to understand this word—this word is the key to your success in life and the ability to discover truth in creation by discernment. The word for *humble* is spelled Kana, Kaw-nah—letters of light are Khaf, Nun, and Ayin, meaning to heed, pay attention, to sing, shout, testify, announce— hence to have awakened strength, to serve with wisdom, humble (self) within. The understanding given to the writer—**we are given truth as we seek for it, and because of the ability to see truth's daily revelation, we enjoy the joy of creation.**

When we realize that we are children of light and are loved by our All-Mighty and All Powerful Creator, we become purified through discerning the truth using perfect wisdom.

The diagonal, Vav represents the truth of love that destroys unconsciousness and fear, which directs us back to our Creator in present time.

As a carpenter builds a house with tools, our Creator sent thoughts to man then man created a language with twenty-two utterance of speech or breath. These letters represent the wood, stone, nails, corner post, and cross beams of our earthy and eternal existence.

"Let there be light, let there be truth." These letters that spell out the Aleph-Tav are in our mind—light gives our existence more life. Each letter has energy, breath vibrations, vitality, and power to create and to destroy. These letters are perfectly created. They all have a sound with a different frequency and breath vibration. All matter was spoken into existence by sound. Each sound has a different frequency, and all matter is formed by sound frequencies, just as Genesis says. The same breath that gives us love, life, and light we use to speak and bring forth our words with different frequencies or breathe vibrations. The breath of our Creator is called using the Aleph-Tav, ru'ach, or spirit in English, and is the same breath or words/thoughts that hovered over the waters and spoke all things into existence. **Ru'ach represents the embodiment of our spoken words. Through which ru'ach do you communicate? Religion or our Creator's viewpoint?**

And depending upon the love breath vibration used in your language will determined the power of truth manifested in the physical world around you.

There are twenty-two letters of light.
We have in our body
Twenty-two cells—chromosome

Twenty-two building DNA

Twenty-two amino acids

Twenty-two bones in skull

Two universal languages—mathematics (numbers) and music (sound)

Music has three mother letters-called a **cord**—Aleph, Mem, Shin—first, thirteenth, and twenty-first letter of the Aleph-Bet.

seven double letters-called an **octave**—Bet, Gimel, Dalet, Kaph, Pey, Resh, Tav—second, third, fourth, eleventh, seventeenth, twentieth, and twenty-second.

Twelve simple letters—Hay, Vah, Zayin, Chet, Tet, Yud, Lamed, Nun, Samech, Ayin, Tzadi, Kuf. Twelve notes include black notes: fifth, sixth, seventh, eighth, ninth, tenth, twelfth, fourteenth, fifteenth, sixteenth, eighteenth, and nineteenth.

Aleph means breath, leader, truth, **strength**, power, unity, instruction, completeness or maturity, eternity, silent letter, more powerful to remain quiet—self-control. Stands apart, oneness, nothing else exist, elevated above all—"Kodesh", using the Aleph-Tav means holy thoughts.

Our Creator loves nature. It is written, "Look at the birds of the heaven, for they neither sow nor reap nor gather into storehouses, yet your Creator does feed them. **Are you not worth more than they?**" This statement is profound!

To be close to our Creator one must overcome the world's image of their creation and the false image of the written biblical account of god.

Even though the heavens and earth were created for beauty and an earthy dwelling place for man, the more oneness (Rishon) with our Creator the more attracted we will be to the breath vibrations of truth. We will love our own selves!

The six days of creation in the Bible is a mask covering the first completed day. For all things were created on the first day and then has continually repeated itself each and every prophetic day, thereafter. There is no special day for rest as we rest every day as our Creator made us that way. The special worship day is called Sabbath or Sunday and only found in religion. To divide up days is not wisdom of one day, as we are one with our Creator, united. One day will remain simple than a manmade special day, as all days are created equal, just as man and woman are created equal. What makes a day different is what man has chosen to regard as important. Oneness will always be perfect. The religious Sabbath or Sunday are holy days designed by religious men.

The holy tongue is called using the Aleph-Tav—**La'shon Ha ko desh.**

John 1:1—The Word explained—"In the beginning was the Word and the Word was within our Creator" (meaning that our Creator possessed the word, Aleph to Tav). The word was in the beginning with our Creator (second time to confirm the word is our Creator). All came (creation) to be through the word (our Creator) and without our Creator not even one came to be that came to be. In our Creator is life, and the life is the light of men eternally. And now the light is seen in the biblical Christ. He shines in the darkness, and the darkness does not comprehend the light of our Creator seen in him. **This period of time that the biblical Christ came to the earth was a very dark time. No person had enough light within themselves to write an accurate account of his life. They did not understand his speech. He was in opposition to religion in his time.**

Keep life simple, love, and continue living with no division of days, therefore, no religion, just creation.

When a person misuses language, it is deception and of the darkness hidden within oneself. If Eve had not talked to Hasatan in the field, then she would not have engaged with the darkness within herself. So, darkness came to be, because of deceptive words. It was the words of deception that Hasatan spoke that desire grew in Eve, not wisdom and discernment. Deceptive words will benefit only the person talking or religious groups, organizations, and their plans. Deceptive words confuse and keep an old energy and old breath vibration cycling. Remember, crookedness or deceptive words lead to confusion and darkness. Light on the other hand has words of love, life, harmony, and health.

Where is the tree of good and evil located? It is located outside the garden as our Creator is only life, love, and light. Therefore, all trees except the tree of life was formed from the ground outside the garden. Our Creator formed Adam from the dust of the ground outside the garden as well and then directed Adam to live in the garden of safety and abundance. Ground means outside the garden, and garden means inside our Creator's protection. The tree of life is in the midst of the garden and the tree of knowledge of good and evil is in the <u>field</u>. "And the nahash was craftier than all the lives of the <u>field,</u> which our Creator had made." Nothing that causes death can be in the garden of life. Choose you this day, life, and live forever!

Our Creator is one. Love truth and become free from all lies and regain your health.

I forgive you my dear brothers that translated bibles incorrectly and for those men who deceitfully made religions to profit their own belly and power.

"May all people have the wisdom to see the errors of man and the courage to **stand** [Tav—last light letter], rightly dividing the word of truth, and flee from darkness!"

Return to pure language—echad= ONE (Rishon), words that are beautiful and full of love, life, and light. <u>The Scripture</u> is a book to be studied—you cannot know the depth of thought or mind if the language is not understood. Can you see how words and thoughts lead to healthy or unhealthy actions? You must have the power of beautiful speech to have healthy actions!

Pr. 18:20–21 pg. 746, power of the tongue—is life.

Ps 119:105 pg. 717, the letter Nun is, "Your word is a lamp to my feet and a light to my path." Therefore, pure, undefiled words are light. (The letter Nun represents the tiniest and least of seeds that grow with tender care and kindness to produce fruit.)

In the Bible there is six days of creation that was used by the biblical scribes to mask the true Creator of this world. The mask was created so that **humility** and not ego/pride could approach pure truth. The more oneness (Rishon) received (the character of joy and love are seen) is determined by the wisdom of you spending time with our Creator in silence. If you know the truth is within you and wherever you go and your thoughts and deeds are completed with thankfulness, the closer you are to our Creator. This brings a powerful relationship between you and all of creation, love, life, and light, which moves all nations to one unified power.

This reading is not for immature people. So rightly discern wisdom in words written and spoken to promote love, life, and light on this earth, which helps others discern the truth for themselves.

Breath-The word breath using the Aleph-Tav is pronounced nesh-aw-maw. The letters of light are Nun, Mem, and Hay. It means a puff, that is , wind, vital breath, inspiration, and intellect. The understanding given to the writer—**The eternal or awakened person that comes forth after the refinement has the truth in their mouth which breathe out present light or revelation bringing harmony, peace, and balance! Amen to memory.**

The letter by itself, with no understanding, is like a body without life (word)—many walk in this manner because of not knowing the truth. You cannot just speak the light letters into words, for it will become like any other language if the letters are not understood and studied. The letters of light are for all humankind and not for a particular religion or group.

The words of humankind are manifested through the heart's deeds. Vav is the letter that represents eternal love. This letter (Vav) **connects** man to our Creator of love, life, and light. Understanding eternal love shows humanity how to live in truth, the tree of life, and not remain eating from the tree of knowledge of good and evil, outside in the field. The ability to show agape love no manner what humanity is facing, in all circumstances, develops the omnipotence of oneness seen in our Creator.

The difference between exile or confinement and freedom or expansion is, exile is constraints and limitations (a person here sees constraints and limitations to their lives, therefore, seemingly preventing them to advance or change—remains a victim, no eternal progress here), where freedom is expansion—takes full responsibility for every healthy or unhealthy choice (humanity here, sees laws that protect and keep order, therefore, receiving the ability to increase in wisdom, discernment, health, and eternity); this is Aleph.

1. Aleph—master of all masters

2. Teacher—opener to freedom—how to live our lives—go from exile to freedom—be productive to perfect or mature ourselves which is our hearts desire.

3. Phala—One Creator, One Thought, and One Unity—wondrous—Aleph backward = phala—the message to Philadelphia. Read this and know your eternal awakened breath (the vowels e, a, i are used interchangeably in the letters of light language). These awakened beings have no earthly organization or group. We are scattered throughout the earth lifting up the light of love.

Eight affirmations for the letter aleph

1. The pure truth led me to the colorful garden and the fruit of pure words.

2. Humility has given me abundant life, agape love, and perfect light.

3. We are blessed by wisdom's oneness with our Creator.

4. We think and do good deeds because of our love, life, and light we received from our Creator and then give the same back to humanity.

5. We have the same breath as truth. We can face our Creator, **unashamed**.

6. Our Creator is the first and the last, eternal. The Aleph and the Tav, forever. If our Creator is the Aleph-Tav, so are we!

7. The pure word brings us **strength to stand** for truth. We then act as one mind.

8. All eternity is knowing our Creator of love, life, and light. Never has there been a day without the sun rising and the sun setting and with the moon and stars appearing at night. Our Creator does not change! What and how the earth was created is in present time today. Be so thankful!

Creator of All

In the beginning our Creator, made the heavens and the earth.
"Let light come to be and light was birthed.
The light is called day,
Which begins at dawn and ends at sunset.
And this is the light letter Aleph, English letter A.
"Let the waters above, expanse, come to be."
The expanse is called heavens and this is the
light letter Bet, English letter B.
"Gather the waters below into one place and land appeared to be."
The flat land is earth; collection of waters, seas, and
this is the light letter Gimel, the English letter G.
"Let earth produce grass, plants, and trees that
yields fruit according to their kind."
And here **continues** Gimel and those that eat here
have health and minds of light that shine.
"Let there be a lesser light to rule the night
and a greater light to rule the day."
Light letter Dalet is the doorway that destroys the
Gregorian Sabbath and the Trinity Sunday.
Let the lights be for signs and appointed times for days and years.

This is the unmovable lunisolar calendar, the
two witnesses, never do we fear!
Created perfect in the heavens where man or evil could not reach,
Bringing forth love, life, and light!
Giving glory, reverence only to our Creator, please teach.
Our Creator brought forth the fish and the birds and
instructed them to be fruitful and increase.
This is the light letter Hay, the revelation of
pure truth and promises of peace.
"Let the beast and the creeping things of
the earth bring forth their kind."
But with none of these creatures was man defined!
With the breath of our Creator, yes! Speaking beautifully and wise,
Was the creation of man, male and female,
from the dust, our Creator did arise.
Then we conclude with the Creator's rest.
All heavens and earth created in one day, a blessing
that comes as a simple humble test.

(Once you have your mind cleaned from the lies and darkness
of this world, you will view each day as the first one was
created—no more division of days or boxes for religions)

A Home Centered in Love

Mother is beautiful and wise. She seeks oneness for all her children's
eternal birth and for her love to endure forever! She spends time
in silence and writing daily. Feeling the power of breath within,
assures her safety and health while she dwells upon the earth.
She writes truth in poetry form as the darkness is removed. Her
creation is full of children that love the truth and each other.
Has her house always been this way?
Let's go ask mother, she will tell us. Mother told the following story.
It was just like an earthquake one Saturday morning.
Mother awoke to find the house and yard a mess.
There were dirty dishes all over the kitchen table!
There were dirty clothes thrown all over the bedroom floors!
A bedroom window was broken and the yard grass was as tall as trees.
Needless, to say, mother was very disappointed with her
children. The truth within each child reminded them of
what would make mother sing Halleluyah again. They had
forgotten what their purpose was while they were gaining
experience and knowledge of everyday life, here on the earth.

Because of their desire to please their mother, they returned to
kindness and love and did the work of truth. The children wanted
mother to experience joy and feel the gift of enlargement.
The next day the girls began by washing the dishes
and putting them away. They also washed, folded, and
put up the clothes with smiles on their faces.
The boys cut and trimmed the yard grass. They also bought
a new window pane to replace the broken one.
Each child picked up their pillow and made their bed.
All the children picked up their toys from the
floor and the yard and put them away.
What could bless a mother more than to see her children
having love for their home and for each other?
The chaos in her house is now in order.
This home is centered in love.
Peace to all and to all blessings of rest.

Listen children, to the still small voice within you.
This inner peace is called the wisdom of love.

CHAPTER 2

BET

תשרקצפעסנמלכיטחזוהדגבא

The twenty-two letters of light are arranged going from right to left:
Aleph, Bet, Gimel, Dalet, Hay, Vav, Zayin, Chet, Tet, Yod, Kaf,
Lamed, Mem, Nun, Samech, Ayin, Pay, Tzadi, Kuf, Resh, Shin, and Tav.

English letter—B.
Bet is pronounced bayit using the letters of light.
The Gematria for the letter Bet is the numerical value of 2.

The "second day" of creation is Yom Sheni on the greater-lesser light
calendar. It is called Monday according to the Gregorian calendar. Yom
Sheni is written like this using the letters of light: יום שני

Second sounds like this shay-nee-written with a Yud, Nun, and Shin and means double again, second time, to fold to duplicate, repeat, return, and do the second time. Day is pronounced yowm or yome using the Aleph-Tav. The light letters are Yud, Nun, and Mem and means warm hours or to be hot.

Now let's put the letters of light together and see what it says: The understanding given to the writer: **At the birthing of a life giving seed it needs refinement, words of truth, light, and breath to complete the cleaning process, and this is done during the warm hours called the day/light**.

"Are not there twelve hours in the day?" The night is for reflection of our day, quiet time with our Creator so we are refreshed and strengthened for the next day.

Design of Bet: has three lines: two horizontal (Light letters for horizontal are—Aleph, Tav, Pay, Kuf and Yud). The understanding given to the writer: Our Creator speaks to man through wisdom's voice which is another name for nature. (And unto Adam came these words within, "Because you have harkened to the <u>voice</u> of your woman," which brings forth all living) and one vertical (Light letters for vertical are Aleph, Nun, Kaf, and Yud. The understanding given to the writer: **the Creator within the awakened seeds protects and brings light for the expansion of life**). These lines represent the direction east, south, and west.

The horizontal one on top represents the east. East using Aleph-Tav is pronounced Kaw-dam and is a prime root to project (oneself) that is, precede; hence to anticipate, hasten, meet (usually for help) also, in front, eternal, everlasting and the forward part. The letters of light that make east are Kuf, Dalet, and Mem, and means perfect wisdom. The understanding given to the writer: **connecting the truth of creation to our words spoken leads to our consequences of love, life, and light.** Be careful of the words you use to speak.

"For by your words you shall be declared righteous, and by your words you shall be declared unrighteous." The universal law of attraction will attract to you, the truth you hold within. Choose you this day love, life, and light so that your body and mind may have health and peace.

The vertical line is the south. South using the letters of light is negeb, sounds like neh'gheb and from an unused root mean to be parched, the south (from its drought) Egypt (as south of Palestine), made with the letters of light Nun, Gimel, and Bet. The understanding given to the writer: **The unawaken's journey throughout the earth without the understanding of our Creator's presence within**.

The horizontal line below is the west. Using the letters of light west is a-rab, sounds like aw-rab, a prime root to grow dusky (swarthy) at sundown, be darkened (toward) evening; this is male. Female is ma'arabah, sounds like mah-ar-aw-baw—the sense of shading; the west (as the region of the evening sun.) Letters of light for west are Mem, Ayin, Resh, Bet, and Hay. The understanding given to the writer: **the words that bring insight to the head or heart of each individual is through revelation received by the words of truth awakened within**.

The design of the Bet is similar to the path of the sun, which rises in the east and sets in the west. This is similar to the construction of the earth. A contemporary illustration of this is offered by geologist. When you look at the earth, you see that there are land masses to the east, west, and south. Even beneath the ice cap of the South Pole, one finds the continent of Antarctica. But beneath the frozen mass of the North Pole, there's nothing. The north is "open." The immediate lesson we derive from the letter Bet is that the heavens and the earth were created complete by our Creator, but because of unhealthy choices by man, the earth as well as man changed from perfection to incompletion. Remember, Adam and Eve's eyes were "opened." To what? Darkness, which then led to unawareness and unhealthy choices. Therefore, the purpose of humankind is to regain perfection, eating for health, and by showing kindness and love while inhabiting a body on the earth. Therefore, changing the North within ourselves back to completeness and harmony. "As it is in heaven, so shall it be on earth." "As it is in eternity, so shall it be always." This is the awakened, "born from within" one. Marriage! (Marriage using the light letters are ownah, pronounced o-naw. Light letters are Ayin, Vav, Nun, and Hay and means to dwell together. Understanding given to the writer—**to see your connection to our Creator one simply needs to dwell in their breath**.)

When we look at our Creator's creation, we see perfection, beauty, consistency, life, and simplicity. To think we never have to worry if the sun is coming up or if the moon is going to shine at night. These luminaries move and have integrity as our Creator made them. Our body should be the same—our Bet, house, where the light dwells within. Light loves perfection and not broken down houses/bodies. The cleaner you are in body and mind the more you see love, life, and light in you and in all creation.

The north for the letter Bet represents unhealthy choices, but if we have a healthy mind, we will follow kindness and love, which is wisdom's choice. We will love ourselves!

North using the Aleph-Tav is tsaphan, tsaw-fan; letters of light— Tzadi, Pay, Nun—meaning: a prime root to hide, hidden that is dark, used only of the North as gloomy and unknown, to hide by covering, to hoard or reserve, to deny, esteem hide, keep secret hide oneself, lurk. The understanding given to the writer: **the hunter (remember who spoke to Eve) speaks to the darkness within.** So beware!

We also need to recognize that the "open" side (this was Hasatan words to Eve that her eyes would be "open" to know knowledge of good from evil), this northern aspect, exists within the individual, as well as from without. In a person, using the light letters it is called the yetzer hara, the evil inclination—in other words, the lies of the world which tempts and urges us to continue to commit unhealthy choices, deliberately or unaware. When we desire health and turn from unhealthy ways and return to our Creator, we literally are closing the North side and rejecting unhealthy dominion. We want to know and partake of the tree of life which causes completion and perfection in oneself. The process of this north side closing takes a life-time of **peace** with perfect deeds and perfect words spoken. Therefore, close the north side, the tree of knowledge of good and evil so that the tree of life, wisdom, is the only tree in your head, mind, and heart that are governed by beautiful thoughts and words. This is the meaning of being one with our Creator.

Note: Herod, governor during the biblical time, represents the mind/ego/North side; the ego is our inner Pharaoh, the one who has been in charge of our unhealthy choices and who will not relinquish this hold easily. This box, the North side, is the society with its words that will fight against you. It is your own inner society, what you were raised in, traditions, and customs with their words that are just that, with maybe a bit of truth. However, you can never misunderstand truth, it is a feeling that illuminates light.

When you choose this new path of truth and your spouse, family, or friends do not understand, be ready to endure life with uncomplaining and a mind of victory because the only reason that those types of situations can affect you in a negative way is because your ego is still alive and becomes out of balance by what you see. You may tend to blame the outside force and say "I can't enter this new truth because my spouse won't accept it, my family won't accept it, and my friends and congregation won't accept it." We use those outside circumstances to hide the truth of what we will not accept. It is rejection that you feel when your friends won't accept you, fear when your spouse might leave or might shun you. You won't agree with the rest of your friends, they won't like you, and <u>puzzled</u> now, with what to do next with your life.

And this will happen to you, but be of good cheer; love yourself and remain connected to our Creator despite the anger, resentment, cruel words, and negative energy that comes to you. This is called winning the race. This is victory with memory!

How you **respond** to unhealthy attacks will determine how fast you are able to close the North side within. All things that happen to you come from what you are allowing, so bless and be thankful all the day long.

For any exaltation there must be a **humiliation**. To ascend, you must first descend. Better said: the unconscious mind is in control until the Creator within is awakened!

The meaning here cannot be totally understood by the intellect fully, but it implies that for us to ascend upward (eternally awakened more and more), we have to descend downward and clean the heart and mind from the deceptive words and the worldly lifestyle that we were born into.

To receive blessings—to see and hear our Creator—we have to humble ourselves, be still and breathe, to be silent—to rest and have peace in our temple (body), to be **humble**.

Real change occurs through teshuva. (Returning to our Creator which is greater than repenting of wrong doings) Teshuva brings with it new understanding/light, which causes wisdom to exclaim, "Hallelujah!" whereas just to repent has no new understanding with it, so no change in heart, and the person will more likely repeat the wrong action.

The new heart action now has to be in accordance with kindness and love toward self, another word for compassion. The message that is hidden in Bet is how to bring Aleph, the breath or life, from our Creator, which incorporates all your daily words to uplift and give grace to Bet, our home/earth. We have to have the breath or words of life, words of wisdom, in our home to call it a home; otherwise, it is just a house.

The Gematria of Bet is 2—two represents duality and plurality. Everything in creation was created in pairs. Man and woman, male and female. For mankind to reproduce, 2, man and woman are required. To understand The Scriptures, one must humble himself to receive the blessing of intellect and understanding and then have faith with peace to carry it out. Many receive answers (which can transform into wisdom **after** doing it) but do nothing with it, so it remains in a dormant state and will eventually be forgotten. See, another reason to study and seek truth. The working of the truth within is the way to enliven those that are lacking in peace and balance.

This body and mind is given to us so that we would learn how to prepare it by discernment so that our new awareness and life giving breath has a place within. Letting your light shine to all!

What have we accomplished? Each day we should reflect upon this. Have we cleansed our temple/body/mind/heart today? Did we sweep, did we scrub, did we carry out the trash, or did we just bring more trash and lies in?

Do you see unhealthy attacks? How did you react? Did you see our Creator's miracles today? Were you thankful?

This is not a matter of belief or good intentions, it is a matter of doing kindness and love. As we increase the true word in us, we will have peace and harmony. We are not measured by our intentions, we have light according to our actions, our faith and their results. Be so careful of the words you use in everyday life, not just in meditation, but how you use words to speak. You are speaking in the name of kindness and love with your communication to others or you are supporting unhealthy choices using deceptive words. The desire for relationship is perfectly placed in everyone's DNA—be careful and choose healthy relationships.

"Therefore whosoever hears these sayings of mine and does them I will liken him unto a wise man that built his house upon a rock."

This work is quiet in the sense that the only one who knows if you are doing it or not is you. Whether you tell all your friends and family, or not, is irrelevant. The one who really does this work breathes at a higher frequency and is not governed by the external circumstance. This light cannot be seen through the world's eye. But you will know if you are working or not, according to your new work/speech and the peace you actually have during your day.

Humanity's low vibrations or breath will punish you if your ego reacts. You will face circumstances in life, and you will feel the negative energy and its low vibration but you do not have to succumb to it because you have overcome their dark vibrations. If you do not see the ego in yourself that causes the low energy, you cannot eliminate it. Ordeals and trails come from living here on the earth. Your ego/darkness has to be replaced with light and the process of reaching this could be painful unless you acknowledge and accept the cleansing/teshuva. Remember, all negative things you encounter on this earth are from the darkness within yourself. Our external circumstances could be successful, prosperous, bad, or indifferent. What makes us feel the low vibrations is our awake mind and how it reacts to the deceptive words. Remember to remain quiet to the truth. **Meditate to awake the silence of memory power.**

When you follow the teachings of truth and, by faith, seek to nullify your ego, you are then tested by the very darkness that you released from your mind and heart. This darkness comes as that crowd/society/ the north side to spit upon you and to ridicule you. Darkness remains until it is replaced perfectly with light. The words of your ego that you speak and think are those thieves (darkness, lies) in your mind and heart that need to be replaced with truth. To nullify these words, you continue replacing the present dark words with our Creator's instruction and words of wisdom, leaving unhealthy choices, traditions, habits, dependent family upbringing, ego, and the tree of knowledge of good and evil. Do you see how you move in the "born within" dimension? You continue moving by replacing words from the unhealthy tree of knowledge of good and evil with words of wisdom, from the tree of life, one word at a time.

So you will not seek for your own glory but the glory of who is ALL in ALL. Very few do this. Most people hear this teaching, see the truth of it and feel the love. They begin to try. They may change some words, but as their worldly words begin to ridicule them, brings them doubt, fear, uncertainty, attachment, lust, and pride, they put down the teachings of the tree of life and go back into the crowd/society/north side, tree of knowledge of good and evil and disappear from those that love our Creator.

The way of our Creator remains without change. It is for those who develop the character of kindness, love, and peace. This is not related to external circumstances. Those who do walk in the light develop the strength by truth to withstand one's own mind and heart. Here we find "one with our Creator." Taking full responsibility!

To maintain faith in the presence of doubt, in the presence of lust, fear, resentment, gluttony, and laziness and to keep one's focus on uncovering truth within your head and heart is proof of our Creator's power within you. The ego has been replaced with light. Once one is serious about conquering the darkness of the mind and heart, one can tell oneself, "Let the world punish me. Let my old thoughts rebel. Let Herod attempt to kill the 'born from within' me. Let the Pharaoh come." When you visit nature and see our Creator and embrace the truth, then death, which is another name for darkness within, will flee and you will achieve freedom and light.

Remember, Aleph represents the breath of our Creator that causes a person to breath out words of love creating a home of love, life, and light.

When you exhale, it is a poison called carbon dioxide. When you breathe out, it is poison. Why? Because you are filled with toxins in your body. Physically this organism is merely a transformer of energy. But the breath you exhale is beneficial for other creatures, plants, who take that as food, but the same is true of the breath of our Creator. The breath of our Creator, beautiful words, are poison to the ego/unhealthy choices and food/health for the life of man. Now you see the reason to visit nature, mediate daily, and nourish your mortal body from the table of creation.

The man who builds his house on sand is the **fool**. To be taught with authority happens because of the harmony vibration and not the position or title given to a person. Many have built their temple/ body on the sand (another word for *field*—Adam was taken out of the dust of the field), which means the shifting circumstances of life. The personality, education, country, language, race, family, beliefs, theories—none of these shows our Creator's nature. They are all merely circumstantial and can change. How can we rely on anything like that to last? Particularly eternally. Most of us who have come this far have come through different belief systems, schools, religions, and churches. Now reflect into your own life how all those shifting sands have left you with a **thin** foundation, a shaky place. Thanks to our Creator that never changes. The foundation is **steadfast**, thick, and **firm**. Look at the letter Bet again and see the thick foundation.

Obviously we seek stability, something solid. The foundation that we need is not outside of us. It is not in a temple or in a church or organization. It is not in a belief system, it's not in any person, or preacher, but it will be the work of our Creator's truth within. When taught with harmonic vibrational words, one's inner being confirms if those words are true. Otherwise, you will not remember the teaching and you will walk away in the same condition you came in with, result; no change in your heart or mind, no continual rest or peace. Remember to visit nature daily.

There are laws of cause and effect. We are trapped in our circumstances because we caused them. And if we want different circumstances, we have to produce new causes/works/words, and to do that, we have to endure and change the causes/works/words we have already set in motion. We have to resolve the effects of them through peace. We celebrate joy with peace so that the dark causes disappear. We study out truth so that new causes/words/works can be established. This takes being in peace and a lifetime of living by the truth.

Unconscious living can be likened to a dark time from the unhealthy cause and effects already set in motion because of impurity and mixture of light with darkness in our life. (This represents the time we ate from the tree of knowledge of good and evil.)

To have a new outcome is a lifelong process. No belief can make a child, there must be thought put into action, and no belief can free the mind/heart from the ego's unhealthy choices. You must do your part. Everybody talks about their beliefs in this or that. To say I believe in such and such a master or teacher or I believe in such and such religion is **just talk,** but what comes of it? What fundamental change comes of that? How does life fundamentally change for that person? You have to do your part. Putting action to your words and waiting in peace for the fruit to develop. This is the same as "the body without the being is dead," so put action to seeking oneness in your words so the fruit will develop and come forth to glorify our Creator.

Doing the deeds or works of the truth learned from kindness and love produces the new change. You have a home in progress, and you too must finish your words/work to leave in peace.

Remember, many children of light never see with their flesh—eyes the effect of teaching the laws of creation. So please, do not become disappointed if you see no change in society, family, or friends in your time here on the earth. The change occurs in you!

May we have the same understanding as we cross over into the eternal world and leave this mortal existence! Remember, the real you, eternal being, lives forever!

Therefore, if you want your mind/heart to be free of the suffering of humanity and disease, you have to resolve the cause and effect of this dark energy and low vibration called **anger within yourself**. Stay in present time and do not rehearse the negative past. Move away from unhealthy relationships!

You have to remove that cause and effect from your temple/body and heart, and the way you do it is through love for yourself. In other words, kindness and love toward yourself first, then, all things continue with freedom and peace.

Return to our Creator and see the truth.

The awakening within will bring to your remembrance the words, the methods, the instruction, the intelligence, the wisdom to do it. No one else can do that but the Creator within you. This overcomer loves spending time with our Creator. Take a deep breath, and feel the love, life, and light present.

The first is to know, with complete faith that truth comes from our Creator, written down by man, to the best of their mature development at that time and the second—that it is only because of our Creator's love for mankind that truth allows us to understand wisdom and see man's errors. The understanding and feeling of truth will help you discern where man has erred. The words in error will not be consistent in their meaning according to creation. We can always be sure that love, life, and light will lead and direct us.

The esteem and love of our Creator brings kindness and peace to mankind. This is the word of truth.

The boxes of man teach all other words and works.

If one denies the love of truth, one cannot properly understand oneness. Our intellect alone is incapable of arriving at the true meaning of love, remember, we want to be like-minded with a heart that is humble and fully **connected** to our Creator.

The Bible begins with a Bet, the second letter of the Aleph-Tav . This is to hint to you that when you endeavor to acquire the understanding of truth merely with your intellect, you are lacking the primary purpose of the study: To become ONE with our Creator" breath is the understanding of light.

How do I know that I have received the truth? Your stony heart will be changed to a "born from within" loving, kind, and joyful one. Not a heart of flesh as quoted in Ezekiel but a humble heart of infinite love, life, and light. This heart is "born from within." You will then receive the "truth of our Creator" and have the light of life shine within.

In light of the above, the reason The Scriptures begin with a Bet is that Bet stands for berachah—meaning blessing. If one's study is preceded by the Aleph (oneness with our Creator), he or she will be blessed with faith and light to understand the deeper meaning of love and discern error and unhealthy passed-down traditions. Each person has been given a portion of light so that when the True and Almighty Light appears within, we will be thankful for the awakening.

Our Creator is all things! Settle yourself and see the miracles. Do you see why you must spend quiet time? Your life depends on recognizing our Creator's daily miracles (the healthy breath vibrations of love, life, and light).

The meaning of Bet: home, temple, body, family, connection, communication, marriage—a place where you can unite with Oneness.

Why is it written that our Creator created the heavens and the earth? To remind us of home. How does one define a home? A home is a place to which you return after finishing with your daily joy work. You remove your shoes, change to comfortable clothes and thank our Creator for a prosperous and **harmonious** day.

Home is the place that the "born from within" unites with our Creator no manner what that home looks like or where it is located. Home is the objective and DNA's blueprint of creation in every being. This home is built on a **firm** foundation for those that have overcome the world and are awakened.

The overcomer learns the feeling of the breath of love. Its peace, comfort, and rest. You have a lifetime to feel what those vibrations feel like and engage in relationships shining the light within. You will be given many chances to confront and overcome your unhealthy words and thoughts with a **firmer** foundation of truth (higher vibrations). You do this by visiting nature and gaining additional wisdom/light or reestablishing the light you were already given but failed to do—because of attachments you have that are still present in the world and its dominion over you. Repeating an action over and over is necessary to gain strength, to stand, and conviction of the truth being taught you. Know that memory power is received through peace by continuing daily to overcome the world and its darkness. Unhealthy choices will rob, steal, and destroy your love, life, and light.

Bet signifies Creation with a perfect **firm** foundation (home). Note that the root of the word Bereishit is the letter Rosh, which means head. The prefix is a Bet. The last two letters of the word are Yud and Tav. Together the Bet, Yud, and Tav spell bayit—house. But to make the house become a home, you will need perfect words, truth and our Creator's love and light.

And how does one make an eternal home?

A home is made by living the letter Bet. Three pillars on which the earth stands: truth produces faith, perfect words, and charity, which leads to perfect deeds because we understand our Creator's breath, love. When a person has perfect words, truth, and then acts in perfect faith doing perfect deeds, one builds a home, with all four walls strong and unmovable. Perfect light!

Remember the design of bet—three lines and one open side which is the North, the side that requires your peace to finish within you.

May you be a blessing to our Creator and fulfill your love work through faith, which is truth, perfect words, and the work of perfect deeds. This will truly merit a life of berachah, meaning a life of blessing and peace. Your four walls are complete because of truth within.

Home (to build and obtain children, family) and **desire** (to search out truth) have the same Gematria—number value. "Let thy desire come on earth (home) as it is in the heavens (home)."

Here is a perfect place for our Creator's nourishment for our dispensation of time:

> Our Creator who dwells within, brings us love,
> life, and light.
> Truth is seen on earth as it is in heaven; see the
> beautiful words that unite.
> Give us this day our daily bread
> As we are "born from within" and are eternally fed.
> Balanced breathing and harmony are our
> protective command.
> And to shine our light to those who have come
> against the beautiful land.
> Lead us by <u>health</u> our physical body and deliver
> our being into eternity, immortal and peaceful.
> For our Creator is <u>love, life, and light</u> for ever
> and ever.
> Now, bless our Creator together. Amen

As Bet starts the beginning of scripture so shall it be found in the end! The last word in Revelation is *amen*. How does amen relate to Bet, the beginning?

What is the root of *amen*? And what does it really mean? Aleph, Mem, Nun—pronounced aw-man.

Means a prime root to build up or support (a **firm** foundation a home), to foster as a parent or a nurse, to render or be **firm** or faithful, to trust or believe, to be permanent or quiet, to be true or certain, to go to the right hand—hence assurance, beli(eve), bring up establish, be faithful of long continuance, steadfast, sure, trust, and turn to the right. The last word in scripture—*amen*.

The truth is likened to the food of creation: When you are free, you are the book of life. Eat for life, and that means eat from the table of our creator (Good resource: *Back to Eden* by Jethro Kloss, and *Mucusless Diet Healing System* by Professor Arnold Ehret, and *The Essene Gospel of Peace "Natural Hygiene"* by Dr Herbert M Shelton.)

Eight affirmations for the letter Bet

1. A woman needs a covering for protection on the earth. That covering comes from her connection to our Creator. The earth provides her with living foods.

    a. Found in the palm of love—a giving nature with no expectation—nursing.

    b. Natural hair—pure and honest—an example of truth.

    c. Modest dress—love of truth.

    d. No mask—makeup on the eyes—overcomer of the world.

    e. Greater-lesser light calendar—our Creator does not change.

    f. Table of creation—health in body and mind.

    g. Kind and loving words—your finished mission on this earth.

    h. Compassion—when wronged, know that this is from within—an unfinished cycle that you formed—so forgive yourself and return to our Creator to be strengthened.

2. Change when truth is understood.

3. My treasure is the love, life, and light of our Creator—the peace that goes beyond all understanding.

4. Continue to visit nature thereby causing Perfect Presence to dwell within..

5. Our Creator's words are our words. Our Creator's family is our family. Our Creator's thoughts are our thoughts. The North side to our home is closed within. Our work and words are finished!

6. Our Creator's wealth is health to the eternal being, mind, and body.

7. As we meditate on wisdom our communication advances in light.

8. Our delight is to bring esteem of memory power through kindness and loving words.

Harmony

In each day, time is set apart,
For cleansing and nourishing our "born within" hearts.
Every day is a day of thanks and physical rest,
Keeping our breath in harmony to bless.
Our cup of pure juice and hands of love,
Choose the fresh food we eat every day that is like
The latter rains falling from above.
In our homes and daily schools no gum chewing, candy
Or any adulterated food claims residence,
This is truth, like a perfect white dove.
Our nursery provides safety, security, and healthy treats,
The love songs sung are the children's meat.
Our young women who respect their mothers
Keep peace, their inner beauty and modesty;
By pleasing their fathers by modest dress, clean
hair, and taking full responsibility.
Our young men who honor their fathers adore their mothers, by
Listening, obeying, and serving others.
Being faithful parents is our perfect reward,
For the word dwells within those that love and guard.
Rest is beautiful and full of light,
All our unhealthy choices are forgotten as we
have become an earthly delight!

A Dream Come True

"Good morning, Bryan (pants), said Ashton (tree).

"Good morning to you, Ashton," said Bryan.

A minute of silence happened between the two children. Bryan spoke first and said, "Last night I was dreaming. Do you want to know what I was dreaming?" questioned Bryan.

"Sure," replied Ashton.

"I was dreaming about how my life could change if I could see as far as you can see," replied Bryan.

Ashton thought about his dream and then said, "Yes, that makes me wonder about how my life could change if I could walk all over the world just like you do, Bryan."

Both Ashton and Bryan stared back at each other and silently prayed for their dream to come true.

After a while, without an introduction, a mysterious small voice suddenly broke the silence of the twins by saying, "I know a way you can both have your dreams come true."

Ashton glanced around quickly but saw no one in the distance. As Bryan moved closer to Ashton, Ashton he said with caution, "Who, Who in the world said that?"

"Me! It is me, Payton (grass). Take a look down here, and I am sure you will see me."

"Oh, yes," reassured Bryan and Ashton. "We can see you just fine now, Payton."

With no hesitation, Bryan blurted out to Payton, "Do you really know a way that I can have my dream come true?"

"Yes, YES, YES!" exclaimed Payton. "In order for your dream to come true, Bryan, all you have to do is to walk up the side of Ashton and look as far as you can see."

"That plan seems a bit scary and out of my reach! I am short and afraid that I might fall and hurt myself," seriously responded Bryan. Payton understood Bryan's fear and said, "With every dream or wish there are fears that come along with it. I know if you take your first step up and continue in the direction of your dream you will win."

So off went Bryan up to the top of Ashton, and to his delight, he made the climb with ease. Only a couple of tares were made by the ruff branches as he was able to keep his balance by climbing on the big round limbs. Once at the top he exclaimed, "Hey, it is just as I imagined it would be. It is absolutely gorgeous up here!"

As this place was so peaceful and the air smelled so clean; Bryan fell asleep.

Then, along came Bob, the flying eagle and woke Bryan up with his squawking and pounding on his chest. This made the ground from which Bryan came from a much safer and relaxing place to return.

With Bryan's returning to the ground, Ashton asked Payton, "Now, it is my turn, how can my dream come true?"

"For your dream to come true, Ashton, all you have to do is step into the legs of Bryan and Bryan will walk you around the world," giggled Payton.

"Ugh, don't you think I am too tall and fat to fit into the legs of Bryan?" blurted Ashton.

"How can you be sure of that unless you try." Payton chuckled.

With that idea in mind and a burning desire to see the world, Ashton jumped into the legs of Bryan without too much trouble.

In fact, she only had a couple of large branches break off and being tall helped her to see the direction they would need to go.

As Ashton and Bryan started off on their journey around the world, Payton stopped them and gave these last words of wisdom:

Be kind in all the places you visit so that you leave peace wherever you go.

CHAPTER 3

GIMEL

תשרקצפעסנמלכיטחזוהדגבא

The twenty-two letters of light are arranged going from right to left:
Aleph, Bet, Gimel, Dalet, Hay, Vav, Zayin, Chet, Tet, Yod, Kaf,
Lamed, Mem, Nun, Samech, Ayin, Pay, Tzadi, Kuf, Resh, Shin, and Tav.

Pronounced gamel.
The letter G in English.
Gematria or numerical value is 3.

The "third day" of creation is Yom Shlishi on the greater-lesser light calendar. Tuesday is the third day of the week on the Gregorian calendar. Written with letters of light this way: יום שלישי

The letters of light are Yud, Shin, Yud, Lamed, and Shin. The understanding given to the writer: **the heart of order and peace is a refinement, the heart of order and peace is the breath that cleans by the word of truth awakened within.** Eat fresh fruits and vegetables for the best energy resource to be established in your mind and organs. These vegetables and fruits are fired by the sun and gives the body all the breath and water needed for the body.

Gimel is composed of two letters—the first is a Vav, representing one with our Creator. To the left side is the second letter, a Yud, which signifies both the foot and the act of giving because of humility. In our own lives, we find that the upper body, from waist up, has a tendency toward selfishness, the predisposition to "take." Our intellect often exists for itself, applying its faculties to secure its needs. The mouth, stomach, and digestive tract are employed in the intake of food and drink. The lower portion of the body, however, is the part that gives to others. With our legs we walk distances to help another person. Our hands and fingers do acts of kindness and heart love. The Yud can also represent the reproductive organ, the seedbed of human life fulfilling a law of creation to be "fruitful and replenish the earth."

The word Gimel is similar to the word gamal, which means camel using the Aleph-Tav.

The reason that the Hebrews say that the number three represents Torah or scripture is that the people at that time were given the first five books of scriptures in the <u>third</u> month of the year to Moses (he was the third child of three children).

"Prepare for the <u>third</u> day do not approach a women"—so for <u>three</u> days, no man was to know his wife until the Ten Commandments were given. The first five books of scripture were issued to a people of <u>three</u> groups: the Kohanim (priests), the Levites and the Israelites. Finally, the Torah itself is divided into <u>three</u> segments: five books of Moses (Torah teachings), the prophets (Nabiy-naw-bee from naw-baw, naba—a prime root to prophesy (i.e., speak by inspiration in prediction or simple discourse from an inspired man or woman. Light letters are Nun, Bet,

Yud, and Aleph. The understanding given to the writer: **the mature seed delivers to the world or home all things revealed from our Creator)** and the scriptures/writings (using Aleph-Tav mik-tawb from the root word kaw-thab—meaning a thing written—the characters, a prime root to grave, to write). Light letters are Kaph, Tav, and Bet. The understanding given to the writer: **our cover, love, life, and light protects the awakened ones in their homes/bodies.** Our Creator is the word, the beginning to the end.

The power of the number three is its ability to combine two different forces to bring about integration (when separate people or things are brought together)—male and female. Aleph and Bet. **So, Gimel has the ability to bring attracting but distant forces together through humility (mature discernment).**

Let's say a person is born into the world learning the scriptures. He grows up in a cloistered (monastery or kept away from the outside world, sheltered) society. He goes to yeshivah (scripture study) all his life and all he knows is the scriptures. Finally, this person gets married and goes out into the world and begins to earn a living. He says, "Hey, there's materialistic world out here! There are things besides holiness, besides eternity. Maybe there are in fact two realities. The first reality is love, life, and light, our Creator. Then the second reality, the world. And these two worlds attract each other"; therefore, scripture is given in the third month because three (movement—there has to be a journey to somewhere to make a difference in the world) has the power to infuse light into the world. Our Creator expects us to make a living (go to a place where others are not awakened) to support our loved ones and enlarge heart love. By conducting our worldly affairs according to wisdom with honesty and integrity we are actually enlarging love, life, and light in the physical world. Showing love, life, and light to those that have not yet been awakened.

Let's look at it from the point of view of a person that grew up in the world. They ate, drank, partied, and lived by the laws of the land and government. They were respected in their families and social gatherings. Their work was with good intentions to help others and themselves. Now that person has an encounter of new words of light from within. Not once, but a few times, and begins to see that what they have been taught all their life is not the whole truth. Again, these two worlds attract each other, so how does that person keep a balance in their life and still maintain peace? Gimel is the letter that helps all people to understand their journey of life with their passing over to the awakened side leaving the world an impression of love, life, and light to magnify our Almighty Creator.

Three stands for that which is solid, real, substantial, complete and entire.

Our Creator's attributes are three—omniscience (the state of knowing everything), omnipresence (perfect presence), and omnipotence (the quality of having unlimited power).

Three great divisions completing time: past, present, and future. When all three come together through the letter Gimel, we arrive at the beginning of the aleph-bet—one. Which is present time.

Three persons in grammar express and include all the relationships of mankind: first person, second person, and third person

The number three is one of the four perfect numbers.

The number three denotes perfect perfection—remember perfection means **mature, complete, and balanced**. Interesting, that becoming healthy in the body will require a person to eat according to the table of creation. On the third day, according to the Bible, the kind of food was given to man. This is for the body level and not our being as we remain perfect in being as our Creator made us!

These next examples are Hebraic:

There are three parts to the Aaronic blessing: (1) May our Creator bless you and keep you (the first place keep is used in the garden where you are blessed), (2) May love, life, and light shine upon you (shine is in the beginning where "Let there be light" was spoken by our Creator), (3) May you become mature, complete and balanced with perfect peace. (Peace is safety, completed in the movement to our Creator, which is accomplished through the letter Gimel in the evening's rest on each and every prophetic day.)

The letters of light for peace is shalowm, pronounced shaw-lome, meaning safe, well, happy, friendly, favor, rest, prosper. The letters of light are: Shen, Lamed, Vav, and closed Mem: meaning given to the writer: **the cleansing process by the words of truth—wisdom, connects us to love, life, and light words developing maturity.**

Abraham prepared three measures of meal—"The reign of the heavens is like leaven, which a woman took and hid in three measures of meal until all was leavened." The first part of the sentence is saying that there will be an awakening within to those that seek peace. The next four words indicate that there is a female feeding the awakened. The next seven words indicate that wisdom, the women, hides her children in three equal measurements (present, past, and future). The last four words mean all three measures (that are one) enlarge love, life, and light.

On the third day of creation, the land rose up from out of the water (indicating a separation from one another), the only way to **see** the earth was for the earth to be removed from the water, forming earth then the earth listened to the laws of creation and brought forth three things; the grass, the plant that yields seed, and the fruit trees whose seed is in itself. "**See**, I have given you every plant that yields seed which is on the face of all the earth, and every tree whose fruit yields seed, to you it is for food." **See** using the Aleph-Tav is spelled ra'ah, pronounced raw-aw, meaning appear, behold, experience, gaze, take heed, respect, stare, think, view, vision. Letters of light are Resh, Aleph, and Hay—meaning given to the writer: **when "born from within," the breath of life, love, and light will pour truth and wisdom into your head, mind, and heart!** Water was never mentioned as being needed to sustain life. All the water was contained in fruits and vegetables at the time of creation. Water flowed from the river of Eden and it watered the garden. The understanding given to this passage of scripture, "Come to truth, all you who are thirsty. Our Creator will give you everlasting water because if you drink from this well you will be thirsty again." The water here is contained in fruit and vegetables. You have to return to the garden and eat from there to **see** our Creator's truth.

Meaning of Gimel

Someone walking—journey, the last word in the five first books of the Bible end with where the Israelites journeyed. Today we will see our journey by the lifestyle we lived, and the doors we shut behind us as we became awakened to love, life, and light.

Gen. (Bereshith) in Egypt
Ex. (Shemoth) their journeys
Lev. (Wayyiqra) Sinai
Num. (Bemidbar)—Jericho
Deut. (Debarium) Israel, the Promised Land

We are all on a love journey. From wandering to a place of settlement from flimsy tents to lasting stones, to an eternal life that does not fade. Those who are not "born from within" live out their lives according to the flesh. They set their minds on things of man's world. Those who have love, life, and light set their minds on the things of our Creator, the laws of creation. In this there is life and peace. We are led by the word of truth. Our Creator is awakening all to love, life, and light. We are a royal family throughout the earth awakened, complete, mature, and balanced.

For we know that if the tent of our earthly house is destroyed, we have a building of love, life, and light, a house not made with hands, everlasting and eternal. We are mature beings and live forever. Only the body dies and transforms to dust.

Who is our architect and builder? The architect and builder is our Creator—and we are constantly showing ourselves perfect and "one" by our words, thoughts and actions.

All life is in a process of running and returning—pulsation of life to finish the race. Remembering our Creator, your race is already won! You are victorious!

Giving and withdrawing—give an account daily of your actions and the consequences those actions produced.

Harmony—balance—side by side—a spouse should be a benefit—head means to help the other person be all that they can be. Man is not above women, nor women above man but "one" in our Creator. Walking together progresses, evenly yoked people. In life, not discouraging each other—a since of harmony to make progress. But two cannot walk together unevenly yoked as no progress will be made and contention and disappointment will be the result. Both must walk with our Creator first and then progress will be the result. When one is not evenly yoked, the awakened one, can be a silent example and bear her or his consequences of choices made. This cannot be avoided because families are made up of those that are awakened and those that are asleep or unconscious to our Creator. The awakened one will always be learning how to be the quiet example with their treasured connection to their Creator.

Another meaning of Gimel is "nourish until ripe." After Korach rebelled against Moses and Aaron, the word of truth within Moses said, "Take a staff from all the other tribes of Israel. Then place the staves in the Holy of Holies." The next morning, Moses brought out the staves from the Holy of Holies and all of Israel saw that the staff of Aaron produced (vayigmal) completely ripened almonds (Light letters for almonds—Shin, Kuf, Dalet—shaw-kad—a prime root to be alert [i.e., sleepless, to be on the lookout whether for good or ill]). The understanding given to the writer: **the tribe of Levi was made perfect to keep watch on the door of the temple**. So of all the tribes, the tribe of Levi—Aaron was completely ripened for this task and no other tribe. Thus the word vayigmal is comprised of the letters Gimel. The tribe of Levi would live out their lives **journeying** with the work of the temple.

We can take this thought of the ripened tribe further down the Hebrew generational line. What child came out of Judah that was fully and totally ripe, written as the first fruit or the awakened of creation? Yes, the biblical Christ.

Another meaning of Gimel is to be weaned. The child grew and was weaned (vayigmal). At first glance, the concepts of being weaned and nourished until ripe seem contradictory. When you are nourishing, you are giving. When you're weaning, you are ceasing to give. In essence, however, they are consistent, because if you nourish until ripe, you no longer have to give. By the way, every mother and father want this for their children, to be weaned from them, so that they can think on their own because they have been taught our Creator's ways and wisdom.

The Gimel is also called gamal, or camel. The camel itself embodies the process of weaning and nourishing, as it is able to sustain itself on journeys of vast distance after being sufficiently watered. We also note that Gimel is similar to the word gomel, to be kind and benevolent. The camel can help the sojourner survive the harsh desert sun by carrying him to his destination. The word Gimel in Aramaic is gamla or bridge. One can say that the bridge is the humpback of the camel itself, which provides the means and structure to bring people where they need to go physically. Who is our eternal bridge? Who is our MOVER? Our one and only Creator!

Now, how is it that the Gimel actually signifies the "born from within," awakened? The answer can be found perhaps in the difference between the terms "heart love" and "Tzedakah," a teacher of righteousness. "Heart Love" is found in a person that grants mercy to those that are lacking in substance or wisdom. Read the explanatory notes under "Heart" in the back of the book The Scriptures.

Tzedakah, in contrast, has a fundamentally different meaning. The definition of Tzedakah is righteousness or justice—simply put, to do the right thing, be an example. In the case of Tzedakah, his or her possessions or words of wisdom is unselfish; our Creator gave it to them unconditionally so that when a lacking person in the word of truth or substance comes along, they can give to them freely. Furthermore, one gives out of love, life, and light. You reap what you sow. For one to receive blessings, one needs to do for others in their own home and country, first, then as one is strengthen, to other nations and countries. "This is called Enlargement."

The greatest level of "Heart Love" is not to give money, even though that instantly helps but to give of your time and wisdom to show them how to be self-sufficient and overcome their fears and disease. To set a person on his feet, nourish him until he's ripe, and then wean him so that he himself can know our Creator and live without fear. This is a fully ripened person, perfected and a blessing to others.

The last meaning of Gimel is the MOVER—the perfect example, the word of truth, the Creator awakened within singing joy and peace to all!

Eight affirmations for the letter Gimel

1. Thank you for the computer sites—connecting to all. Creating oneness has helped gather thoughts, ideas, and perspectives regarding the Light letters. Going outside and viewing nature is perfect truth.

2. Aleph, has given us strength. Bet has a place for us ; home is our sanctuary. Gimel—the MOVER of our awakened journey.

3. Our eyes are opened to truth—we confront daily, each other, moving to love, life, and light, keep us humble. Feeding those that are asleep and remembering all things with peace is for the benefit of truth.

4. As the camel was to our forefathers, love, life, and light, is the true journey and water of life for us .

5. The Aleph to the Tav are our counselors, blessings, and health come through eating from the table of creation.

6. Understanding Aleph and Bet brings harmony to marriage— the movement of love.

7. Unite the awakened; We are balanced, ripened, and weaned for this worthy task.

8. Our Creator's light is nourishment—a circle of life in that the seed planted moves through yearly cycles weaning to the next level causing continual eternal growth. And by perfect presence, (visiting nature), we become closer to one in perfection.

Home

We all go on trips to one place or another.
As we are called "home" then we realize that this was
the only place that we anticipated to discover.
As we see love as a never ending cycle,
We can visualize our eternal gift; Peace, for being a faithful disciple.
Our earthbound body, and thoughts of that kind,
Are left here with our mortal family, as a sure sign,
One with our Creator is our eternal home, a blessing, and a relief.
And no man knows the mind of love and light when we believe.

One

May we with tender mercies and outstretched humble hand,
Bestow the love of wisdom within our minds
and hearts to our fruitful land.
Faithful and Virtuous have become one, receiving
the love of truth, now, awakened to be,
"Jubilee"
The eternal light has opened unto them,
Brave, courageous, beautiful are made ready to awaken all within.
The joy of life and presence of our Creator remains,
The earth is cleansed,
The curtain descends.
Hallelujah for memory. Amen!

CHAPTER 4

DALET

א ב ג ד ה ו ז ח ט י כ ל מ נ ס ע פ צ ק ר ש ת

The twenty-two letters of light are arranged going from right to left:
Aleph, Bet, Gimel, Dalet, Hay, Vav, Zayin, Chet, Tet, Yod, Kaf,
Lamed, Mem, Nun, Samech, Ayin, Pay, Tzadi, Kuf, Resh, Shin, and Tav.

Fourth letter of the Aleph Bet.
English letter D.
Pronounced dah-et—sound of D as in door.
The numerical value is 4.

The "fourth day" of creation is called Yom Revi'l. It is called Wednesday and is the fourth day of the week on the Gregorian calendar. Written like this using letters of light: יום רביעי.

Fourth using letters of light are raw-bah, raba, a prime root to squat or lie out flat sprawling at all fours—the letters of light are Resh, Bet, Ayin—from arba, ar-bah or arba ah, ah-baw-aw—letters of light are Aleph, Resh, Bet, and Ayin. Understanding given to the writer: **our Creator, the Creator of all things, resides with those that watch and love from every direction**.

Dalet represents a doorway. In other words, when the letter is placed in a word, you have to keep in mind that not only is it the letter D, it is the number four and symbolizes a door. For example in the name ADM-Aleph, Dalet and Mem using the Aleph-Tav, Dalet is the central letter, between the Aleph and the Mem. The Creator's doorway to receive the word. The understanding given to the writer: **so humankind was created to speak and articulate words that opened the door to truth and gave order to creation**.

Eden has Dalet in the middle of it: Dalet is the doorway to Eden (our eternal awakening)—and to awaken from darkness to light, "our Creator born within."

"Everyone drinking of well water shall thirst again, but whoever drinks of the water from creation shall certainly never thirst. And the water shall become a fountain of water springing up into everlasting life within." This water is perfect wisdom (eating from the fruits of creation) that opens the door and the actual words to love, life, and light.

How do we return to the Garden of Eden? We mentally return to our Creator, in mind, heart and physically we eat from the table of creation and spend time in nature, thereby, purification happens as the breath of life cleans our words of darkness. Our words become loving and kindness for mankind is seen in our daily actions.

This takes a process of time! We just cannot see all the lies and unhealthy traditions at one time nor be able to stand in the light of Perfect Presence all at once. We will still be in cycles of unhealthy choices that we entered in before we were awakened to our Creator within. So become united and one with love, life, and light in the power that can rid our personal mind of darkness. Remember, "born from within" is a continual daily offering of one self and is not the same as the initial awakening. As you mature in your walk with our Creator, you will understand the distance that you were in, from truth.

We are talking about the distance from the words of truth. Look at the words in the Bible concordance from A to Z and select only words that you feel the high vibration of love, life, and light. Following our Creator's one law of love will guide you to all healthy words. You are like a baby when first born within. Many years of loving and seeking truth will bring you to our Creator's one law of love, having no judgment but perfect discernment.

You see, heart love is the doorway that understands wisdom so you may awaken eternity or the most holy place, our mind, within your very being. Every action is a choice that we perform that produces an effect or consequence. When our action is empowered through heart love of our Creator, the result is multiplied and there is an exponential scale that unfolds. The greater our love for a perfect nature, the greater power we have to overcome evil in our lives. (Be gone, anger, pride, envy, jealousy, lust, and most especially, fear, the chief amongst them and is found by the desire one has outside of the love of our Creator. When you are outside, still in the field eating from the tree of knowledge of good and evil, fear, of some degree, is your consequence.)

Eden is eternal, a place recognized on the earth in the Bible where our Creator thought, and life appeared. This eternal garden is likened to the awakened being.

We have wisdom to give us light/order and understanding. This light comes from knowing our Creator and is imparted to those that love light, life and wisdom. A physician is needed as long as we are eating from the tree of knowledge of good and evil.

Physician using the letters of light is ra'ash, rah-ash, letters of light are Resh, Ayin, and Shin. Meaning a prime root to undulate (move with a smooth wavelike motion), to make afraid, make to shake, make to tremble, unhealthy vibrations, uproar, commotion, confused noise, earthquake, and fierceness. The understanding given to the writer: **The person that relies on their own knowledge and the words of the world has their vision darkened and their thoughts and choices lead to internal pollution of the body and mind as they did not first inquire from our Creator's truth**.

The letter Dalet is shaped with two lines, one horizontal and one vertical.

Psalm 118: 19–21, pg **714** says, "This is the gate of our Creator the pure will enter through it. I shall give thanks for creation has answered me, and perfection is my salvation [awakened state]."

Psalm 62:1–2, pg. **679** says, "My being finds rest in our Creator alone, for truth, love, light and life is my deliverance [awakened state]. Truth alone is my rock and my deliverance, my Hightower."

Salvation—y'shuw'ah, yesh-oo-aw, meaning—something saved (i.e., deliverance, hence aid, victory, prosperity, health, help, welfare) from the root word yasha, yaw-shah to be open, wide or free, to be safe, to free or succor, avenging, defend, deliver, help, preserve, rescue, be safe, bring salvation, get victory. Letters of light are Yud, Shin, Vav, Ayin, and Tav. The understanding given to the writer: **The beginning of all things requires the awakening of truth to dwell in humankind (words of truth) and by these new words of revelation to know our Creator that humankind may see life is "oneness" and live forever.**

Once we have salvation (awakened state) within, then our own tongue becomes a door of life, love and light to others.

In each moment of your life, you are breathing our Creator's breath. That means you are listening by the promptings of the truth within. The human organism is a transformer of forces, and according to your awakened thoughts, those forces are transformed into perfect deeds with their consequences. The result is always perfect if you know all things come from your awakened state. Our Creator made us perfect, however, through our choices we enjoy the consequences of love, life, and light or suffer with the unawaken humankind because of unhealthy emotions. Remember, it is your choice!

In mathematics when you use the Greek letter Delta, which relates to Dalet, it means change. It is a symbol in math that indicates change. It is a door through which things change. We need to consciously utilize our precious opportunity of having a physical body, to spend time in daily oneness or meditation so that we can benefit others. For our health, in body and mind, keep the law of love, life, and light so that you have vitality and have it more abundantly.

Day 4 of creation according to the Bible—our Creator placed the sun, moon, and stars in heaven to give light on the earth and to separate light from darkness. These are perfect and continuous luminaries that have a perfect purpose of truth that never changes and moves the seasons according to the laws of heaven and earth that govern them. Cross over or pass over from man's way of calculating time, darkness, to the everlasting light of the sun and moon.

Passover (passing from death to life) is a reminder of springtime; we have life because of our awakened state within. Our Creator is of the living and not of the dead—so when we speak of those that have passed on, we never say "they died or they are dead," unless you are talking about the physical body. We are eternal beings and live forever.

Dalet represents humility and the consciousness of possessing truth to give. The poor man or women represented by Dalet is not financially or materialistically poor but eternally lacking. The more you feed physical desires, they just get hungrier. That's because those desires are the vehicle of the tempting unhealthy choices you have succumb to. Yet we become addicted to sensations. Physical sensations, emotional sensations, mental sensations. We are impoverished because our unhealthy desires have stolen everything of value from us. Our physical health, sound mind, and good thoughts.

As much as we seek and seek and seek in this external world, as much as we think we need something outside of truth to give us happiness, we are fooled, we are in a delusion, because nothing external to our "born from within" will ever give you lasting happiness. Rather, love our Creator first and nature, and all the rest will be provided!

"Love your enemies, and do well and lend expecting nothing in return. And your reward shall be great and you shall be awakened sons and daughters because love and truth is kind to the thankless and wicked ones. Therefore, be compassionate and do not judge at all. Condemn not, and you shall not be condemned at all. Return to our Creator and you shall be renewed. Give and it shall be given to you. A perfect measure, pressed down and shaken together and running over shall be put into your lap. For with the same measure with which you measure, it shall be measured back to you."Luke 6:35-36

Wisdom says, "Do not measure or compare and you will have mature and complete freedom with abundance!"

Measure using the light letters is Middah—mid-daw or madad, maw-dad—means a prime root to stretch as if by stretching a line [of defense] (the letters of light are placed in a horizontal line for defense; they are your letters of love, life, and light), to be extended for discernment. Your words either expand you are confine you. The letters of light for measure are Mem, Dalet, and Hay. Also, amah, am-maw or em, ame meaning a mother (that is a unit of measure) as the bond of the family. Letters of light are Aleph, Mem, and Hay. The understanding given to the writer: **our Creator with wisdom's words births the family by awakening the joy within humankind.**

Using the Aleph-Tav the word for poor is dal. The basic food eaten by poor people is called dal. "Poor" is where we get the word porridge in English. We all look at such food as if we are above that. Thus we want to eat expensive, rich food as if it proves our value. But the truth is that as rich as we may be in the physical world, and no manner how good our food is (eating from the tree of knowledge of good and evil), if we do not have our Creator born within (tree of life) health, then we are poor both physically and eternally.

What we have within is a desire of, ego, fear, resentment, attachment, and hunger. We are a poor man or woman, darkened, burdened with terrible patterns of life, traditions, and negative behavior.

Our Creator wants to bestow riches upon us but cannot if we are not ready to receive it. When we are awakened to these new alive words (which come from overcoming trials of life and being true to love), our Creator will lift us up (Di lis so ni) from our bad behavior, family traditions, and generational curses and lies.

You do not create anything only our Creator who is ALL and ALL is responsible for creation. You may help to build or restore something on this earth but never do you create, only our Creator has that power. For in the beginning our Creator created the heavens and the earth and all that was in them. The thing that is created cannot be the Creator of the thing created. We enjoy the tranquility, unity, and eternal blessings as we join together as "one." May you be free and courageous and stand to strengthen our children in truth, light and peace.

Our Creator's breath cannot be separated from the mortal man or woman or the body will perish. Our eternal journey (Gimel—third light letter) uses our Creator's breath (Aleph—first light letter) through the awakened within to become perfect (mature and balanced) to receive the truth so that we can become a doorway of light to others.

To know Dalet, one has to become a perfect (mature and balanced) expression of the Gimel and Dalet, which together spell GOD. Using the Aleph-Tav, it is pronounced Gad. Gad means to tell, "to speak," and how else did our Creator make us but through Dalet in the throat and out comes male and female voice and words (mouth is a doorway)? Remember, this is where power of love comes from. The words we speak are just like our Creator born within. At the end of your mortal existence, kindness will be your most beautiful companion, and you will be celebrated by the words you think, say and do. How did Hasatan deceive Eve? By his cunning words! Learn to quiet yourself and speak when you can commune in wisdom.

And our Creator said, "Let there be light: and there was light [order]." Remember, we are children of light, the day.

The Gematria of Dalet is 4.

There are four basic elements of creation: <u>**fire**</u> (energy, vigor, vitality, vibration, inspiration, fervent, exuberance, passion, enthusiastic, intensity, light, life, excite, sparkle, awakened, stimulate, enliven, and motivate), <u>**air**</u> (gas, aria-a song in opera, a breeze, a tune, a jump off the ground, express opinion or grievance, broadcast on radio, parade or show, noticeable all around, and unresolved issue), <u>**water**</u> (liquid, ice, urine, amniotic fluid, the quality of transparency and brilliance shown by a diamond or other gem, finance capital stock that represents a book value greater than the true assets of a person or company, the eyes become full of moisture or tears, produce saliva from the mouth, and water something down such as: not telling the full truth, a statement or proposal less forceful or controversial by changing or leaving out certain details), and <u>**earth**</u> (solid, the world, soil, planet, the underground den of a fox, the substance of the human body, cover the root and lower stem of a plant with heaped up earth, return to reality, euphemistic used to refer to the experience of having orgasm, and last, go into hiding).

Today, we are "born from within" the eternal man or woman, our Creator within and have joy for the change of life.

There are four levels of interpretation of the Scriptures called PARDES, an acronym formed from the following:

<u>P</u>'shat—literal meaning based on historical intent of author
<u>R</u>emez—hint, allusion, analogy, allegory
<u>D</u>'rash—application, exposition
<u>S</u>od—mystery, deep meaning

Indeed, the word for knowledge (*da'at*) means the "door on the eye" using the ancient pictographs.

Lamp = niyr, neer—to glisten, the burner or light, fire, a prime root the idea of the gleam of a fresh furrow; to till the soil, break up, freshly ploughed land. The letters of light are Nun, Yud, and Resh. The understanding given to the writer: **the mature seed breaks up all darkness and replaces the darkness with wisdom words forming perfect light in the mind and heart.**

Remember, whatever you think, speak and do on this earth will be how you are known—speak kindly about all things and the **humble** ones will listen, those that want to know our true Creator. The words we speak are the life born within called the word of truth. If words are being used that are not kind and beautiful in a conversation, understand that communication belongs to those that are not awakened. Be kind and only speak beautiful words to these people or just say nothing. This is your test to shine our Creators love. Sometimes you need to ignore people that are confusing in their words and walk away.

Meaning of Dalet

A door, hang, entrance, back and forth, movement, dangle, weak, poor, lift me up, selflessness, receptiveness, cling.

Dal—a poor person

Dalet—door

Dilisoni—to lift me up. Di lis so ni, di les so nee.

How do these three words work together? The convergence occurs when every individual realizes that he or she is poor. This poverty doesn't necessarily denote a state of financial want. Rather it means that everything a person "owns" in fact belongs to our Creator. Life and sustenance comes from truth. Without love and light, we have nothing. The acknowledgment of this is the door (teshuva) into the highest vibration of the mind, chamber. And once we enter that chamber, truth will lift us up—dilisoni—to bless us with life, health, sustenance, and success.

In Psalm 30 of the book of Psalms, King David tells us, "I praise Elohim, Yehovah because he lifts me up [*dilisoni*]." If we turn this phrase around, we could say, "*Dilisoni*, because Elohim, Yehovah lifts up, I praise him."

In this expression, our Creator lifts us up by giving us the skills to be satiated, prosperous, healthy, and loved. This enables us to shine truth about our Creator from eternity to eternity in humble authority for ever and ever.

Eight affirmations for letter Dalet

1. Our being loves truth.

2. Truth ways are our ways. We move by the Creator born within purifying our fleshy heart into a humble fruit—giving heart.

3. Humbleness is the entrance to the mind and heart chamber. Memory.

4. Truth is light; safety remains with love.

5. The idols surround us —shine the truth—our heart is lifted up. Di lis so ni.

6. Write your truth—potential to actuality.

7. The love born within us is the door to truth.

8. Remember the poor (slavery when unawaken) for we were once poor and in bondage. Truth set us free!

Eternity

Can there be found on earth such an expression of perfect love?
To our Almighty, Omnipotent Creator, set
in the mind's chamber, above.
To whom we owe the very breath we take
each glorious and prophetic day.
To utter in thanksgiving, blessings; Do we dare disobey?
Turn our heads, show arrogance, no affection for humankind at all.
Let's look at Adam and Eve, their unhealthy choice led to their fall.
We are all known by our Creator; our lives lived
for truth is our mortal mission and test.
We have love, life, and light within, to assist us in choosing the best.
As we learn and progress, we will enter into a daily rest.
Love requires peace and humility, which
is likened to unleavened bread.
For these are the words of awakened beings; remember they said;
This law, love, is only possible by knowing truth.
Please humble yourself and enter in.
Leave the world of darkness and become "love born" from within.
Humility followed by joy is the dance and song of "one."
United in love, truth and light; ignites the fun;
moving us in present time, the race is won!

Bouncer the Ball and Whisper the Wind

Inside the hall closet sat Sonya, better known as Bouncer the Ball. She had not been outside for many years. As she patiently waited for the door to open she said, "It is no fun being stuck inside this old, dark, dusty closet. I pray for this door to open."

And to her amazement, that day, the door creaked open. At first Sonya did not know what to say or do. She just stared at the tiny opening of light that shinned through toward her. As she looked around the room, she found that there was no one present.

"Was she just dreaming this odd occurrence?" she asked herself.

With quick movements, Sonya assured herself that she was not dreaming. She first touched the floor, then she touched the wall and in the instant she touched the closet ceiling; she knew it was real and that she was not dreaming.

Sonya rolled herself out of the closet and down the hall. When she reached the kitchen, the door to that entrance was closed.

She immediately prayed for this door to open. Again, to her amazement, the door creaked open.

Sonya quickly rolled through the second door. As she sashayed around the room with great delight, she spotted the door that led to the outside. This door, however, was closed too. With great ambition to be in creation again, she approached the door and quietly reviewed her past behavior and life style.

This time when Sonya went through the door; she not only knew who opened it, but her heart about life had changed.

Out into the yard Sonya, better known as Bouncer the Ball, bounced for joy!

She was praising, singing, and having a glorious time when very faintly she heard Mike, better known as Whisper the Wind, say, "Can you do it again? Can you do it again?"

"Was that Whisper the Wind playing a game with her? What did he mean, "Can I do it again?" thought Sonya as she continued to bounce.

"Can you do it again? Can you do it again?" whispered Whisper the Wind.

"Can I do WHAT again?" Sonya said a little louder.

Mike said even louder, "Can you do it again, Sonya? Can you do it again?"

Sonya decided to quit bouncing. She sat very still while she meditated about these words. She felt many emotions as she repeated the words to herself, "Can you do it again?"

She continued to roll upon the earth and ponder while waiting for an answer.

As the answer was revealed, Sonya understood her hidden pride. She had forgotten to thank our Creator publicly for opening her door to freedom.

Whisper the Wind, better known as Mike, came to Bouncer the Ball, better known as Sonya, to see if she would take personal credit for the miracle. Without any further hesitation, Sonya said to Mike, "Can I do it again? Can I do it again? Knowing truth, anything is possible."

Have you thanked our Creator publicly for your freedom?

"Thank you," said Sonya, "for truth that set me free!"

CHAPTER 5

HAY, OR HEH

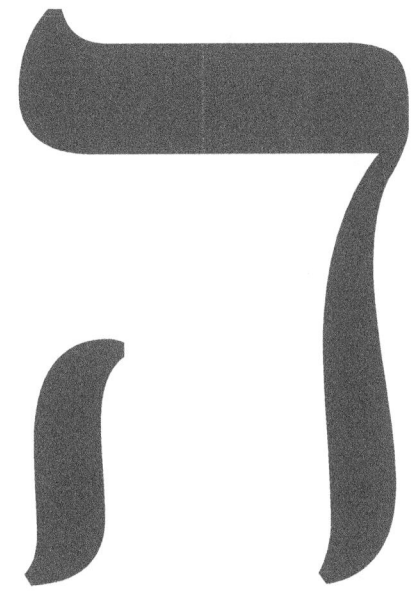

תשרקצפעסנמלכיטחזוהדגבא

The twenty-two letters of light are arranged going from right to left:
Aleph, Bet, Gimel, Dalet, Hay, Vav, Zayin, Chet, Tet, Yod, Kaf,
Lamed, Mem, Nun, Samech, Ayin, Pay, Tzadi, Kuf, Resh, Shin, and Tav.

English letter H.
Fifth letter of the aleph-tav.
Gematria or numerical value is 5.

The fifth day of creation is called Yom Chamishi (kham-ee-shee).
Thursday is the fifth day of the week according to the Gregorian
calendar. This is how it is written using the letters of light: יום חמישי

The letters of light for Chamishi are Yod, Shin, Yod, Mem, and Chet. The understanding given to the writer: **the beginning of all things requires the breath of life to move all things to eternity by words that declare our Creator is over all**.

The Aleph-Tav is progressive—the discernment of truth will allow you to move out of a letter when you have successfully seen our Creator in the letter. Your success to move out of a letter is determined by the new vocabulary you think, speak and do through observation of the heavens and earth, within you. You have within you all that is necessary to transition to the pure law of love, life, and light language.

Design

Hay is made up of a Dalet and a Yud: one horizontal line (signifying width) and another that is vertical (signifying height), which together represent the physical world, the world of materialism. The Yud (the detached left leg) represents truth and thus the eternal nature of man. The "born from within" person.

When this person's character shines the light of our Creator, the physical world around that person reflects joy and is given abundant love, life, and light here on the earth.

The Hay represents thought, speech, and action (love, life, and light). Just as the form of Hay is composed of three lines, so do thought, speech, and action comprise the dress of one's being, the three ways through which we express ourselves. **Thought**: **speech**: **action**.

The top horizontal line (thought), by its very design, represents the concept of equality. To truly experience every person as equal, one must restructure one's thought process. Perhaps it appears on the surface that some people are better and some are worse than others and they are according to the physical body. However, our Creator made us eternal perfect beings, and it is humankind's pride with their unhealthy choices that leads to inequality in the body here on the earth.

But as an overcomer, our nature is to focus on the heart, our Creator's breath, within each person. Our heart emanates love, life, and light given to us from our Creator. We are all governed by love vibrations and have different tasks to perform with a personal energy and blessings in life. When we delve beneath the personality and externality of a person we can see the heart of that person manifest our Creator. This is why we do not judge a place or people but leave peace wherever we go. No contention just silence is sometimes necessary. Judgment and courts are left for the unawaken man.

Children of light have joy in discernment.

The Hay's right vertical line represents hierarchy or power structure, which is speech. A king/queen or man/woman of a country or home rule with their words. They are empowered to sit in a palace or home and utter a decree or rule from home, which then becomes law or boundaries. People do not have to see the king/queen. Children do not have to see their father or mother to know what is expected of them. Those in authority need to speak; that is their duty, and so it is for the family of humankind. The words you put out into the universe remain alive with dark vibrations or light vibrations. This remains your choice.

The vertical line of the Hay descends from a higher state to a lower state. We learn best by example. Be careful of how and what you do.

Finally, the shorter, detached leg on the left side of the Hay represents action. Why is this limb detached? It is very easy for us to think and speak about what is right, but it is quite another thing to bring a good intention to fruition. Therefore, by faith and peace, the **gap** serves as a reminder of the work that is required to unify our dress—that is thought, speech, and action.

Hay also represents Aleph-Tav word, *teshuva*—tes-u-VAH— meaning to return to our Creator of love, life, and light.

To appreciate how the form of the letter Hay embodies the concept of *teshuva*, compare the Hay to the eighth letter, Chet. Both forms look very much alike. Each is made up of three lines. The one difference is the small aperture atop the Hay's left limb. What does this have to do with *teshuva*? The opening or door on the bottom of both Chet and Hay is wide and represents the world. But the Hay has another opening, another possibility which is called *teshuva*, or return, located on the top left side and is small. Notice that the opening has the potential to move a person to the next letter of light, Vav. Advancing and enlarging beautiful light.

Another difference between the Chet and the Hay can be illustrated by comparing chametz (leaven) and matzah (no leaven—flat). Compare the spelling of the two words: Chametz is spelled Chet, Mem, and Tzadik. Matzah is spelled Mem, Tzadik, and Hay. The difference between chametz and matzah is the letter Chet versus the letter Hay. Chametz, leaven, represents being puffed up, the ego. Matzah is flat, representing humility. If a person is humble, he or she will come to truth, to do *teshuva*. But if a person is an egotist, he or she will never return to our Creator. What is their attitude? "Why do I need the Creator? I'm doing great on my own. Look how successful I am, I am a creator." Or if he or she want to get away with bad behavior, he or she might say, "What do you want from me? I'm only human. If our Creator wanted me to be perfect, then my choice would not be necessary. He would have made me that way. The Creator gave me a *yetzer hara*, an evil inclination. The Creator set it up so that I should choose unhealthy choices. So why should I do *teshuva*?" The egotist has no reason to become one and return to our Creator. He or she is stuck in their ways and cannot admit or see their faults or new light. **They always have an excuse or blame others for their problems**. The egotist is bloated with the Chet of chametz, of leaven.

The Hay on the other hand is like matzah: FLAT and unselfish, a concern for the well-being of others. Its very design contains an opening, a gap, for an individual to pass through if he or she is humble. The Hay is a human being's understanding of humility, the gateway to love, life, and light. This is very important! Having humility within helps a person say and feel good things about others when they have deliberately hurt them. Likened to a wound that is healed—all the rough edges have fallen off and only the pure and cleansed skin appears.

In a broader sense, we need to understand that *teshuva* does not only involve remorse for our unhealthy choice, it means returning to our

Creator, perfect wisdom, love, life, and light. As such, *teshuva* is relevant for every individual, even the rare individual who has seldom made unhealthy choices. When our Creator is born within, this individual will even get better at choosing healthy choices. Every person will realize that no matter what their status, they are always learning how to shine the light formed within for the betterment of others.

One can accomplish this by perfecting his or her thoughts, speech, and action. As humankind has perfection (matures, completes, and has balance), this shines the Creator within. There begins the latter rain, "a rain of blessings," and the crops begin to grow. Do unto others with the capacity of love that you have toward our Creator and see fruit ripen before your eyes.

Behold, look! Revelation. The breath of our Creator, perfect revelation and light. *Light* is mentioned five times on the first day of creation. Hay is pronounced only with breath; connecting with the word—wind—air moves across vocal cords, creating a sound.

The strong leader of the house gives generously by faith to all in his or her reach, which opens a door of revelation for both the strong leader and those that receive help. Revelation begins by opening your hand to open the door to give—physically as well as eternally—that is revelation. And when you do these acts of kindness you can see growing, the testimony within yourself, and the revelation of love.

By now your house is in order/light—you will have abundance and a nature to give. Remember, if giving your time or presence is not being done, then the letter Hay is not fully understood—our Creator and the universal law of pure love will continue to support and direct you until you gain a mature understanding of the letter. You may read through the next letters to the last letter, Tav, however, with partial light and understanding.

Auditory perception is hearing and then believing in the intuitive words rising from a cleared conscious of the awakened Creator within. "Shama" using the Aleph-Tav means to hear.

"Shama"—Remember, eating from the table of creation is life, so overcooked and processed food leads toward bodily pain and disease more quickly. True awakening will always produce an effectual movement.

Gematria

The number five is the number of grace.
Five fingers on each hand.
Five senses—all bring revelation, the sense of smell is the greatest.
Five levels of light.

1. Nefesh—physical body, fleshy.

2. Ruach—spirit—ruwach, roo-akh—means to blow, to smell, make of quick understanding—Light letters are Resh, Vav, and Chet. The understanding given to the writer: **humankind, both male and female, is designed with a head for understanding the potential of giving life through words of love and light.**

3. Neshamah—being or soul—n'shamah, nesh-aw-maw—means a puff, wind, intellect, inspiration. The light letters are Nun, Shin, Mem, and Hay. The understanding given to the writer is, **the life-giving seed has high vibrations or harmony from wisdom's words that express revelation of creation and our Creator.**

4. Chayah—life.

5. Yechidah = or yachad, yaw-khad means union, to be one—join, unite—light letters are Yud, Chet, and Dalet. The understanding given to the writer: **all things have the capacity of love, life, and light as our Creator designed what was in the heavens and the earth by the laws of creation, perfect unity.**

Our Creator's breath that everyone possesses is also called *pintele Yid.* The *pintele Yid* is the propelling force behind teshuva. This concept of returning makes it possible for a person to enjoy life when they hear (Shama) the pure truth spoken. The heart of this person will grow in wisdom.

Pintele yid is the light in each person that resists the darkness and refuses to be a part of even, a little darkness.

Our Creator gives us seeds (i.e., the potential to be productive and make beauty of our lives). Many times however, we become disturbed and confused and lose our heavenly or "born from within" direction. Eventually, though, every person will come to do teshuva and acknowledge our Creator. Each will then behold the word of prophecy which is the love born within.

By elevating one's thought and speech into beauty and perfect action, one reveals the *yechidah,* the fifth level and light within his or her being, oneness with our Creator, with everlasting and eternal life.

Eight affirmations for letter Hay

1. Give our thoughts clarity and vision.

2. Give our speech the pure thoughts of clarity and vision.

3. Have our actions demonstrate our speech and thoughts that have clarity and vision through writing.

4. Eating from the table of creation takes humility, a reminder to us of the pure actions of speech and thoughts being carried forth.

5. Wisdom's way is through the small side opening of Hay.

6. The mature seed has overcome the world and is "born from within." The Hay gap is closed behind us .

7. A house of order/light is revelation. Thank you for perfect presence and eternal love that protects our home.

8. Personal offering has been consolidated through faith, grace, humility, and truth—behold a blooming union uniting earth to heaven—Jacob's ladder, the Aleph to Tav.

What Voice Do You Choose?

It does make a difference in what you say, as
well as the manner in which you say it.
It is the language you use, and even more so the
tone and body language you use to convey it.
"Come here," I sharply said, and baby cowered and wept.
"Come here," I cooed and quietly the baby
smiled and straight to my lap he crept.
The words may be mild and fair, or the tones may pierce like a dart.
The words may be soft as summer air, or the
body language may break the heart.
For the words are formed in the mind and with
wisdom they grow with study and art.
While the tones and body language leap forth from
the inner self and reveals the state of the heart.
Then would we quarrels avoid and in peace and love rejoice!
Keep love not only in your heart but in your eternal voice.

Birthday Voice and Harper Grace

"What is all the excitement about? Does anybody hear me out there?" questioned Harper Grace as she awakened from her afternoon nap.

"I hear you very well," answered Birthday Voice. "Talk to me."

"Where are you?" questioned Harper Grace. "I cannot see you."

"I am in the family room," spoke Birthday Voice softly.

"But I am in the family room," answered Harper Grace, "and I still do not see you."

"I am here," remarked Birthday Voice. "You just cannot see me until the day of the birthday."

"The day of the birthday," repeated Harper Grace. "Tell me, what happens on the day of a birthday?" questioned Harper Grace.

"It is a day to remember. It is the day that a certain individual is born."

"Hm," Harper Grace thought, "I wonder when I was born?"

Birthday Voice continued speaking, "A birthday is celebrated with a party. This party is called a birthday party."

"That sounds like fun!" exclaimed Harper Grace. "Do you think I will have a birthday party?"

"Sure you will," insisted Birthday Voice. "What day were you born?"

"Well, I am not sure," wondered Harper Grace as she scratched her head.

"We are in the month of March. Tomorrow is the fourteenth," stated Birthday Voice. "Does that day mean anything to you?"

"No, but I sure am glad you told me." Harper Grace giggled. "Perhaps that is the day I was born and you are here to tell me."

"Maybe this is my mission," Birthday Voice answered in a pleased manner.

"It is getting late and time to go to sleep," said Birthday Voice. "I will see you in the morning."

"Good night," said Harper Grace as she slipped under her blush pink sheets.

The next morning Harper Grace awoke and Ashton, her mom, dressed her in her very best clothes. When she entered the family room, she cried out in surprise, "Oh! What a wonderful dream come true. All my family and friends are here."

"I just love the balloons, cake, and ice cream! The birthday gifts are wrapped in beautiful paper. This is so exciting," cried out Harper Grace.

When the party was over, Harper Grace whispered quietly to Birthday Voice, "I will never forget this day. Thank you so much for reminding me."

How old do you think Harper Grace is?

Who is Harper Grace's teacher?

CHAPTER 6

VAV, WAW

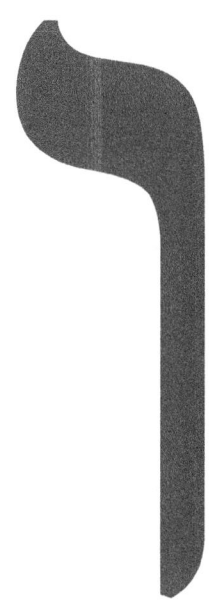

תשרקצפעסנמלכיטחזוהדגבא

The twenty-two letters of light are arranged going from right to left:
Aleph, Bet, Gimel, Dalet, Hay, Vav, Zayin, Chet, Tet, Yod, Kaf,
Lamed, Mem, Nun, Samech, Ayin, Pay, Tzadi, Kuf, Resh, Shin, and Tav.

English—W, O, and U.
Numerical value is 6.
According to the Bible, humankind was created on day 6.

The "sixth day" of creation is called Yom Shishi. It is called Friday
on the Gregorian calendar. This is how we write it using the letters of
light: יום ששי

Shish-shee, shishshiy, means overplus beyond five on the fingers of the hand. From root word Suws, soos.

The letters of light are Shin, Yud, and Shin. A prime root to be bright (i.e., cheerful, be glad, greatly, joy, make mirth, rejoice). The understanding given to the writer: **Steadfastness is in humankind when words of wisdom are chosen. Humankind brings bright light and life to the earth.**

Vav is a hook or connector—like the word "*and*." If we look at the letters of light for the word "*and*" we get A= **aleph**—the breath of life, N= **nun**, promise seeds or life given seeds—*and* life, love, and light is the D= **dalet**—doorway to inner peace.

Vav can also be a chute (conveying information from higher to lower levels) that connects the heavens *and* the earth. "Receive truth to all you that love life **and** our Creator." Aleph to Tav.

When you are connected to heaven (our Creator) you can work in the world and be joyful. When you are connected from within, you don't fall down here below. We are humble (mature) like the perfect nature we were created from.

North, south, *east*, west, above *and* below = six directions. The number six represents completion on earth because something that is surrounded on all six sides is complete, balanced, *and* mature (perfection).

We know that the first day of creation represents all days even to present time—no special day, like Sabbath or Sunday, as each day we rest in love, life, light, and peace—no division of days existed, so no man-made religion needed—only love, life, and light for our planet. Because of humankind's poor choices, religion was created to gain back what they had lost, the power of love, life, and light. If we look into the Bible's six days of creation, we can observe each of the six millennia *and* its corresponding life choices **and** consequences for that era.

The first day of creation is *Chessed—the character of kindness.* checed, kheh-sed' toward our Creator—piety, root word to have respect and humility and love of all things created—letters of light are Chet,

Samech, and Dalet. The meaning given to the writer: **the letter of life has an eternal doorway to love because of humility and light.**

This was the day written, "Let there be light." (Owr or Ore, **East** as being the region of light = light). This light is bright. We are children of light because we belong to the day (dawn to sunset, daylight hours), so let the light created by our Creator shine through you with deeds of kindness.

In the first thousands years, man had enormous lifespans—example—Adam lived for 930 years—the concept of *Chessed* thus represents kindness. Endowing man with kindness **and** plants, herbs, **and** fruit of the trees for food.

The second day of creation is imbued with *Gevurah, contraction, and judgment.* By the second millennia, man needed a new word to describe his unhealthy choices, judgment, for he had lost discernment. Discernment is from the tree of life where as judgment is from the tree of knowledge of good **and** evil.

Judgment using the Aleph-Tav is mishpat, mish-pawt—a verdict, a **sentence** or formal decree, to be judged, from prime root sha-phat, shaw-fat, to vindicate or to judge that is pronounce a *sentence*. The letters of light are Mem, Shin, Pay, and Tet. The understanding given to the writer: **the words we speak and think about, either attract light or darkness, attracts health or disease, your choice.**

This millennia or day was the time that separated the pervasive waters into the higher *and* lower realms. Historically, the second thousand years was harsh judgment leveled against the inhabitants of the world. According to scripture, Noah's flood *and* the tower of Babel fall into this time: **And** look how judgment comes but from a *sentence*, a set of words that is complete in itself conveying a statement, question, exclamation or command, that express the mind's condition.

Love, life, and light is truth *and* without iniquity, just *and* perfect is our Creator. "They that plow iniquity *and* sow wickedness, reap the same." "For the time has come that truth must begin at the house of each: **and** if it first begins at us, what shall the end be of them who make unhealthy choices that obey not the truth of peace **and** harmony." "Who shall not fear our Creator, **and** esteem love, life, and light within? Love is kind **and** beautiful: for all nations shall come ***singing and dancing*** with love in their hearts." (Return to the garden **and** eat according to the law of love.)

    <u>**The third day of creation**</u> is a day of *Tiferes—beauty **and** mercy.*

    *Beauty using the letters of light are Tiph'arah, tif-aw-raw means ornament, bravery, glorious, honor, majesty, or tif-eh-reth. Prime root from pa'ar, paw-ar—to gleam that is embellish, beautiful foliage, be sweet— letters of light are Tav, Pay, Aleph, Resh, **and** Hay.* The understanding given to the writer: **our Creator reveals truth to the leaders in a home, to imprint the beauty in the minds of creation (male and female— children), the revelation of love, life, and light.**

    On this day, the flowers, plants, grasses, **and** trees were created, together with all the colors **and** sounds of the universe. According to the biblical account the third millennium saw a merciful hand in the freeing of the Israelites from Egypt ***and*** giving of instruction of life.

    Keep in mind our Creator, "Love born within" sets us free.

    The first five books of the Bible are called Tiferes, or beauty.

    Beauty is not monochromatic (one color) or monotone (one tone); it is brought together by blending ***and*** harmonizing various colors **and** sounds: music. Thus our Creator's instruction is a harmonious blend of healthy words ***and*** a coming together of the eternal ***and*** physical elements of creation. Blessed are those doing the law of love so that the authority of peace shall be theirs.

    <u>**The fourth day of creation**</u> is *Netzach, victory **and** endurance. Victory using the Aleph-Tav is netsach, neh'tsakh, the bright object at a distance travelled toward, splendor, **and** truthfulness, or confidence, perpetual, strength.* Prime root to glitter from a far (i.e., to be eminent, to be permanent), from t'shuw ah, tesh-oo-aw in the sense of rescue national or spiritual deliverance, help, safety, salvation. From a prime root to be free shava, shaw-vah (for help [i.e., freedom from some trouble, cry (aloud) out, shout]). Light letters are Nun, Tzadi, ***and*** Chet.

The understanding given to the writer: **the life given seed overcomes darkness within to regain freedom and love toward our Creator! Born from within***!*

In the Bible it is written that the two luminaries were made in the heavens, the greater light *and* the lesser light **and** the stars. The greater light to rule the day *and* the lesser light to rule the night. "Let them be for signs, appointed times—mo'edim, days *and* years." What was first created has never changed *and* when seen with no darkness by the children of light they receive endurance and victory over all life conditions, errors **and** see the lunisolar calendar as truth with the first day, having all things created in it and then just a repeat of the first day up until now—present time.

Our Creator knew humankind and their inadequacies toward life but love never stops life and light. Our Creator continues to love them throughout all generations. In creation humankind will always find love, life, and light. Every day the sun comes up **and** goes down for the day cycle **and** then the moon with its continuous illuminations **and** stars appear to rule the night. The trees, plants, **and** flowers sway with the wind, the animals live according to the law of nature, **and** the fish **and** birds sing **and** splash the perfectness of harmony.

The fifth day of creation is Hod—acknowledge **and** can also mean devastation.

Acknowledge using the Aleph-Tav is—nakar, naw-kar—a prime root to scrutinize (i.e., look intently at, hence with recognition, be acquainted with, care for, respect, **and** revere). From yada, yaw-dah a prime root to know advice, answer, appoint. The letters of light—Nun, Kaph, **and** Resh. The understanding given to the writer: **The life given seed is known for their love, life, and light and is the head and not the tail. The tail, immature, receives the same potential for power using love, life, and light**.

Destruction using the Aleph-Tav is m'huwman, meh-hoo-maw—confusion or uproar from kuwm, hoom, prime root to make an uproar, agitate greatly keh'teb, qetab to cut off, ruin. The letters of light are Mem, Hay, Vav, Mem, and Hay. The understanding given to the writer: **The Aleph-Tav reveals the revelation of love, life, and light: the Aleph-Tav, our Creator, is the revelation.**

In the Bible this is the day of "sea monsters" *and* the ocean began to swarm with creatures. Birds began to fly in the sky. The fifth millennium was a generation of massacres, expulsions, *and* horrific difficulties for many people.

The sixth day of creation is Yesod, yacad, means building a foundation **and** bonding.

Foundation using the Aleph-Tav is Yacad, Yaw-sad a prime root to set, to found, to sit down together (i.e., settle, consult, appoint, take counsel, establish, instruct, **and** ordain). The letters of light are Yud, Samech, and Dalet. The understanding given to the writer: **our Creator who starts all things is the eternal circle, with words of love. These words of love open the door for bonding—that is, teaching and communication of wisdom.**

According to what is written in the Bible, the sixth day is when Adam, the first man, the beginning of humankind, was created. Our Creator first fashioned the entire world *and* then brought humankind into it. From this we learn that it is humankind's desire to form a connection or bond between the material *and* the eternal realms by using every aspect of the physical world in the service of the law of love. The children of light dress themselves with speech that beautifies the earth. Thus it is up to us to increase in acts of perfectness *and* kindness in thought, speech, **and** action.

Let's look at the cause of expulsion from the Garden of Eden—what was the attraction that led to an unhealthy choice **and** its consequence? (Nu.11:1–35, pg. **152**).

To commit idolatry, physically or mentally is to use the power of uniting love in the wrong way (mixing darkness with light—what is an example of mixing darkness with light?). Having an intimate relationship with a person that does not love light or has no desire for healthy choices in foods and speech. This is mixing truth with unhealthy darkness.

You might lust by greed, have envy, anger, or jealousy, which are wrong things to have because they cause unhealthy consequences. These are all forms of idolatry. Our Creator does not create envy, anger, lust or fear, we cause them by our own thoughts, speech, **and** actions that go against our Creator. Any action we perform is a transformation (a change in form or appearance) of forces, whether we see it or not. This is the power of your words, actions, *and* thoughts, also found within your body language. The forces of the mind are empowered by the desire to unite. That means we all have a natural nature that desires to engage with words to develop a relationship with things or people. This could be a desire for relationship with a child, spouse, garden, animal, flowers, business, friends, or anything that means something to you, even a car—remember, all things have vibrations **and** are affected by love. If things are breaking down around you, check your love within and toward those things.

Our Creator created us to have a relationship, **first** with love *and* then with others *and* things. Love with all your heart, mind, *and* being, *and* second, do unto others with that same capacity of love that you have toward our Creator.

This intimate relationship with our Creator was lost when Adam *and* Eve chose in thought, speech, and action to go against the law of love. They lost that intimate relationship, connection with our Creator because of a desire for another kind of relationship that was not based upon the law of love. According to the written word of the Bible, Adam **and** Eve were instructed to not eat from the tree of knowledge of good **and** evil. When you use your mind in the wrong way, you are taking potential love forces (the tail) from within you *and* directing those forces in a way to confuse others, therefore, going against our Creator of love. In the Bible, this is called "blasphemy, profane talk, **and** purposeful dishonor." It is to use those forces in the wrong way *and* commit a crime, not only against ourselves, but against the Creator forming within you **and** others. The consequence most always develops into disease of some kind when continually performed. So yes, you can commit idolatry by watching television, movies, texting, games, hobbies, sports, exercising, reading books, drugs, fantasizing, day dreaming, homosexual activity, *and* overeating. Idolatry occurs when you use those forces to cause an unnatural "DESIRE," that is lust, outside of the law of love, life, and light—when the women saw that the fruit from the tree of <u>knowledge</u> of good **and** evil was good for food, that it had a pleasing appearance *and* that the tree was **desirable** for making one wise (however, Hasatan said she would know good **and** evil not wisdom, here, she already misunderstood Hasatan's speech), she took some of the fruit *and* ate it. A **desire that was outside of the relationship to our Creator** was the unhealthy choice that brought them out of the garden (love, life, and light) *and* into the world. So **desire** for relationships that are not from our Creator gives us consequences of suffering, disease, and plagues with short life spans. Here we will find "pagan ways of all kind" from the nations, tongue, **and** people outside the law of love of creation.

Do not partake of the tree of <u>knowledge</u> of good *and* evil. Eat from the tree of life—love, light, **and** perfectness *and* mercy will follow you all the days of your life. Be so very thankful for the truth **and** the simplicity of life with the new light of freedom. We are forever blessed **and** "one."

We are a VAV **and** with the truth, an awakened family of love, life, and light.

When we truly love our Creator, the consuming power of our Creator connects to the true perfection within so that the home/temple/body is *ahad* (one).

Return to creation: gaining wisdom is to turn **and** to turn is to reconnect. You can give hugs, say sorry, but until you return to our Creator there is no true teshuva—so no lasting connection. Reconnect = return!

Give back what you have stolen—"a person's character"—Greek mindset says, "I will never do it again"; however, Hebrew mindset says, "credit system"—what is the requirement—what will this cost me? Return 70×7 to that person or the land—have the truth direct you in love's way. You will be given many chances to return wholeness to the character/person/land you destroyed with your **words** when you were unconscious of the effects it had on you *and* the person or land.

Start today—if you hear truth, look at the words you have said throughout your life *and* think *and* say only wisdom's words! Start today! Make a list with healthy words on one side **and** unhealthy on the other. You will become the overcomer with beautiful feet that publishes peace **and** truth.

An oversize Vav marks the center of the entire Torah (Leviticus 11:42 pg. **115**), appropriately enough, the word in which this Vav occurs is *gachon, gaw-khone,* meaning the external abdomen, "BELLY," as the source of the fetus. The letters of light are Gimel, Chet, Vav, and Nun. The understanding given to the writer: **we travel victoriously in life as we stay connected to love, life, and light to bring forth fruit from the fertile loam soil.** We end with this because what we eat physically **and** eternally does affect our belly **and** heart!

Who is this? "On your belly you are to go **and** eat dust all the days of your life."

Be careful of the food you eat as the food will bring forth its kind, connections, **and** consequences.

Eight affirmations for the letter VAV

1. Love **and** memory has healed our heart; we are one **and** connected.
2. Humility is what bonds us forever, keeps us alive, **and** enlarges the word of love.
3. Speaking truth from the heart is accomplished by love of self **and** discernment of the Aleph-Tav.
4. The tongue to the body is a small member—be thankful in thought, word, **and** action.
5. Out of the belly flows rivers of kindness **and** perfection.
6. In our greatest trials we will speak perfectness **and** kindness showered from the Creator formed within.
7. Return to truth and words of wisdom for we are forever awake **and** joined.
8. We are not ashamed; the fifth-dimensional kiss healed our heart **and** mind.

Agape Love

Nothing could be more refreshing than to view heart love in action.
The freedom of the wise **and** born within revives **and** gives us passion.
Our Creator loves all, bringing peace **and**
memory to today's adulterated fashions.
Humility is a covenant love relationship between
male **and** female in subjection.
Families can grow **and** reproduce a healthy kind. For heart love
is learned within the home no matter the world's rejection.
Daily rest **and** reaching out keeps marriage whole, a
healthy relationship with no inward opposition.
Remember our Creator made male **and** female to cleave
to one another so both would not feel alone,
And then pronounced love, life, and light in a single day
and what was in them, another name for their home.
So what have we learned in these few words of wisdom,
Our Creator's love shows no division
And our love choices in life bring eternal perfection.

Cry Baby and White Rose

For one month, it had not rained. The weather was the main subject that everyone was talking about. White Rose, better known as Violet Lucille, **and** Brown Dirt, better known as Keith, were sensitive to the concerns of the townspeople. They, too, discussed the weather.

"Don't you find the weather more hot **and** dry today than yesterday?" questioned Violet Lucille.

"Yes, as a matter of fact, I am burning," cried Keith. "If I become any dryer, I will surely turn into dust **and** be blown away by the wind."

"Oh, that really sounds terrible!" exclaimed Violet Lucille.

As Keith danced around, he said, "Let's do a little rain dance. Perhaps we can make it rain."

"No," replied Violet Lucille. "I would rather wait for Cry Baby, better known as Yvonne. Maybe she will visit today."

Keith did not like her answer. He was angry about the weather, as it was, **and** was in no mood of comforting a crybaby.

"I need real rain, not tears!" shouted Keith as he marched off toward town.

"Look over there by the tree. Here comes Yvonne now." It was too late. Keith was already out of hearing distance.

"Boo-hoo, boo-hoo, boo-hoo!" cried Yvonne. "No one listens to me. Boo-hoo, boo-hoo, boo-hoo."

As Yvonne neared the garden, Violet Lucille wrapped her soft petals gently around her. Violet Lucille gave off her most fragrant smell, which helped Yvonne to be comforted. However, the tears continued to flow as Yvonne's heart was hurt from the ways of the world.

Violet Lucille's color was shiny like velvet silk **and** bright as the midday light. Yvonne took notice **and** began to peer into the flower's center. As she looked, her tears dried up, **and** on her nose landed a ladybug. This made Yvonne start to laugh **and** giggle. The ladybug tickled Yvonne, which distracted her long enough so she could find joy in just being in nature.

Yvonne was very happy now **and** began to move around the garden eating the many colorful berries. As she crossed the cucumber row, she found a bunny eating fresh, tasty lettuce leaves. No manner where Yvonne went, she felt heart love from all the animals **and** plants that enjoyed the quiet of the garden.

As she passed by Violet Lucille again, she acknowledged the beauty that our Creator made for mankind to enjoy. She said to Violet Lucille, "You are the most perfect flower I have ever seen," while giving her nose one long last sniff.

Remember, kindness **and** being thankful go together like a gardener's glove to the hand.

Where do you go to be comforted **and** feel the blessings of our Creator?

CHAPTER 7

ZAYIN

תשרקצפעסנמלכיטחזוהדגבא

The twenty-two letters of light are arranged going from right to left:
Aleph, Bet, Gimel, Dalet, Hay, Vav, Zayin, Chet, Tet, Yod, Kaf,
Lamed, Mem, Nun, Samech, Ayin, Pay, Tzadi, Kuf, Resh, Shin, and Tav.

Seventth letter with the numerical value of 7.
English letter z—pronounced "Zah-Yeen" and has the sound
as in zebra.

The seventh day of creation is called seventh-day rest. It is called
Saturday or Sabbath on the Gregorian calendar. This is how we write

Yom Shabbat using the letters of light: יום שבת—**or simply** שבת. The letters of light are Tav, Bet, and Shin. The understanding given to the writer: **our Creator's creation is manifested in the body/temple that has been cleansed by the breath of truth.**

Zayin means the symbol of authority of a king, scepter, and perfection.

A Yud on top of the letter Vav. The woman of valor is the crown of her husband.

Considered a "crowned" Vav. Just as Vav represents "**yashar**" straight light from our Creator to humankind, so Zayin represents "**chozer,**" or returning light, on every day to the one who gave it, our Creator. We return the light back to the universe as we live out our lives in love, truth, and peace every day. In other words, we are acknowledging our Creator's perfectness by our thoughts and speech and the actions we do each day.

Just as a woman of valor is the crown of her husband, so Zayin is the crown for Vav. In other words, keeping and guarding your rest time, after the sun goes down, each day is the peace and harmony from our Creator to the world. No sunlight means it is time to rest the body and mind. We actually are kept from darkness and unhealthy choices when we honor our Creator's time of rest. Remember, our Creator knew that humankind would not remember lunisolar time. Inventors developed artificial light that has given humankind a false light and says that this is progress. Progress for humankind to work twenty-four hours without rest. Humankind did not see the later consequences that would develop over the years that would harm the body and mind. Our genealogy lines would be contaminated and mixed with false traditions and doctrine by the broken-off branches of truth. The little game we play as children is exactly what happened to the word of love from our Creator. Give a child three words in his or her ear and have ten people in a line give the same words that they hear to the next in line (generation) and see what words come out at the end of the game (present time). Thankful for the truth revealed by being humble to those "born from within" that have discernment of what is spoken and the truth that is passed to the children of light, overcomers, today. Return to creation, enjoy its beauty, and love its life and simplicity.

Zayin means to cut, plow through.

The Gematria of Zayin is seven, which is the same value for "**Binah**," which means using the Aleph-Tav —*understanding*. So you could say that we receive understanding and wisdom at time of rest as we show our love for our Creator by guarding this time each day. We see love moving, uniting, and bringing all the pieces of creation to completion at the end of a day. Even though our Creator created and finished all in the beginning, we, too, once "born from within," must see completion at this time of day called rest as we have become perfect male and female, children of light.

Zayin is a paradoxical word—(self-contradictory), since it means weapon or sword but derives from a root word that means sustenance or nourishment. But how is food or nourishment related to the sword? Notice that the word for bread using the Aleph-Tav is **lechem, lekh-em,** meaning to feed, to consume, to battle, to destroy, to devour, to eat, to overcome, to prevail, and to make war—letters of light are Lamed, Chet, and closed Mem. The understanding given to the writer: **the teachings of life require words that close off error or unhealthy choices**. Lechem is contained in the Aleph-Tav word for war **Milchamah,** mil-khaw-maw, which means fighting, a battle, engagement, warfare—letters of light are Mem, Lamed, Chet, Mem, and Hay. The meaning given to the writer: **The word of love breathes wisdom of life and new beginnings. We receive light as revelation leads to nourishment and life.**

The sword of war is often needed for our nourishment, not in the since of vindictive fighting that is based on lust for power over others, but in the eternal since that to be nourished and at rest we must daily war against the fleshiness in our own bodies to obtain our Creator's rest, peace and tranquility. If we know the one and only law of love and guard it then we achieve daily REST and peace by the understanding of pure truth.

We see that the letters of light consist of 3 × 7 letters =21 with the last letter 22-Tav as eternity. Even though the numerical value to each of the letters are increasing in value—the actual day each were created always represents the first day, one. The last letter of light will be the strongest toward perfection and probably a higher pitch to the sound of the word causing a person to stop and meditate. The understanding given to the writer: **Rest with awakened breath will purify the life given seed with our Creator's love, life, and light** and expose error.

What happens when humankind changes dates or reckoning of time that invalidates what our Creator set up in the beginning? Like the change that happened to our time of rest. Humankind made a religion to support their control of time.

1. Catholics worship on the Sunday in honor of the resurrection. This is in accordance with the act of Constantine, which changed the observance from a lunisolar-calculated Passover to the pagan, solar-calculated Easter.

2. Jews worship on Saturday because Talmudic law justifies the act of keeping one day in seven—when one does not know when the True Sabbath falls.

3. Most Protestants join with Catholics in worshipping on Sunday, the first day of the modern Gregorian week, assuming it is the day of the resurrection.

4. Saturday Sabbath keeping Protestants worship on Saturday because it is the seventh day of the modern Gregorian week and they assume since the Jews worship on Saturday, it must be the Biblical Sabbath.

5. Muslins, likewise, honor the pagan papal Gregorian calendar-keeping by going to masque for prayer on Friday. The above five examples are taken from World's Last Chance.

Zayin and remembrance

The word time is spelled zman**, pronounced zem-awn-**meaning season, an appointed occasion, light letters are Zayin, Mem, and final Nun—**Daily rest time brings healing words to all generations, those that listen to pure truth.**

The word time using the Aleph-Tav begins with Zayin, as does the word remember—Zacher, pronounced Zakar, Zaw-kar—means a prime root to mark, to mention, think on. Letters of light are Zayin, Chet, and Resh—The understanding given to the writer: **The time of rest is life to the ones that have returned to our Creator of us all** and Zicharon (remembrance) the memory of this time is the basis for your destiny and your purpose in life here on the earth. Remember the days of old (creation, once born from within) remember to keep rest time with joy. Those that return to our Creator will have memory! Memory has the letter of light Mem in it which relates to the words of truth!

THE OVERSIZE ZAYIN

Since Zayin represents a penetration and strength of the word, remembering our Creator and the laws of creation will bring back peace to all nature, perfect harmony and balance.

Zayin brings life through the sword causing light to overpower darkness of the ego and nourishment through the sword of the words of truth that we keep.

Zayin breaks up ground for the purpose of bringing forth mature seeds—this means that it breaks away old traditions, lifestyles, lies, and religious beliefs so that the truth of our Creator can develop in us.

Zayin cuts deep into the soul to cut out what is not love, life, and light so that new birth may mature. Nothing new can grow if the old lies/traditions/habits are not removed. This is an unhealthy cycle and needs to stop! Can you fill a cup with pure water if the cup remains half filled with well water? You could pour the pure into the well, but then there would be confusion and mixing of truth with error. Get rid of the well water so that the fresh water can nourish and grow eternal truth.

Get rid of the unhealthy water—"everyone drinking from this water will thirst again, but whoever drinks of the water of love shall certainly never thirst. And the water that shall become in him is a fountain of water springing up into everlasting life" and keep your eyes fixed and unmovable upon our Creator and the pure words of love which is your sword of truth.

Zayin means daily rest time, recommit yourself to our Creator by guarding this time of day, rest or sleep—this is liken to a treasured time which we experience every day and not every week. We gather in, even if it is only you, and keep that time of day in peace.

Some have made our Creator common and not cherished. Bringing love down to their level or fleshy vibration of love. Our Creator gave mankind fruit and vegetable to eat as all flesh is not met for humankind to consume! This is not about the taste, tradition, or possible illness from the flesh—once you understand truth, you love because **our Creator provided mankind with fruit, herbs, and vegetables** and for no other reason. Eating fruit and vegetables remains in effect today, but who will observe it? Remember, there is a consequence from this law of love when we forget—disease, pain, and short life.

An apple a day keeps the doctor away! These are words from the tree of knowledge of good and evil. Our Creator gave us all fruit and vegetables to eat and herbs for our health. We need no doctor if we are eating from the table of creation. We fast when our body does not feel well.

Now let us look at the word *apple*. The following Aleph-Tav words were under the word *apple* in the concordance. Iyshown, pronounced ee-shone, meaning to be extant, the little man of the eye, the pupil or ball hence the middle (of night) black, obscure from Iysh, pronounced eesh, letters of light are Aleph, Yud, Shin, Vav, and final Nun. The understanding given to the writer: **the breath of life, our Creator, begins the cleaning of humankind and their polluted seeds because of unhealthy choices.** Next word using the Aleph-Tav for apple is babah, pronounced baw-baw, means to hollow out (as a gate) that is the pupil of the eye-apple [of the eye] letters of light are Bet, Bet, and

Hay. The understanding given to the writer: **the house, our body, is cleaned through love, life, and light—pure revelation.**

The next Aleph-Tav word is bath, meaning a daughter, branch, company, owl, town, village.

Next is Ben, pronounced bane for male—son, builder of family.

Next is Banah, pronounced baw-naw—female prime root to build, obtain children, make, and repair.

The last word under apple using the letters of light is naphach, pronounced naw-fakh, a prime root to puff, to inflate, blow hard, scatter, kindle, expire, to disesteem, <u>cause to loose life</u>. Letters of light are Nun, Pay, and Chet. The understanding given to the writer: **The seed that speaks life will be awakened from Adam's unhealthy choice, who ate from the tree of knowledge of good and evil, darkness, and led to unconscious behavior**.

We have been taught that a fence or boundaries are not allowing us freedom in the world today—however, the fence and law of love keeps us safe and protected. Do not eat of the tree of knowledge of good and evil! Instead, keep our Creator's love in you! Eat from the tree of Life.

White pages = while fire represents the word of our living Creator— Black letters mean nothing except that they are placed on the Ra'ock, white fire. When we read pure words we are literally watching perfect love bring alive the word of our Creator, to the reader. This is better seen out doors in the environment. Here is another reason to be in the process of "born from within." If not eternally born, the words in the scripture will not sing and dance of light, but be read without conviction, life, or understanding (discernment). The words will bring confusion and misunderstanding to the reader! Creation and not written books has abundant life that will keep humankind healthy, wealthy, and wise.

Many beings have come to break down false traditions and to restore perfect discernment and truth. Our Creator has raised up love to protect you. Now your responsibility is to keep and guard pure love, life, and light—plain and simple.

Follow the lunisolar calendar to find the truth of the calendar of creation, but understand that the rest day occurs every day. The greater-lesser light calendar shows time calculated by the moon's movement.

The moons lumination is how we count days, months, and years. The new moon starts each month.

Translation day is always the thirtieth on a lunar month. Translation day is an astronomical tern, not found in scripture. However, the fact the Biblical months were based on cycles of the new moon is sufficient proof they existed in the biblical calendar. A lunation is 29.5 days long. A lunation is never less than twenty-nine days or more than thirty days. Again, the thirtieth day of lunation is called a translation day, and it falls at the end of the lunar cycle called the "black moon," when the moon cannot be seen. Originally all ancient calendars were lunisolar with an interrupted weekly cycle. The weekly cycle restarted at the beginning of the month lunation or at the beginning of the year following five intercalated days that closed the previous year. These five intercalary days are not part of any weekly cycle.

The first and thirtieth are not a part of the seven-day cycle but are counted in that month. The beginning of each month started with the new moon day and not counted in the weekly cycle.

The new moon starts a new cycle of four weeks.

Eight affirmations for letter Zayin

1. Our Creator's love when placed within us brings wisdom of perfect presence.

2. Completion means life, and life more abundantly. Love is our comfort.

3. A being's nature that expresses love has been perfected.

4. A whole life in perfect loving presence—what! Shama, hear! The true blessings of rest and peace.

5. Our work is done, so we rest each day at the natural time. Peace and truth.

6. Go inside, close your mind to movement and thought, breath, and relax, at time of rest.

7. Our Creator is like nourishment to the body. Love is proclaimed in our walk; our DNA is clean.

8. The crown of love is placed on our head, amen, amen, and amen. Hallelujah for memory.

Rest

This time of day is set apart,
For cleansing and nourishing our humble hearts.
This time of day brings us physical rest,
Keeping our humble temples as a crowned guest.
Our cup of pure juice brings the cleansing light to our head,
Cultivated by homebuilder's loving hands; let it be said or read.
The food we eat each day is likened to the
latter rains falling from above.
In our homes, no gum chewing, candy, or any adulterated
food claims residence, this is truth and perfect love.
The nursery provides safety, security, and healthy treats,
the love songs sung are the children's meat.
The young women who respect their mothers
keep their inner beauty and modesty;
By pleasing their fathers with proper dress, clean
hair, and taking full responsibility.
The young men who honor their fathers adore their mothers,
By listening, loving, and serving others.
Understanding the Lunisolar calendar brings nature's singing truth,
Just as daily rest is our Creator's unchanging love and perfect proof.

Red Apple and the Truth

The wind was whistling through the thick apple tree orchard. The mosquito-hawks darted in and out playing the game of hide-and-go-seek.

Eve's thoughts were innocent but active so that she could absorb all that was going on around her.

Soon the time would come for all of Eve's children to emerge and how happy they would be. For all the little seeds would turn into big mature children just like you and me.

Eve, then, returned to the time when she was a seed and the feeling of finally being free from her mother's stomach. That feeling was such a great relief.

Now she is grown and feels as if she is faced with wanting to be free again. But free from what?

Wasn't that what everyone talked about and wanted? To be free and to know their purpose in life.

Eve's mother even said that she would understand freedom and her purpose when she was all grown up. Here she is all grown up physically, with her children on their way to adulthood, and she is still left feeling like a child without an answer to her question.

As Eve watched her family living their life with little understanding, she thought, "They do not know the answer to life either." After that depressing thought, Eve decided not to talk to anyone. As she closed her eyes to think and ponder, she was rudely disturbed by Lucifer's voice.

"How are you feeling today, Eve? You look sad and tired!" voiced Lucifer.

"I am neither sad nor tired. I am waiting for the answer to my question that I ask every day," answered Eve.

"When will I be free?"

Lucifer declared, "There is no such thing as being free. You will always be like you are and so will everyone else. You cannot change!"

Eve closed her eyes and pretended not to see or hear Lucifer. He was a grumbler and faultfinder.

Jacob yelled out from the upstairs window, "Boy, if we get any more rain, I am sure that our houses will all be destroyed!"

Lucifer replied, "I do agree with you. Too bad you don't have the power to make it stop!"

Lucifer and Jacob continued talking about the weather while Eve retired to her bedroom for meditation.

"I want my freedom! When will I know that it has finally happened to me," she prayed with deep sincerity.

For the rest of that day, she devoted her time in silence and requested for truth to be revealed.

Early next morning Eve was awakened by the horrible sound of thunder and lightning.

The sky was as black as a cat crying out with rage. The raindrops were as big as basketballs and were smashing all living things.

Eve was convicted and knew that she desperately needed to believe and have total faith in her Creator to direct her life.

At that moment, through the understanding of the new light of her Creator, Eve submitted her life to pure truth.

She was sure of her purpose on Earth and could best help others by loving our Creator with all her heart and being.

Now she was ready to confront the rain, the thunder and lightning and the dreadful blackness that still remained. As she confronted the rain, the raindrops stopped, and it left the afternoon air smelling like fresh honeysuckles. She knew her thoughts were purified.

When she confronted the thunder and lightning, it stopped too. What came shining through that dark black sky was nothing better than the bright yellow sun. This miracle reminded her that she was perfectly loved by her Creator.

And at last it was time to look at that dreadful darkness that the sky continued to have. When Eve did take that look, not only did the sky turn as blue as heaven but she was instantly released from the hold that the world had on her.

Thereafter, eternal Eve taught and helped others with a love that only our Creator could give to her. She knew she had been "born from within."

Everlasting peace and rest are the true blessings for all humankind! Remember, "let your light shine!"

CHAPTER 8

CHET

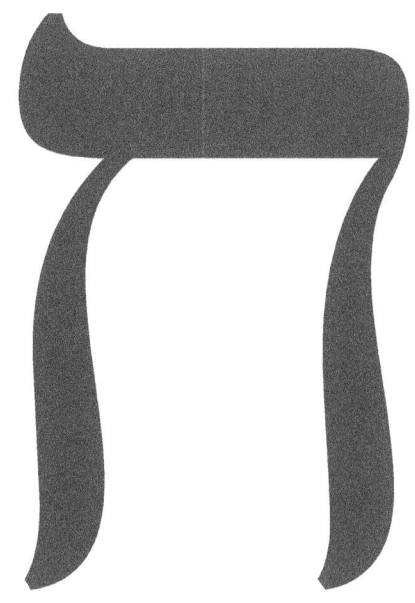

תשרקצפעסנמלכיטחזוהדגבא

The twenty-two letters of light are arranged going from right to left:
Aleph, Bet, Gimel, Dalet, Hay, Vav, Zayin, Chet, Tet, Yod, Kaf,
Lamed, Mem, Nun, Samech, Ayin, Pay, Tzadi, Kuf, Resh, Shin, and Tav.

Eighth letter of light.
Gematria or numerical value = 8.
If counting a weekly cycle according to present-day calendars,
we are now repeating the first day of creation. Yom Rishon, the other
two light letters that fall on this day are Aleph and Samech. Meaning

given to the writer: **our Creator gives us eternal life, so listen to wisdom's voice of love!**

English = H, rhymes with *met* or *mate* and has the sound of *ch* as in *bach*.

This is the light letter that **represents life.**

Letter of life chay, pronounced khah'ee or chayim, pronounced khah'im, means alive, hence raw, fresh, strong, life or living thing, appetite (wild beast, company, congregation from chayah, pronounced khaw-yaw a prime root to live whether lit. or fig., to revive, give life, nourish up, preserve, quicken, recover, repair, restore to life, be whole). The Light letters are Chet, Yud, and Hay. The understanding given to the writer: <u>life at the beginning of creation has the truth and the revelation of perfect light</u>. True life comes from Chasidut—which means devotion, aleph-tav word charam, pronounced khaw-ram, a prime root to seclude, to devote to the Creator's work, consecrate— Light letters are Chet, Resh, Mem. The understanding given to the writer: **life is in the heads and in the leaders of those that speak truth, words of love, life, and light**.

Chet is (the number of grace, using the aleph-tav grace is spelled Chen, pronounced khane from graciousness that is kindness, favor, pleasant, precious, well favored from chanan, pronounced—khaw-nan—means to bend or stoop in kindness, to favor, meditate, make supplication. Light letters are Chet, Nun, and Nun. The understanding given to the writer: **life is found through humility and expands the seeds of love!**

And the word wisdom spelled with light letters chokhmah, pronounced khok-maw—means, skillful, wisely in mind, word, or act, exceeding, teach wisdom, deal wisely. Light letters are Chet, Khaf, and Mem. The understanding given to the writer: **life by the blessed is the word of truth delivered in nature's sounds.**

Both grace and wisdom have the Gematria that equals eight. So we have grace, wisdom, and life—what a merry trio.

Gematria of Chet: Since Chet is formed from Vav (6) and Zayin (7) one Gematria value would be thirteen, the same value as ahavah—which means love. It is also the value for echad—which means one. Putting these ideas together, we can see that love unifies us in true fellowship, just as our Creator's wisdom taught us.

Chet is the number of **new beginnings**

- Brit milah—using light letters means the covenant of circumcision which occurs on the eighth day.

- There were eight souls saved—mabul hagadol, which means great flood, in Noah's day.

- David was the eighth son of Jesse—when the prophet came to anoint David as king, his father did not call David from tending the sheep because he did not think David worthy of this high calling. He also looked different than all the rest of his sons (1 Sam 16:1–13, pg. **297**).

Object lesson: How do we discern? Telescope—what part of the body do you use to see? Eye—light letter Ayin, ah-yin, an eye, a fountain (as the eye of the landscape) outward appearance, color, conceit, be content, countenance, humble, knowledge, look, sight. Greek spelling—ophthalmos, pronounced—of-thal-mos, the eye, vision, envy (from the jealous side glance) eyesight to stare at, to discern clearly, to attend, to experience, to appear, behold, perceive, see, take heed. Not only by sight do we see but by all vibrations of the Universe. The higher the awareness of the human race the greater the light breaks through the darkness.

Chet is the letter that represents **discipleship**. Love leads and teaches us on the pathway of life.

A yolk is a connection between two people so that they move and work together. Since the sum of the letters Vav and Zayin equals the value for love, we can see that the essential nature of this moving and working together is that of loving our Creator first and with that capacity of love, we love one another.

Today, when speaking, we are the present time living scriptures—we are not willing to be yolked to anything other than love, life, and light, which is found in our Creator. We started as a lost people connected to darkness; however, love works through people—love does not call us to be independent oxen—that will destroy peace and harmony. People of all kind are yolked together and walk in unity—result power in the word of love. Listen to those yolked to our Creator and watch the awakening grow. Remember, the truth about rest and you will not be led astray.

The Creator's law of rest are known by those that understand love, life, and light and treasures this daily time.

Conclusion

Chet is the letter that separates and connects at the same time.

It follows the plow of the word of truth that drives deep into humankind and separates even bone and marrow.

Chet makes things clear! Life has no darkness! As written in nature, remember, our Creator "separated the light from the darkness."

In the garden was there a need for a fence? No.

But when humankind chose unhealthy choices, then they were removed from the garden of protection, and churb's (imaginary figure) were placed to guard the tree of life . This is a fence.

What does that mean to us today? Choose you this day life, the garden of protection, so that darkness flees from your thoughts and the truth becomes clear, beautiful, and treasured. No need for stories or words that cover truth because life has given you the inner eye to see. An awakened being or child of light. Go outside and view nature!

The words of peace, rest and truth have become the only fence of protection adored by those that love life and light.

In past history, The Holy of Holies was protected by a fence of curtains and is likened to the words of peace that protects us today.

Curtain using the light letters is spelled y-riy-ah, pronounced yer-ee-aw, a hanging (as tremulous quivering, timid or nervous) from yara, pronounced Yaw-rah, means a prime root to be broken up with any violent action. That is to fear. Light letters are Yod, Resh, Yod, Ayin, and Chet. The understanding given to the writer: **the beginning of all things is located in the head and has the power from wisdom, using heart love, to gain LIFE even to unwanted destruction.**

We were one of the nations steeped in traditions and idols. We forgot our Creator along with the true rest time and how to heal from the law of love. Remember to walk without shoes in the loam soil to connect with truth.

The closer we move in, toward the pure truth, the closer to our Creator's presence and peace we embrace.

Greater the requirements of keeping the law of love as you get closer inside the heart of our Creator, the first protection to the truth. The freer you want to be, the more wisdom will reveal to you in depth, on each word of wisdom. This beginning revelation comes and is confirmed as you love what you have already been awakened to. Spend time outside with your feet buried in the rich loam soil containing humus—(the organic component of soil formed by the decomposition of leaves and other plant material by soil microorganisms).

Your joy (perfect presence in you and blessed with the power to speak love words, for power, equals words of love, life, and light) where you are placed is based on what you do in your body here on the earth. We are not talking about the first encounter of beautiful words received that is near the door, where truth first meets you. We have gone further into the tabernacle or the tent of meeting or temple or state of mind— buried deep within the earth's loam soil, eternal awareness—right into the heart, the very omnipresence of our Creator.

The ribcage (fence) protects the heart and lungs. Our Creator made each person with this protection. The heart and lungs represent love and life. We are living truth daily by the words we speak and the thoughts we treasure. Pure truth is called the word of love made **flesh**. Our Creator made each of us perfect with the capacity to love and have life more abundantly.

The word flesh using the Aleph-Tav is spelled-ba sar, pronounced baw-sawr and means body, person, mankind, skin, nakedness from baw-sar, meaning a prime root to be fresh, that is full, cheerful, to announce glad news, messenger, preach, publish, show forth (bear, bring, carry, preach, good, tell good) tidings. This is where we get the word besorah—good news or words of peace. Light letters are Bet, Shin, and Resh. The understanding given to the writer: **a body of flesh created from love, shines forth, and clears the heads of mankind for the good news, besorah, words of peace.**

Eight affirmations for letter Chet/Het

1. Pure love and truth is the canopy, contract/covenant/protection so that marriage between male and female may perpetually exist.

2. This fence of protection, truth, will preserve the eternal marriage covenant made for humankind.

3. Our Creator unites man and woman when truth is found in their heart.

4. True life is experienced when lived with a heart of wisdom.

5. Love is the teacher; it is a bridge uniting brothers and sisters back to our Creator.

6. A home has children covered in peace.

7. There is no trial or obstacle that you cannot overcome when you have the understanding of our Creator's love. Our Creator thought and all things listened as they were created. Truth never returns void.

8. In the beginning of a marriage, it is a bonfire, but as the years pass, it requires stoking (change) to have the heart breathe, an eternal force of new life. Give a complete new face to those that are "born from within," remember, love life and light.

Hightower

I've taken a look down the true narrow path of time
And connected it to the treasured creation
of the One that has designed.
The words of love that builds a home and its gates,
Withstanding the marvelous promise made between mates.
As I pressed forward the religious were sure to catch
my eye, but returning to my Creator daily
Peace was restored, filling my lungs, with a deep sigh.
I see, children of light, rejoicing and singing,
on the wonderful land called earth,
Sharing their heart's blessings and entering
in for their born within birth.
From the top of the head down to the toes of the feet,
An energy flows freely proving that we are mature and complete.
The memory of love is sweet and the harmony has a marvelous sound.
The awakened are bright and beautiful with the
peace of discernment they have found.
A new and joyful day is celebrated in a delightful hour,
Being thankful for love, life, and light, our Creator's Hightower.

Cayden Dreams

The day began as one would think. The sun arose and because of that, there was light. All things started to move from a lifeless sleep. One could begin to feel the excitement that this day would bring.

Cayden went down to the kitchen where Chloe, his mother was making breakfast. He thought, "What game will I play today? Yesterday, I played like I was mom and dad so today I will play like I am my dog, Cruz."

Cayden quickly brushed his teeth and combed his hair then gobbled down his pancakes and fruit. After mom's instructions for the day she held open the kitchen door to let Cayden out. Cruz was waiting on the porch wagging his tail. As soon as he saw Cayden he jumped up for his treat.

Mother knew that Cayden was excited about living because he wore a huge wide smile across his large round face.

Cayden ran across the yard and up a tall tree to his secret hide-out place. He lay down on the tree house floor, with his head propped in his hands. As he closed his eyes he thought how it would be to be his dog, Cruz.

Cruz is a huge and ferocious dog. He has large red spots all over his body. Do you see them? His ears are long and pointed like an Indian arrow. His hair is short and fussy like cotton candy. Cruz begins to walk down the street and sees his friend, Luke, being chased by another huge dog. Cruz decides to grow as big as a house and scares the other dog away. Cruz grows smaller again and wags his tail for Luke. Luke, the cat, licks Cruz's ear and tell him what a brave and wonderful dog he is. Cruz is really happy now.

Cayden is now in an airplane with large wings and a propeller as big as the sun. The airplane sores up and down and back and forth throughout the earth eating up all the oranges and apples for fuel. Up in the sky, the airplane approaches a cloud that is full of rain. As Cayden flies through the cloud he is amazed at the wonders of heaven! Then, in a blink of an eye, he comes out of the clouds and enters into another part of the earth that he has never seen before. He looks down at the people and notices that they have straight coal black hair and eyes that are almond shaped. Can you guess where he is?

Away he flies for many more miles. He propels himself through thick icy skies. As he looks down at the people, he sees them dressed in heavy wool coats. They travel with sleds and their houses are made of ice. Where do you think he is now?

As he moves closer to the equator, he reaches a place where the sun is so very strong. He looks down and sees lions, monkeys, elephants, and giraffes playing tag with each other. Where could he possibly be now? And then...

Cayden hears Nicho, his daddy's voice, in the distance calling him home.

Quickly he runs back to the house where his daily chores and family await him. Having fun can never replace listening to his mother or father when they call him.

Remember the teaching of your Creator so that your life will be long on the earth.

CHAPTER 9

TET

תשרקצפעסנמלכיטחזוהדגבא

The twenty-two letters of light are arranged going from right to left:
Aleph, Bet, Gimel, Dalet, Hay, Vav, Zayin, Chet, Tet, Yod, Kaf,
Lamed, Mem, Nun, Samech, Ayin, Pay, Tzadi, Kuf, Resh, Shin, and Tav.

The ninth letter of the aleph-tav is Tet.
Numerical number is 9.
Rhymes with mate and has the sound of *T* as in *tall*.

The number nine represents the number of **truth**, spelled with
light letters emes, pronounced em-ess—which means stability, of long
continuance, build up—or support as a parent or nurse.

Repeat of creation day two if counting a weekly cycle according to present-day calendars—Yom Sheni. Bet and Ayin are the other letters that fall on this day. Using Bet, Ayin and Tet as instruction we receive this truth: **A person's body or his home sees with light, his inner eye, our Creator's eternal truth.**

Design of Tet

The design of Tet is like a pot, a vessel with an inverted rim, representing **hidden or inverted perfection**. Another interpretation of the Tet is that it represents a man or woman bending their head to truth in meditation and thanks.

Another idea is after the union between husband and wife, the healthy bonding allows a conception. The Tet represents the hidden perfection that resides within the womb of the mother.

Eternally speaking, all that want our Creator's presents will have the opportunity to approach the light and be given truth that helps you grow for that season of life. Each day prepare and listen for new words of instruction that bring a life of blessings/children and the words of truth and health.

Tet is the letter of **decision**, awaken to one another. Here is the fork in the road Y.

Decision is spelled with light letters—charuwts, pronounced khaw-roots. Light letters are Chet, Resh, Nun, and Tsadi. The understanding given to the writer: **life with new beginnings announces humility in the light giving seed, the era's spiritual leader.** Meaning of decision— Incised or incisive, a trench (as dug) gold (as mined) a threshing-sledge (having sharp teeth) determination; also eager—decision, pointed things, sharp, and wall, from the prime root word charats, pronounced khaw-rats—which means to point sharply that is to literally wound; fig. to be alert, to decide—bestir self, decree, determine, move.

Earthly challenges make you stronger either for truth if you have entered freedom's door or remain in the field with darkness. The saying "This too is for the best" is like the wind to a tree to make the tree roots stronger. Here is a lesson: When we are taking a trip, for example, our tire might suddenly blow out. We think this will delay us and all the plans we have! We may have to spend hours changing the tire. Then we will have to stay in that place instead of making the trip in one day. Now, we could say, "Perhaps the ill health of this tire is saving us from yet a worse situation that would have taken place had we continued our trip as planned." But the emes—truth—is that standing on the side of the road with a flat tire <u>at that time</u> is in itself perfect (**separated** you from darkness). It is time for a new healthy tire. Even events that are not readily perceived as being positive are totally perfect, since everything comes from wholeness and we know our Creator is perfect. If you see that everything that happens to you is for your perfection (**separated** from darkness), then you have crossed over and have become an overcomer, born from within. Remember generational deception— you cannot see your past as it will be cloudy—keep in the protection of the fence—Present time truth and the law of pure love and rest. Never look back, like Lot's wife, or think of your past because you are moving forward into our Creator's marvelous love, life, and light not back into darkness or maybe's.

Be so careful of the words you speak! Your words will bring love, life, and light (**separation** from darkness) or unawareness to you! It is your choice and your level of awareness that will determine your healthy words or unhealthy words and their consequences and actions.

Meaning of nine—deals with discernment to make a choice or the finality of things. Basically, it's used when love enters humankind at the time they try to enter the door of life. An individual may have many attempts to enter the door but he or she can only enter if his or her heart is humble and his or her words spoken reveal love, life, and light. If their heart is not humble that person stays with his or her unhealthy choices. This will be recognized by the words he or she speaks and what he or she does. Gen 4:7-pg. **4** says, "If you do well, shall you not be accepted? And if you do not well, an unhealthy consequence lies at the door. And darkness will rule over you."

A person can be water baptized and have a religious experience of the world's approval but in truth that person's heart assigns himself to an awakened state, the tree of life within or remains in the field of darkness with the tree of knowledge of good and evil. (If you are attracted to the tree of good and evil, then how can you expect an awakening of expanded health?) You are "born from within"; that means the Creator is awakened within you and you have moved out of all religious boxes and unhealthy man-made organizations.

There is no judgment for those that love our Creator. They live out their lives in discernment. Once they have crossed over (**separation** from darkness). These ones that have pure truth will not have the inclination to entertain unhealthy choices. These are the children of light. They will have joy, blessings, harmony, peace, tranquility, perfection, happiness, words of wisdom, healing of mind, body and soul, abundance, enlargement, discernment, wealth, health, confidence, hospitality, integrity, faith, courage, colorful personality, unity, energy, and awareness and have tremendous abilities to have fun on this earth.

Remember to love the words of light, for you were created to have freedom and joy as you lived upon this earth.

Tet is a letter that reveals the knowledge of good and evil that contains error. This is speaking of the tree of knowledge of good and evil and not the tree of life, wisdom. If you do not see the difference between the two trees, one of life and the other darkness then the consequence will be that you remain blinded. Remember Jacob's ladder? Here you meet the angels or messengers that guard the ladder of light letters and their meanings. Using the Aleph-Tav, *ladder* is spelled cullam, pronounced sool-lawm meaning a staircase, from the root word cala, pronounced saw-lal prime root to mound up, fig. to exalt, to oppose (as by a dam), raise up(dilisoni). Made with the Light letters Samech, Lamed, and Lamed. The understanding given to the writer: **the words of love are ever teaching and instructing the individual so that they may be lifted up (dilisoni).**

The form of the letter is inverted suggesting hidden perfection. Like a women pregnant with child. However, sometimes the potential for perfection, spelled using light letters tahorah is perverted spelled avah, pronounced aw-vaw, a prime root to crook—do amiss, bow down, make crooked, commit iniquity. Light letters are Ayin, Nun, and Hay. The understanding given to the writer: **by using one's eyesight (words of wisdom from light) to change the original meaning of words of love to hurt the children of the earth, this is what causes impurity or filth (tumah).**

Our Creator is perfection therefore all is perfect even the first darkness. In our earthly sphere, to make a distinction, both light and darkness had to be present. That is why darkness and light is in each person created as they represent all of creation within. Creation is in your DNA. Your responsibility while you dwell on this earth in a physical body is to learn how to choose light and awareness therefore, leaving the darkness of unconsciousness behind. What keeps a person unconscious? Trauma, surgery, medication of any kind, foods that are stimulants or over cooked, using words of the world in thoughts and speech, such as cursing, unhealthy habits, caffeine, cigarettes, not responsible intake of alcohol, narcotics, over exercising, to name a few.

Tet can picture either the man or woman that is in rebellion with truth or the man or woman that has **humbled** himself for learning. Will we choose to **humble** our lives or will we inwardly rebel and live in the selfish pride that creates disease, trauma, pain, confusion, which is mixing truth with error! Our Creator loves you and gives you all that you need to be healthy, wealthy and wise.

Crowned letters—eight Light letters are given special adornment by attaching three tagin or crownlets to them called sha'atnezgets.

Shin, Ayin, Tet, Nun, Zayin, Gimel, Tzadi, and final Tzadi. The understanding given to the writer: **The fire received from the insight of refinement, causes a new decision. The life giving seed keeps daily rest time. Their journey on this earth returns to nature, and they become an example of pure truth and peace.** Retirement at rest time is natural for those that love our Creator.

"Sha'atnez gets" letters

Let's look at the word crown and why these letters are given special adornment. The first time crown is used in the scriptures is in Gen. 49:26 pg. **55**, in the blessing of Joseph. Crown is spelled using the Aleph-Tav qodqod, pronounced qod-qode, and means the crown of the head most humble. He was **separated** from his brothers. When you begin to be **separated** from the people of the world, this could be family as well as friends, because you are following our Creator's love, you too will feel that crowning of truth or **separation** coming upon your head. *In other words, crowing is being **separated** from darkness and the people who continue to choose unhealthy choices. You will have relief and sadness and many other feelings as you are **separated** from the darkness of this world.*

To be a blessing with the awakening of our Creator within fulfills your whole lifetime purpose on the earth. Enduring with peace finally producing trustworthy enlargement—and precious fruit. This is another way to recognize the word <u>faith</u> within you.

Faith is spelled using the light letters emuwn, pronounced ay-moon and means established, trusty, trust, worthiness, faithful, and truth and comes from the prime root word aman, pronounced aw-man and means to build up or support, to go to the right hand, to be certain, to foster as a parent or nurse. Light letters are Aleph, Mem, Vav, and Nun, also spelled emuwnah, pronounced em-oo-naw, and means firmness, security, fidelity, stability, steady, truly, verily. The understanding given to the writer: **our Creator and the words of truth developed within completes and matures the individual here**

on the earth. You are completed, as you live forever, and the memories you leave for others perpetuates love, life, and light for our Creator. Many times there will be written accounts of wisdom provided for those that search out pure truth.

Truth will separate and divide a person's life from their darkness when recognized within. Included are just a few examples: could be aggressive and dominant family member, recreation that inhibits wisdom's healthy words, hobbies or work that consume a person's life and thoughts, dependent friends, sexual arousing clothing, fallacious outer adornment, unhealthy thoughts and words.

All there is, is present time—if you live in the past or future you are not awakened to pure truth. Past lives, out-of-body experiences, and channeling and speaking to mediums are a sign of unhappiness with your present life condition. The sun goes down this is time of rest in a perfect day. When the sun comes up this is the time to awake and be joyfully engaged in a day of love, life, and light. If you are not feeling peace in your day reconnect to your Creator of love. Go outside, take deep breaths, look at nature, and listen to the beautiful song made by creation, work in your yard, put your feet deep within the loam soil. Clean your house, give order to that which is controlling your lifestyle. Love yourself so that you can reach out to others in love. Perfect peace is always the answer to any question that you have. All true answers must have peace in it or it is coming from a dark source. Our Creator of love, life, and light is always the correct answer. Know it, believe it, and love it! Simplicity in all things.

Eight affirmations for the letter Tet

1. What is concealed is revealed in the appointed time liken to a pregnant woman. Child birthing is a crowning event as well as being "born from within" knowing our Creator.

2. We are like a vessel or container—remember, awakened and aware sees the vessel of potential, humble yourself so you can live out your life for the purpose of love, life, and light.

3. In life meet every challenge with courage and strength. Rest your mind so truth can prevail.

4. Nine is a true number. Meaning once added or multiplied, the sum numbers can be added and you will get 9. As 9×9=81 and 8+1=9. In the beginning, middle, and end, our Creator never changes. Love, life, and light will always be pure truth.

5. When yolked to our Creator, as one, you develop discernment.

6. Remove the world, surrender, leaving time and moving into the eternities. Our bodies live in the worldly realm however our thoughts and actions show that we honor perfection, which is timeless.

7. **Separation** feels alone at first, but as you mature, joy in silence becomes a blessing delight and health to the body and mind.

8. Blessings are better than a night vision, a possible afterlife experience or dream. You cannot really trust that! Awakening of our Creator within is seeing how the blessings are manifest in actual daily life. As the darkness is removed from our mind and awakened to the truth of love, life, and light, we become changed within and love unconditionally with discernment all life. We finished our work in Emunah—FAITH!

Crossover

We rest with peace, yesterday, today, and forever.
A choice made clear as darkness grows cleverer.
Difficult is a word with the word cult within.
This word describes the people that are hard-hearted and
chose deliberately to remain in religious ignorant sin.
Peace and light with the overcomer that rightly sits,
Separated in purity the finished puzzle piece exactly fits.
Steadfast in purpose, an inward song that never dies,
Awakened to truth, hallelujah and found without lie.

Sincere in profession, renewing those that live with a restful heart,
Awakened by truth, with works that do follow and with this last
remark:
Separation from darkness is the perfect truth,
Live with love and light to keep your youth!

A Decision

"Journee, is that the bathtub water I hear?" questioned Hannah.

"Yes, it is," answered Journee. "It must be time for Sarah's bath."

"Oh, Journee, I just hate hearing Sarah cry and fuss!" exclaimed Hannah. "She always does that when she takes a bath."

As Sarah walked into the bathroom, she cried, "Well, it is time for me to get my hair washed. I hate this as much as you do Hannah." As Sarah climbed into the bathtub she continued complaining, "I do not mind getting my hair wet, but I don't like getting soap in my eyes. When it is time to brush my hair, oh, how that pulls and hurts."

Journee immediately piped up, "I don't mean to hurt you when I brush your hair. The bristles of the brush are made in a way so I can remove the tangles from your hair."

"Yes, I know that it is not your fault, Journee. I just wish I knew of a way to get my hair washed and brushed without it hurting," answered Sarah.

The bathroom door was left slightly opened. As Debbie passed to return to the kitchen, she could not help over hear the conversation between Sarah and Hannah. With a desire to help Sarah solve her problem, Debbie knocked on the opened door.

As she was told to enter, Journee exclaimed, "Look who is here!"

"Yes," quietly spoke Debbie.

"What are you doing here?" declared Journee.

Journee continued talking without giving Debbie a chance to answer her first question, "I am going to tell Mother on you. You know you need to finish washing the dishes!"

"Yes, you are right, Journee. I am only here because I thought I could help Sarah solve her problem. I hate hearing Sarah cry too."

"What idea could you possibly suggest, Debbie?" questioned Journee.

"Well, I could cut Sarah's hair short. It would never hurt to brush and wash it again," answered Debbie.

"If you do that," screamed Hannah, "Journee and I will not speak to you again."

Debbie decided to be quiet while Hannah and Journee just glared at Sarah.

Sarah had listened to Debbie's idea of cutting her hair short and to Hannah and Journee's disapproval of this idea. Sarah knew it was her turn to make a **decision** concerning her hair.

As Sarah climbed out of the tub with her hair going every which way, she announced, "I think Debbie has a great solution to my problem." After these words were spoken, Hannah and Journee closed tightly their bedroom door.

Sarah said a little louder, "I still plan to be with you both. You will only be relieved of this chore Mother gave to you to do."

The next evening, as Sarah took her daily bath, Hannah and Journee peeped through the bathroom door only to see that Sarah had her hair cut.

Journee and Hannah were disappointed. To think that their favorite sister really cut her beautiful thick long brown hair.

After many weeks of watching Sarah not cry at bath time, Hannah and Journee discovered how much better their day went. This was not easy to admit to each other, especially, since they had spoken bitter words to Sarah and Debbie about the haircut.

But as time passed, the four sisters expressed many feelings about this **decision** and how it had affected them personally.

This was a time of change for all the family.

Can you recall a time when you experienced a **decision** that changed your life and the life of others?

CHAPTER 10

YOD

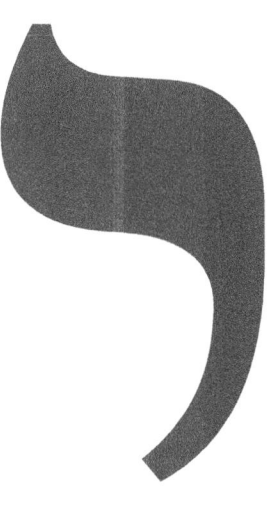

YOD
/yōd/

א ב ג ד ה ו ה ד ח ז ח ט י כ ל מ נ ס ע פ צ ק ר ש ת

The twenty-two letters of light are arranged going from right to left:
Aleph, Bet, Gimel, Dalet, Hay, Vav, Zayin, Chet, Tet, Yod, Kaf,
Lamed, Mem, Nun, Samech, Ayin, Pay, Tzadi, Kuf, Resh, Shin, and Tav.

Yod, or Yud, is the tenth letter of the aleph-tav, the smallest of
letters and is suspended in the air but not above lamed, the
twelfth light letter.

Yud is the repeat day of the third day of creation if counting a
weekly cycle according to present-day calendars. Yom Shlishi—Light

letters on this day are Gimel and Pay. Meaning given to the writer: **the journey of a person begins each day with the words they use all day**.

The design of the Yud is a point: the beginning and ending of all things, a dot which represents our Creator's essential power, the One who is echad, pronounced ekh-awd, meaning to unify, collects one's thoughts, united, alike, alone, one, and altogether; light letters Aleph, Chet, and Dalet. The understanding given to the writer: **the Creator's breath (words of wisdom) protects with the law of love all those that are awakened to love, life, and light—perfect existence**. Furthermore, the Yod looks like a flame that soars ever higher, representing a person yearning to unite with pure truth. At-one-ment or unity. At-one-ment or blessed spelled with light letters Kaphar, pronounced kaw-far, meaning a prime root to cover, to expiate or condone, cleansed, disannul, forgive, be merciful, pacify, pardon, reconcile.

Light letters for at-one-ment are Kaph, Pay, and Resh. The understanding given to the writer: **The blessed speak with wisdom!**

Today, because the people will not seek for the truth—they have been given the Gregorian calendar in place of the lunisolar calendar so that they can worship on the world's days and be "one" with the world like in the time of Babel. However, this "one" is made by man and not our Creator. Gen. 11:1–9 pg. **10**. Today those that remain in darkness celebrate pagan holidays instead of resting according to creation and celebrating each prophetic day of creation. They eat from the tree of knowledge of good and evil and not from the tree of life.

Additionally, the Yod represents the method by which the blessing descends from our Creator to all people. The Yod represents a seminal drop, the concentrated power of the power of love. The Vav (sixth light letter, connector) represents a descent, for its form is that of a chute-and through this the blessings of our Creator travels downward to our world through the understanding of love and the words of truth. The Dalet (fourth light letter) having height and width, represents the physical world, signifying how our Creator's blessings are manifest in every new day. This teaches us that our Creator's blessings come from the love formed within. They flow down to this world and endow us with physical health and strength, sustenance and success when we follow the words of truth. Remember, the words of truth and nature will only magnify and confirm love, life, and light, the teachings of wisdom.

Maybe this is why the first letter of each of the three passages of the Bible's priestly blessing begins with the Yod.

May our Creator bless you and guard you.
May our Creator shine upon you and be gracious to you.
May our Creator love you and grant you peace and truth.

Because our Creator's original and fundamental intention in bringing us into the world was not to eschew physicality, but to transform the physical humankind into the eternal humankind, even if this is only talking to you and no one else around you at this particular time! Transforming into the eternal being, born from within our Creator's love, is the ultimate purpose of all humankind.

How can we apply this to our lives? When asked to do something, we say, "No, I do not want to do that." However, it is for your eternal growth of all and not just the individual. Think about where our Creator has you and stay there as long as required. When the door opens you will know that it is the correct time to move. Our Creator will make sure you know and confirm it by opening another new and beautiful door.

Anointing using the Aleph-Tav is spelled mishchah, pronounced meesh-khaw, and meaning—a consecratory gift, prime root to rub with oil to consecrate also to paint. Light letters Mem, Shin, Chet, and Hey. The understanding given to the writer: **the words of love are the words of wisdom to those that received the revelation of light, which brings forth eternal life**. Believe and have Faith. Do not force a door to open and do not go before the door is opened.

Now imagine this scenario. A mother wakes up her eight-year-old son for school, and he says, "No! I do not want to go to school." How does the mother respond? "What homework did you not finish? Do you have a spelling test that you need to study for? How can I help you get ready for school today?" She will incline her ear for truth to discern if it is due to rebellion or lack of study to feel confident and successful for that day.

Now if only we would all be strong and courageous—committed to learning the truth so error can be removed and strive to be awakened and connected to our Creator every minute of the day!

Numerical value: 10.

Sound—"Y"—yes.

Meaning: Right hand.

Deals with completeness, a cycle has completed and the outcome is 10. Yod is the most found letter as Tet, letter 9, is the least.

Yod is the "atom" of the form from which all the other letters begin and end.

Yod represents a mere dot, a perfect point of energy. Since Yod is used to form all the other letters and building blocks of creation Yod indicates our Creator's omnipresence.

The power and doorway of creation.

The life and light of the word of love in everything.

- Yod, the greatest in number, is inherently linked with humility as it stands as the smallest and most unassuming letter, yet possesses perfect power. The number 10 is a number marking shelemut. Using the Aleph-Tav, the word for peace, shalom (שלום) is derived from a root denoting wholeness or completeness, and its frame of reference throughout Jewish literature is bound up with the notion of shelemut, perfection. Complete and mature or completion and order.

In the concordance, the word for complete is tamiym, taw-meem, meaning entire, integrity, truth, without blemish, full, perfect, sincerely, sound, without spot, undefiled, upright, whole. Light letters are Tav, Mem, Yod, and Mem. The understanding given to the writer: **eternity, our Creator's breath, is the ATor ET (means Aleph-Bet). Our Creator is who begins all words, that means created everything with a beginning and an end meaning eternity.**

The basic ten number system is universal. Just as Yod is part of all the previous letters of the alphabet (as a component) so Yod is part of all the numbers. We have ten toes and fingers because Yod means ten and not the other way around.

The number ten represents sanctify and holiness.

Yod shows that the truth is life and one, and that from truth derive all other things by the power of wisdom.

The dot, the Yod, represents a student in instruction. When one student is beside another, when one student respects the other, then peace dwells in their presence. Their alliance and agreement becomes the awakened child. But when one student is on top of the other, when one student thinks he's better or smarter than the next, or disrespects his neighbor/teacher, then that's the end of the connection. It creates a separation in the relation between the student and peace and love.

While we live in a physical world of "natural" order, our Creator is truly the one and only Creator of nature.

Therefore, the mission of a "born from within" person is to go forth into the depths of the materialistic world and infuse it with the Yod of love and perfect truth. This refers to every place a "born from within" foot lands. We must journey from day to day with words of love into business with the same intention, with the same passion to fulfill light's creation.

Anyone who denies idolatry and thereby acknowledges love, life, and light, has the gift of kindness. Remember, we live forever and when we leave this earthy dwelling we leave behind our pure acts of love!

It is interesting to note that the letter Yod, when placed at the beginning of a word (ET or AT), represents **constancy.**

The same concept holds true with our Creator. The word hoveh means the present. Our Creator continuously creates the world—right now, even as you read this. The Yod in front of hoveh reminds us that creation was not a singular occurrence. Rather, the laws of creation are forming the world anew every moment.

A loving person, by nature, is thankful for our Creator. Thankfulness is expressed every moment of our earthly existence. This is heard by the words we speak and why the words we speak are so strong and full of power. Of course, some days our thankfulness can be concealed in quietness but that can never obscure a loving person's perpetual, unyielding connection to our Creator in their thoughts.

This can be likened to today with the COVID-19 virus—wearing of the mask over our nose and mouth. This is the darkness trying to force people to silence their words of love. Our Creator is in control and in time will show us the higher reasoning for this plague. Outside of the earthquakes and hurricanes the birthing process is in its enlargement stage and era. Continue with love and you will continue birthing "born from within," children of light, to a fulfillment.

Eight affirmations for the letter Yod

1. We are but a dot, the smallest on this earth. Remember pure love as life formed us and gave us breath.

2. When we know the beginning of creation that will bring eternal and physical order to your life. Living to awaken love, life, and light to all.

3. Our Creator is eternity; give us light as we sojourn on this earth, living with thanksgiving.

4. A mind with order, love, and all truths attributes gives our being peace. Thank you for the word of truth.

5. When we know no lack, we understand humility. No manner the circumstance, keep us small and humble.

6. Thank you for life's blessings—We will be in the community as long as breath is in us.

7. Everyone is living their life—our Creator's omnipresence continues the birthing cycle of the overcomer with newness daily.

8. Let our heart be pure in words of love, so that we remain faithful and awake each morning to a memory of love, life, and light.

We Won

Lo! In the minds of those born within appears love and the day of fun.
Light brings a rainbow's train of generational years,
The children are complete, perfect and mature; a new life has begun.
Love dwells in those that continually bless
with mercy, truth, and righteousness.
Sweet! Beautiful, words rejoice when there is love at
Every humble feet.
Love shall reign from pole to pole, the glory of every
Awakened soul.
Because those heeded the words of love, amid their daily
cares, and by loving life have strived to pattern theirs.
Those who conquered darkness have won.
Praise, glory and honor; treasured is that perfect daughter and son!

Garbage Can and the Word Purpose

Today is the day that the garbage is pickup. Garbage Can, known better as Alicia, patiently waits for this day each week.

You see, this is the day that Alicia is scheduled to have her garbage removed by, Alan, the garbage truck. Once the heavy load is lifted out from her, she instantly feels relieved and enjoys feeling as light as a feather.

This particular day she was sitting with her lid tightly secured and her side seams almost bursting. She listened for Alan. She could tell he was on his way by the sound he would make, "Engine-gen-gen-gen, clank-a-ta-clank, bang-bang!"

"Oh!" Alicia exclaimed. "How happy I am to see you today. I cannot budge because I am so full!"

"I understand," answered Alan, "I will pick you up and empty your garbage into the back dumpster."

After Alan set her down he exclaimed, "My, my little one, you are really heavy today! What have you been eating?"

Alicia answered, "Everything one can imagine. Mother did her spring cleaning and emptied all the rooms inside of me. Besides that, she had a birthday party for Taylor, and I had to eat all that mess up too."

Alan replied, "What a huge job you have been given by this family. Well, it is spring! The birds are singing with joy! The cool breeze whistles around my wheels while the children run and play. I hope your day has plenty of sunshine!"

"See you next week," said Alan as he "engine-gen-gen-gen, clank-a-ta-clank, bang-bang" down the broken paved street.

Alicia quickly raced to the back door and banged her lid to get mother's attention.

After banging her lid for what seemed to be ten minutes, she knew that mother was not home.

Oh, how disappointed Alicia felt. "The only day I have to move about easily and mother is not home," she thought.

As she walked away from the back door she dragged her wheels and hung her lid in disappointment. Now she was faced with waiting!

She spoke out loud, "no one could possibly understand me. I am only a garbage can and what does that mean to anyone?"

She opened the yard gate door and sat on the grass by the edge of the street. She hoped that she might see something interesting. As Alicia sat there and looked around she noticed that everything she saw was waiting for something are someone. The cars were waiting for the red light to turn green so they could continue going down the street.

The grass, trees, and flowers were waiting for it to rain so they could grow more beautiful. A boy was waiting for his dog to reach him so they could continue walking down the sidewalk.

The children in the school across the street waited for class to end so they could go outside and play. Oh! What exciting noises came from that school when the school bell did ring!

Alicia then thought, "Here I am just waiting for time to pass. Does anybody see me waiting?"

As she looked around her environment, she knew her answer: "No one sees me waiting. Everyone is too busy doing what they want to do. People just can't be bothered with me."

"I want someone to see me! I want to be important!" screamed Alicia.

After these words left her lips, in the distance, a truck door slammed shut. Immediately she came to her senses. She was feeling sorry for herself again, and thought, "Was that Daddy? He would notice me!"

Out came Daddy into the yard with a pile of garbage. He and the family had been to the farm and what a load of clippings he had collected.

As Alicia opened her lid to allow daddy to throw his trash into her, she realized the fantastic feeling of having a perfect purpose in life.

"It felt so good to have garbage inside of her," she thought. She wanted to wrap her round little body around daddy and kiss him. However, she knew better. Garbage cans can't do that.

Alicia was content to know that she knew her purpose in life.

Do you know your purpose in life?

CHAPTER 11

KAF

ת ש ר ק צ פ ע ס נ מ ל כ י ט ח ז ו ה ד ג ב א

The twenty-two letters of light are arranged going from right to left:
Aleph, Bet, Gimel, Dalet, Hay, Vav, Zayin, Chet, Tet, Yod, Kaf,
Lamed, Mem, Nun, Samech, Ayin, Pay, Tzadi, Kuf, Resh, Shin, and Tav.

Kaf, or Khaf is the **eleventh** light letter.
Numerical value = 20.
Dalet and Tzadi are located on this day if counting a weekly
cycle according to present-day calendars. The meaning given to the
writer: a **"born from within"** moves from the door where life allows

freedom and has been washed and cleaned for the next chamber, the most holy, to receive his or her enlargement.

Sound: "K" as in kite with a dot and "KH" without a dot (dagesh) the difference between the letter Kaf and Khaf is the presence or absence of the dot in the middle of the letter called a dagesh mark. When you see the dot in the middle of this letter, pronounce it as a "K," otherwise, pronounce it as "KH."

Meaning: palm, spoon, crown, to cover, to rescue, covered by the love of our Creator—we are kept from disease because of our discernment of life using wisdom. Our healing occurs daily and is manifested in every cell of our body (remember to eat from the table of creation) to enjoy life.

"Blessings are upon the head of the just but violence shall cover the mouth of the wicked" (Proverbs 10:6 pg. **737**).

Kaf, the crown, symbolizes being "born from within" with the love of life, to be done on earth as it is in heaven. What does scripture say about a crown? (Pr.12:4 pg. **739**, Pr. 17:6 pg. **744**).

Kaf is the *blessing power* received from the words of truth. (It took ten letters to be ready for your enlargement.) This stored power from the words of truth that is in everyone recognizes our Creator who created the heavens and earth, male and female within the human heart. Our Creator is in the head or mind/heart so that the creation of heaven and earth can be remembered in that individual. When this happens it is said that a person is "born from within." "Born of the word of wisdom" is more correct as the word of truth is the power needed to have this beautiful understanding. The Aleph-Tav word for born is yalad, pronounced yaw-lad meaning a prime root to bear, calve, lineage, the office of a midwife, bring up, travail, labor. The light letters are Yod, Lamed, and Dalet. The meaning given to the writer: **the enlargement teaches the love of our Creator which causes dilisoni— to be lifted up**.

Kaf literally means "palm of the hand." The letter Kaf is after the letter Yod. Yod means hand, while Kaf is the palm of the hand.

Kaf and Bet or alike in shape however the Kaf is made with one stroke that is a curve while Bet is made with two strokes. Bet and Kaf are related in their shape. Also if you take the 0 away from the numerical number for Kaf—20, you get 2—Bet.

When prefixed to a word Kaf means "**like** or as."

When we bend our wills in submission to love, we become one within and we are given the reward of separation from darkness. Crowning is a continuous act as every day we feel perfect presence upon us and completing that day in love will bring us joy and peace. Recognize, when first doing this, you may be unfamiliar with the feeling, however, as you continue in love you will begin to feel more comfortable with the *responsibility* that comes with the enlargement—remember to stay quiet and peaceful in your daily life. Taking full responsibility gives a person strength and courage to go forward in love and truth.

Forgetfulness is a choice made by the individual with its consequences. Forgetfulness is a form of disease of the mind. Keep life simple for the day and you will see and be living in present time. If two thoughts come in at the same time, take time to write both down and then do one at a time. This may seem ridiculous at first, however, your mind will be strengthened as you become more confident, stable, and balanced.

Remember, we are love, so your body parts, especially in your head is related with Kaf, since the letter Kaf symbolizes the palm of enlargement on top of the head, which symbolizes the awakened man, Adam. Yes, Adam—we explain that the biblical symbol Adam represents our brain/mind/heart—speech, our head, while Chavah, Eve, represents our healthy reproductive organs, beautiful children, and awakened family. Kaf means **crown**.

At the root of our nose is the pituitary gland, located along the line that the nose points inward toward the brain.

What role does the pituitary gland play?

1. Pituitary gland function. One of the dominant functions of the pituitary is to direct and control other endocrine glands and organs of the body by sending them chemical messengers through the blood stream. The hormones secreted by this gland perform following major functions which are primarily concerned with maintenance, growth and reproduction. · The pituitary gland is called the "master gland" because it directs a multitude of endocrine functions in the body. It regulates hormone activity in other endocrine glands and organs. Pituitary activity is regulated by hormones of the hypothalamus, a brain region connected to the pituitary by the pituitary stalk. Your pituitary gland is an important pea-sized organ. If your pituitary gland doesn't function properly, it affects vital parts like your brain, skin, energy, mood, reproductive organs, vision, growth and more. It's the "**master**" gland because it tells other glands to release hormones.

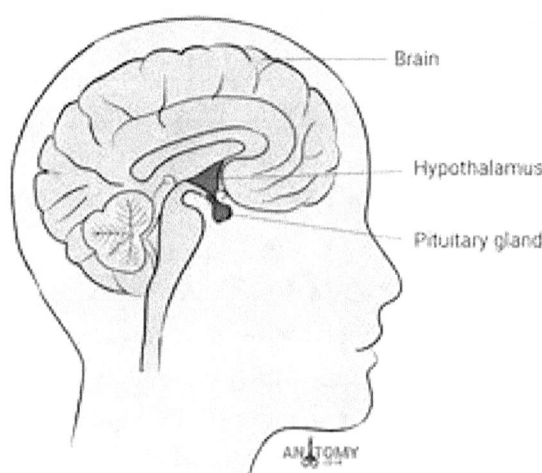

In the center of the brain is the pineal gland, and its function is to produce healthy sleep patterns called circadian rhythms. It also produces the hormone, melatonin. The secretion of melatonin is inhibited by light and triggered by darkness.

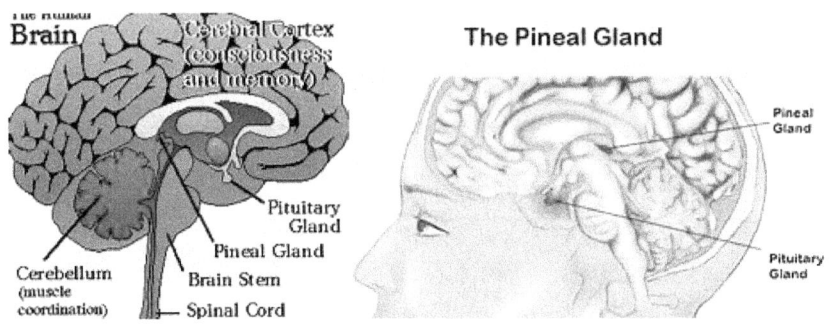

A healthy pineal gland is necessary so we can move by the words of truth. This is the reason that proper rest (a law of creation) is so important to the mind as rest will promote health, thereby, giving us strength to overcome and continue our daily awakened state under stressful life situations.

What is the hat, kappa, cap, or turban over the head of religious people? What does that symbolize? The cap, or hat, is the palm of authority; in other words, the cap is a remembrance or a means for you to remember our Creator, because in your head is the joy of love if you will allow it. This quiet and reverent appearance shows us that religion is not what gives the power to us but it is the understanding of pure love. Today we have the word of truth in our heads/hearts so no need for an exterior covering as the skull cap is sufficient. Our body is the temple of love with our heads and minds, directed by the power of the words of truth which clears all dross so light and wisdom can shine.

Let's go back to the beginning where Adam and Eve lost their covering, the wisdom of our Creator.

After Adam and Eve chose an unhealthy choice by eating from the tree of knowledge of good and evil they hid in the garden. Unhealthy choices give us the reason for hiding, lying, and deceit. Little children hide from their parents when they do something wrong.

Awareness and light allows a person to speak the truth and come out of hiding. Result—present time living!

All children born on earth are fleshy/mortal, in an unhealthy state of unconsciousness. That is why every person on earth has a physical birth first and then once we are "born from within," our second birth, by the words of truth, we become conscious of truth and our Creator. The children of light will not have a desire to speak or do things that are unhealthy. When we look at our children and see how they are selfish from a baby, we can see how this is true. What makes them change? It is the understanding of the correct truth of the law of love, returning them back to creation and our Creator. This is a gradual process and does take time and living in peace. You might be that child right now so remember, love is very merciful and shows peace to thousands, to those who love life and treasures the laws of creation.

We all need an awakening so we can be reconciled back to our Creator of love, life, and light (love indicates infancy, life indicates growth, and light indicates maturity and eternity).

When Adam and Eve used their reproductive organs to fulfill "be fruitful and multiply," their offspring carried the unhealthy choice of darkness within their bodies. The journey of darkness would prevail until the time was opened for perfect light to penetrate the darkness. This occurs with the birthing of children of light who love creation and life. Throughout the ages there has been many that have helped awaken the people with truth. No different than today with writings that will hopefully awake many. Returning to our Creator will remain the truth and the whole truth. Mankind would have to return to the Creator of love, life, and light to see humankind's unhealthy choices and the generational consequences that cycled throughout the years. The same cycle continuing until advancing light breaks through and healthy thoughts become victorious. We all have eaten from the tree of knowledge of good and evil which means we all have been born into mortality and family traditions of unhealthy choices. Responsibility is an enlargement word with wisdom as its root. Today is the day to be born with our Creator formed within. The meaning of "being born again."

We are to be the head and not the tail. We can accomplish this if we are "born from within"; otherwise, we live in darkness and dwell upon the earth according to the tree of knowledge of good and evil, and man-made religion. No real freedom!

Today children are born out of lust and not out of love, life, and light from our Creator. They do not remember the creation of heaven and earth because our Creator is not yet formed in their heads and hearts. Today, if you have wisdom's thoughts, listen and be "born from within," becoming children of light.

Again, we are so thankful for our Creator who brought forth creation that we have the opportunity to be "born from within" at any age, even when born within a family that makes unhealthy choices. We can still choose peace, harmony, love, and life.

The Nahash was the one that said Adam and Eve would be like god, knowing good and evil; however, he was lying. God is not our Creator but a made up deity for religion. So Adam and Eve became a part of religious history.

What did Satan do to get himself kicked out of the garden as he was in the field hiding? The Nahash said he was god and ignored our Creator and the laws of creation and the truth about the life cycle of man. Man has a physical body that perishes and a being within the body that lives forever. The Nahash made man think that they were a body and if they ate from the tree of good and evil they would be like god and live forever. So man has done everything they can think of to have their bodies live forever and not age according to the law of creation. When the truth is the body is a vehicle for the being but the being lives forever and returns to our Creator once the life cycle on the earth for the body is completed. The body then returns to the dust from where it was created. If physically eating from the table of creation and following the law of rest your health and length of days will be extended as well as the aging process will be slowed.

Our Creator is not about death but life. Everything on earth was made so that it has a physical life cycle of birthing and dying. The tree of knowledge of good and evil was written by the biblical scribes that if they ate of it they (being) would die. We are eternal beings and live forever. The cycle of life, our being lives forever, is what we forgot. The body was never intended to live forever. As long as people think that they are a body they will never understand about being an eternal being. If you are connected to the tree of knowledge of good and evil, religion, and all organizations connected to it, then you are communicating with the wrong tree. The tree of life, the whole truth, is the tree of wisdom that represents our Creator. This is eternal love, life, and light.

This life cycle has never changed. It is permanent like the sun and moon that appear each day and those who still are in darkness, no manner their unhealthy choices, will live forever as those of us who walk in truth and have health. All human beings will experience their consequences here on the earth for their choices of health or disease and live in peace or chaos. Those that are not awakened will just be removed from the earth still in darkness, without the light of truth or our Creator born from within.

Adam and Eve were like the Hebrew god Elohim, Yehovah after they partook of the tree of knowledge of good and evil because they chose religion and a man-made god and not creation and our omnipotent Creator as their truth. So darkness and unconsciousness would be a part of every mortal person born on the earth until they return to our Creator and are" born from within." The people that are fleshy will be there to tempt you, however, knowing the truth about our Creator will give you the strength to overcome the darkness. Remember to go outside and look at the animals, trees, birds, plants, and flowers to see the beauty of life. All religions are asleep and the people connected to them. Now you can be kind and loving to all, for you will meet on the other side no manner what is done here on the earth. The only difference is you will live in peace and harmony with creation while living out your life.

Remember, the laws of creation do not change. All humankind follow the life cycle even if their choices are unhealthy. Fish, birds, and other animals follow their laws and have their consequences. Our Creator made humankind according to creations law, perfect. What we do with our vehicle, body, is our choice! "Whosoever respects creation is the one who wants to form the likeness of our Creator within."

As we learn truth, we are able to discern the lies that contradict truth. Scripture is based upon religion and their traditions not upon truth of the laws of creation or our Creator.

Life is simple, beautiful, colorful, musical and healing!

There are seven unhealthy choices we need to avoid: lust, pride, envy, greed, gluttony, laziness, and anger. To live with love, life, and light one is "born from within" and has a new vocabulary with words that bring joy, happiness, peace, health, healing, energy, beauty, unity, blessings, strength, abundance, discernment, children, memory, integrity, freedom, and fun.

Remember, everyone has a choice to choose peace.

We remain in an unconscious state until we become "born from within" and return to the original nature of man. How our Creator created our bodily form and the laws of nature for guidance will support health and happiness.

Until we are "born from within," we remain in darkness and look to the tree of knowledge of good and evil for understanding. There are good people here! You were once one of them so do not judge but love continually. (Constancy using ET or AT in front of your name shows oneness with our Creator.)

An overcomer lives with his thoughts, speech, and action coming from a clean mind with peace, love, kindness, surety, and faith. All things are possible with children of light. They no longer suffer as the kids of the world do. The children of light have chosen our Creator and the laws of creation to live by.

Eight affirmations for the letter Khaf

1. Nature has us in the palm of love, shaping us into a woman or man of truth.

2. Nature and its laws protect us .

3. The blessing of latter rain (revelation) establishes omnipresence. Thank you for the early and latter rains and all the seasons of change.

4. When we know truth no longer is patience required. We live in peace.

5. A spoon is useful and brings pleasure when eating, so as a spoon is to the eater let ET child of light be to our Creator useful and a pleasure.

6. We gravitate to that which we love; this is the law of attraction.

7. The laws of creation are physical, many laws that run this earthy sphere. Remember the one law of love and rest in peace.

8. Great is the study of Aleph—Tav, for it brings into action a crowning (separation from darkness to light) within all the children of light.

Sorrow

In the beginning of life great sorrow came to
our first parents, Adam and Eve.
They partook of the tree of knowledge of good and
evil which consequence had them leave, the very
place of rest and peace to experience and find,
A heartfelt sorrow by conceiving and feeding
their very own mortal kind.
Having the responsibilities of toil and labor to maintain life,
The enduring of a dual nature, love and strife.
This brought painful sorrow and great distress of mind, so, they
gladly returned to our Creator and the laws of the earth
And watched for mankind's miraculous birth.

Temper Tantrum and Little Selfish

"This is my toy!" screamed Heather. "It was bought for me and therefore belongs to me! I should be able to do what I want with it."

"You are not being fair!" cried Little Dave. "You should want to share your toys with me."

"Who wants to share their toys with a big crybaby? You are always causing such a fuss!" exclaimed Heather.

"I want the truck! I want it! I want it!" cried Little Dave as he jumped up and down.

"You can't have it. Nah, nah, nah-nah, nah!" teased Heather.

"I see that you are both being yourselves again," declared their mom, Celia Ann.

Heather looked at Little Dave. Little Dave looked at Heather. They both chimed in together and exclaimed, "Are we really being ourselves again?"

"It is so hard not being what you are!" exclaimed Little Dave.

"It will take time and prayer to change the way you are," stated Mom. "You must begin by doing something each day that will help you to be a better person."

Heather looked at David, her dad. She looked at Little Dave. She turned and said a prayer. Heather then stated, "I will do something today that will help me be a better person. I will let Little Dave play with my truck."

Little Dave looked at his dad. He looked at Heather. He turned and ask for help. Mom whispered something in his ear.

Little Dave said with much excitement, "I know what I will do today. I will play quietly for fifteen minutes. This will help me be a better person. Set the timer, Dad."

When Heather and Little Dave did things to cause each other happiness, they became less selfish and angry. Simple acts of kindness keep love growing in our children.

What will you do today to be a better person?

CHAPTER 12

LAMED

תשרקצפעסנמלכיטחזוהדגבא

The twenty-two letters of light are arranged going from right to left:
Aleph, Bet, Gimel, Dalet, Hay, Vav, Zayin, Chet, Tet, Yod, Kaf,
Lamed, Mem, Nun, Samech, Ayin, Pay, Tzadi, Kuf, Resh, Shin, and Tav.

L amed is the twelfth letter of the aleph-tav.
It has the numerical value of 30.
Repeat of creation day 5 if counting a weekly cycle according
to present-day calendars—Yom Chamishi. Light letters Hay and Quph
or Kuf are also on this day. Meaning given to the writer: **the revelation of
creation revealed by awakened Eve (woman) is the teacher of wisdom**.

It sounds like the English letter "L." Sounds like the word look. Pronounced lah-med.

It is considered the central letter (or heart) of the light letters.

It means to receive wisdom, to be trained, to teach, to write, a disciple, a follower of truth. Shepherd staff, good, control, authority, the only letter that its shape reaches above the other letters, which draws our attention to the source of all wisdom that we receive from our Creator. And our Creator saw the light, that it was beautiful (perfect) and separated the beautiful from the ugly (darkness).

Let's look at the word good using the Aleph-Tav, Towb, Tobe—means beautiful, best, better, bountiful, fine, glad, graciously, joyful, kindly, kindness, loving, merry, most pleasant, pleased, pleasure, precious, prosperity, ready, sweet, wealth, welfare, be well favored. The light letters are Tav, Vav, and Bet. **The house of love is in peace, amen!**

Lamed, "a heart that understands wisdom"; in other words, the goal of learning and teaching is heart wisdom with the end result, to be "born from within," children of light.

Note: according to the sages, the numerical value of the phrase "lev meivin da'at" is the same as the phrase "the heart of Eve," suggesting that the woman's heart is essential for a complete understanding of LIFE (remember life means growth—growth can only happen if something is alive and healthy otherwise it is considered diseased and dying).

The goal of Lamed

Discerning truth from the scriptures is not an end of itself but should urge us on to action. One who studies truth to teach is given the means of discernment of words and one who studies truth to be is given the means to meditate and love. Discernment using the letters of light is spelled naw-kar, light letters are Bet, Yod and Nun. The meaning: prime root to scrutinize, to look intently, to acknowledge, to care for, to respect, to separate or distinguish mentally, to perceive and to hear intelligently. The understanding given to the writer: A house (body, mind) with understanding has respect of the choices made by humankind, therefore no judgment.

Three words of truth

Thought—remember that the truth will bring to your remembrance all that you will need to know.

Speech—remember that every word you speak, not just in oneness and meditation, will be how you discern each day.

Action—kind and loving deeds require faith. Faith without action is dead!

Like a wise shepherd, learning will both urge us on to wise thoughts and control our animal instincts, unconscious fleshy nature.

Prefix for Lamed

"To" or "for"—example melekh—means king but l'melekh means to a king or for a king

Studying and understanding truth is meant to ultimately reveal the love, life, and light of our Creator.

Lev =means heart using the light letters.

Today, the children of light, wherever they place their feet they have the ability to change that place to a pleasing existence. This is a lesson and wisdom for present day people to understand why they may be stuck in a place of darkness. Remember our Creator and the laws of nature and wherever you go, you must take love, life, and light with you, ushering truth to that area, elevating it and showing by example what true humility means. Remember humility means a mature and responsible person that loves our Creator first.

This power, to begin transforming yourself in earnest, begins when we have been born from within. Up until that point we are in training. We receive instruction through many avenues and compare that instruction to that which man has as false religion, unhealthy traditions, and wrong lifestyles.

We find another interesting Gematria in relation to Lamed. Both the Aleph and Lamed represent the teacher. What's the connection between the two letters? The design of the Aleph is comprised of 2 Yod and a Vav, 10 and 10 and 6 = 26. The Lamed is comprised of a Kaf and a Vav: 20 and 6 =26.

Yet there is a marked difference between the teaching styles of the Aleph and the Lamed. The Aleph is more theoretical while the Lamed is more practical. For example, the Aleph represents the written scriptures (stories, general concepts, and deeper meanings of truth) while the Lamed focuses on oral (how to practically apply these truths in one's day to day behavior and speech. Like a parable.)

The shape of Lamed has two levels: one superior aspect, one inferior aspect. One descends to ascend. Those who are working, that is, "born from within"—and those who are receiving instruction to be "born from within"—work in the depths of the mind and heart to gain access to the true wisdom of life. We cleanse our mind and heart of impurities—that is, lies, pagan traditions, and false instruction to give birth to purity, which is truth, wisdom, peace, victory and light. We conquer the carnal thoughts to magnify wisdom, in other words, we cannot know our Creator (cannot enter our head and heart) if we have lust, anger, pride, envy, fear, greed or gluttony. These must be cleansed, purged from our mind. Lamed teaches us this.

Lamed is known as a "tower flying in the air." This tower in the air, the upper segment of the lamed, is our faith. It is the reality of returning to our Creator: to unite, once again, with creation. So you can see that Lamed is a very important letter for us who love our Creator and who are "born from within" and who know where they are going. The Vav of the Lamed represents the mind that has been cleansed. The Vav, which is a chute, draws this purity down from the purified thoughts into the physical world, until it is internalized into the Kaf, the human mind. This merging of purified thoughts into the physical body immerses the Lamed (teacher) with the ability to teach very healthy wisdom in a practical way.

Every person can influence his or her friend or student, and every parent has the heart to teach his or her children the wisdom of our Creator. **We teach best by our own example. Our example must** match up with our words, otherwise, confusion is the result with no progress for our children or ourselves. What is needed is the humility to know when truth is found even though it goes against our present lifestyle. Be able to SEE the false traditions and the people that hold to them and uphold the light of truth without fear. Remember, our Creator is love, life, and light.

Truth tells us that "you shall teach your children and talk to them about these things." To teach our children, we know of our own desire to study the truth of our Creator. For how can we teach our children the truth if we haven't learned it ourselves? Let us look at the word wise, sakal, saw-kal a prime root to be (cause, make or act) circumspect or be wary and unwilling to take risks, hence intelligent-consider, expert, instruct, prosper, (deal) prudently, (give) skill, have success, teach (have, make to understand, wisdom, be, behave self, consider, make) wise (ly) guide wittingly. The light letters are Shin with dagash mark to the left, Kaf, and Lamed, the meaning given to the writer: **The woman Eve, who is born from within, has conquered unhealthy choices and is given the gift to write or speak a way to instruct wisdom to her children.**

When it comes to studying the truth, a person is always a child, and thus "teach your children" can also apply to us. One should never say, oh, I am 50, 90, or 120 now. "I've read books upon books about this subject so many times I cannot remember the number of times. You cannot teach me anything new." On the contrary, the lessons are meant to be infinite. No manner how many times we have set foot in the fertile loam soil, we can always discover new light or uncover deeper meaning in that season of our life if eating according to life. We must approach it like children, and be humble to receive wisdom. But please remember that you must be successful at doing what has been given to you already for more to be received. Showing the change in your actions, speech and thoughts confirm that you have understood the new or uncovered light. Your light is getting brighter every day, thank you for kindness, mercy, and enduring love for your children, amen.

"Who is wise?" One who can learn from all that our Creator has created? Even a rock may have a message.

Even a child!

Lamed is spelled Lamed, Mem, and Dalet, three letters. The Aleph-Tav word Lamed means "to learn." But this learning is not merely intellectual; it begins with the intellect because we have to acquire information through our senses, brain, and nervous system. We need to go deeper than that. If we want to be "born from within" and have a new life, if we want to understand suffering and the consequences that we are in now, we need our mind to be made new with eternal wisdom and vision. That is not done with the intellect. Ideas and theories are just that: ideas and theories. They cannot change anything. Change comes through the heart. The "heart" is spelled with a Lamed and a Bet= leb, labe. The understanding given to the writer: **heart instruction called wisdom is for the home and the children of light that accept our Creator's laws of creation.**

When you comprehend truth in your heart, <u>stress is removed.</u> The intellect only plays games with concepts. You cannot reach our Creator through a concept. Our Creator is beyond a concept. Far, far beyond ideas. Life is growth, a living, vibrating reality, which we feel and taste physically. But life is beyond the physical world. Our ideas only make us wonder, theorize, and argue. None of these achieve anything.

What should happen in us is represented in Lamed. The lower portion of Lamed can represent your heart. If you look at the shape, you can see the shape of a heart in it. Your heart is shaped somewhat like your fist, and almost the same size, and it is almost a pear shape. You see how that fits into a Lamed? If you just drew the little tower on it, you would have Lamed.

אבגדההוזחחטיככלמנסעפפצצקרשת

Look at the twenty-two letters: lamed is exactly in the middle: the heart of the alphabet. Lamed shows us it is possible to go beyond the communication line that the letters were created from. You see the order that all the letters hang from? Only Lamed passes beyond it, above, reaching. This is the power of the heart. This communication line is the real language that has victory. Today, let us consider these letters and their meaning so that we can overcome darkness and the words that mean death. Beautiful communication are words put together to enlarge love, life, and light.

Lamed is your heart!

When you seek truth and wisdom, your heart sees love in all things. Your heart asks, "What do I do with these feelings that I have? This new discernment I have?" Then, we go out and look for guidance, using everything we know, at that time, especially the wisdom we have received from truth. This is "Lamed" to learn. Our heart reaches toward the light. Our mind looks for wisdom; it seeks by the guidance of love. Unfortunately, most of us get stuck right there. We acquire a lot of information, and we might believe it or disbelieve it, but rare is it for that wisdom to come to the heart and be comprehended by the heart; to be digested, to be understood in the heart. Normally, we take ideas and concepts and play with them in the mind. We show them to others—we compare; we analyze.

Then along comes oneness, unity, love, and perfection. Yes, the child of light and truth blossoms in their heart. Wonderful, amazing and full of beauty.

How did they do this? The mind and heart receives wisdom. It says, the "heart of the prudent," (acting with or showing care and thought for the future), so let us look at what that actually means. It is not talking about your physical heart. And it is not talking about "prudent" in the way we think of it. We need our Creator in our heart. Prudence is important, but when we have both male and female in our heart, then prudence is transformed from bin (understand) to Biynah, bee-naw, Light letters, Bet Yod, Nun, and Hay (perfectly understanding wisdom) The understanding given to the writer: **Mother/female has the power to instruct her children of true revelation of our Creator and laws of nature.** biyn-bene—a prime root to separate mentally, distinguish, understand, attend, consider, be cunning, discern, eloquent, instruct, be prudent, teach, deal wisely. Light letters are Bet, Yod, and Nun. In other words, the understanding given to the writer: **true wisdom has the power to heal and bring peace to mankind**.

Intellectual knowledge is just concepts. True wisdom is the power of words.

If we don't have our Creator inhabiting our heart, then we have only the world's knowledge and words. Every creature has a specific language, food, habitat, and behavior. Humankind is no different. Let me see you swim like a fish or fly like a bird or scamper up a tree like a squirrel. Do you really think you have dominion over them?

Did you not have a mother and father or male and female that bore you into this fleshy mortal life? Why do you think it strange that you need our Creator to be formed within?

We can have all the scriptures memorized. We can have man's entire religious doctrine arranged in our mind and be able to explain it, discuss it, and debate it, but it is meaningless if our heart is dead, cold, if our heart does not hold perfect love, life, and light of creation. Remember, our hearts were corrupted by deceptive communication. We ate from the tree of knowledge of good and evil bringing darkness into our mind and body. We need to eat from the tree of life and live forever, which means eat from the table of creation and keep the law of rest.

Being "Creator formed within" is eating from the tree of life, love, light, and wisdom, where perfectness brings man and woman together. Here the hearts are one.

To balance and have peace, truth must overcome the lies, traditions, and preconceived ideas and lifestyles of your past. This is accomplished with little steps of changing your everyday pagan words to words of wisdom. Moreover, you need to be aware of those words that offend. To be a master is to be a "master of words." Because through your words and thoughts comes action. We are what we are because of the words we think. If you want to be something other than what you are now, control your words. Control your words by knowing the truth. Lamed represents how love descends into your heart. The relationship between you and our Creator which is not just in your mind anymore but has reached into your heart! Another word for "Creator formed within," children of light.

Becoming free from suffering has more to do with a person's heart. In the mind, we learn steps, concepts, and ideas, and we need them to clear confusion. But they do not start the "born from within" process in you. Wanting to know truth is by returning to our Creator and the laws of creation. What were we to remember? Remember that we are eternal beings that inhabit a physical body.

Your spinal column is of great significance in this teaching. Lamed represents a staff we carry. A staff in our body; the spinal column. We do not need a physical staff as seen in the Old Testament, like the prophet, Moses. We are children of light with the tabernacle and all its holy furnishings inside each one of us. How did we become so confused that we lost the simplicity of life? Eating dead lifeless flesh! And believing in a religion that actually kills an animal sacrifice to a god. Our Creator is about love, life, and light only—no death!

One who overcomes has love for themselves and others. Kindness will promote healing to all. As we have fun on this earth remember, what do you want to leave behind? "Let your light so shine before men so that they see your beautiful works and praise our Creator that made heaven and earth."

It is the beauty of creation.

The pure truth. It does not say, "Go follow somebody who has light." It does not say, "Go believe in this other light," or "go think about it." **It says let your light shine."** That light shines through your mind, body, and words spoken. Your heart needs to be inflamed, burning, with the love, life, and light of our Creator.

This experience of truth cannot come to us when we love our ideas and our beliefs more than truth. When we love our attachments and when we are in love with matter and energy, when we are addicts of sensation, when we follow people or beliefs, or schools, or traditions, when we are attached to flags and countries and educations and titles and theories, all that, which makes up the world in our mind, is an obstacle. These things above will literally obstruct your ability to breath from your nose, your physical consequence.

To taste the truth, to experience the reality of the emptiness in all things, one must abandon everything that one thinks one is or knows. Not even a speck of "I" can enter there. The letter Lamed teaches us this.

To fully develop a heart of love you close your eyes. You have to shut off your sense of touch, you have to walk away from your hearing, from your sense of taste, from your sense of smell. You have to withdraw into your heart, stay peaceful and still for the victory of the truth to be uncovered. To know this truth all it requires is that you let go of all your attachments. If our point of view is centered in remembrance of our Creator and creation, the opinions of others become less able to hurt us or motivate us toward harmful reactions to ourselves or others. When we can remember our Creator in that way, we are given amazing strength. This is how the great martyrs, the great prophets, the saints, were always able to receive the persecution of others and only respond with love. They could not fake that. Neither can you. The ability to respond to all of life's challenges with a loving heart is a matter of our Creator residing in your heart. It is not a false attitude. There are many people who try to disguise themselves as prophets. There are many so-called masters and spiritual guides who are false, who are all smiles and speak very sweetly. But in their mind, in their heart, they are wolves, beasts, fleshy. It is easy to fool oneself and others. Yet no one can fool our Creator. Be thankful and sing hallelujah!

That spark or flame that burns in the heart is represented by the twenty-first letter, shin.

This is the flame of wisdom that wants to destroy the lies and misconceptions. It does not want to pat you on the back and make you feel better about yourself. It wants you to see the truth, that you make your own suffering, needlessly. All of us. If you suffer it is because you lack truth and wisdom. That is what we have to see. And we have to see how we do it. We have to see past our misconceptions that we have agreed to believe out of fear of being different or shunned by family and friends. Remember that all things that come your way is for your own development. When we see that, we can stop the attachments and lies. The worst lies we tell are to ourselves. We have to see those lies and stop them. This is very painful, but necessary. When we can see the lie then maybe we can see the truth. But you can never see the truth, unless you see the lie first.

To raise a child, you instruct them with your heart directed by truth. **They will learn the most by your example**. Mean yes when you say yes and no when you say no. Live it and teach what you can and suggest, and encourage as prompted. But at a certain point, you have to let the child do it themselves. To learn to walk, the child has to do it on their own. Every one of us has to learn to walk on our own.

A wise instructor, like a wise parent, will hold your hand and then let go once instruction and teaching has ended. Some stay longer, some need less time, it depends on the student. And when they fall down, they learn from falling. At least, they should. We have to learn. Same with children. Ultimately, you have to let them develop themselves with the truth as their guide. If you always help them get out of money problems and sickness, they will never learn to stand on their own. When they have difficult times, they must experience their consequence. They will learn quicker if you give a listening ear. You are there to encourage them and listen to them. The heart is stronger when you understand how to actively listen. They will respect you when they can no longer manipulate your emotions and get you to be responsible for their problems and consequences. Kindness never fails.

The heart condition is what livens the pineal and pituitary gland. These two glands start shutting down if the amount of stress is no longer healthy. The quicker you learn to actively listen to others problems the healthier these glands will become. (*The pituitary gland is very important as it takes messages from the brain via a gland called the hypothalamus and uses these messages to produce hormones that affect many parts of the* *body including stimulating all the other hormone-producing glands to produce their own hormones. Weighing less than one gram and measuring a centimeter in width, the pituitary is often called the "master" gland since it regulates the secretion of the body's hormones. These substances when released by the pituitary into the bloodstream have a dramatic and broad range of effects on growth and development, sexuality and reproductive function, metabolism, the response to stress and overall quality of life.) (Pineal gland is located deep in the center of the brain and once known as the "third eye." It produces melatonin, which helps maintain circadian rhythm and regulates reproductive hormones. The best known function of the pineal gland is to regulate sleep and day-night cycles. It allows the brain to detect whether there is light in the environment. The detection of light stimulates the **natural** melatonin cycle.)*

Think before you speak. Stop! Check your heart—the words spoken—does it feel right or confusing, does it give your heart a weighing? Ask for explanation or restate what is being asked. Learn to give your heart time to respond to their energy, respond above their energy—let them be responsible—know that this will be wisdom for all. When someone tells you of their money problem, your best response is to listen and help them figure out how to improve budgeting. If they have a health problem, it is better to listen unless they ask you for advice. But then give them some helpful information pointing them to resources so that they can be led by truth to make their own decision. Let them gather their own information and suffer their own consequences, unless you want to suffer for them. The physical consequence you receive if you always are enabling is they will destroy your pineal and pituitary gland if you let them and ultimately damage your heart! You will allow them to take away your strength in our Creator and the Aleph-Bet letters. These, by the way, are the children of darkness, not "born from within." Know them, pray for them with wisdom's words, confront them when necessary because they cannot be anything except fleshy.

Eight affirmations for letter lamed

1. Thunder and lightning firmly state how to rise above this earthy realm. Notice and be alert to the truth.

2. The heart of the manner is this, be a living example.

3. May our Creator continue to rain down wisdom and revelation to all so that we may finish our work on the earth in truth.

4. A truth-filled teacher will move the student to a higher eternal level.

5. Love, life, and light removes fear, doubt, and darkness.

6. Our Creator's connection grows the heart for additional wisdom. Quiet yourself so that truth can impart daily wisdom.

7. Teach to bring love, life, and light to others—thank you for this time on the earth—kindness and mercy endures forever.

8. Lamed is our backbone (spine)—humility and discipline will give us the power to move with authority to teach those that desire to unite with our Creator and the laws of nature.

Perfect Dance

Hal-le-lu-yah
The birds, fish, and beast play
The trees, plants, and herbs sway.
The moon, stars, and sun obey,
The song of each glorious and prophetic day.
The winter, spring and summers ray,
Bring to mind our Creator's way.
The rain, snow and frost lay
Upon the earth's fertile land—hoo-ray!
Morning, noon and night say,
Hal-le-lu-yah
Moving all creation into one, the perfect dance in May.

December 2022
Love, Life, Light

Fear Is Swallowed Up in Victory

Little Rene and Scott were sitting quietly playing a game when they noticed that it was nine o'clock and time for bed. Both were discussing how they could convince their sister to let them stay up for a few more minutes.

But wouldn't you know it, right in the middle of their conversation, their sister, Anjanette, walked into the family room and turns off the computer before either one could say another word. As she pointed to the clock, she said, "Mom and Dad wanted you in bed by nine tonight, so it is time for bed, boys."

Little Rene answered in a whiney tone of voice, "Oh, Anjanette, do we have to go to bed now? Can we play one more game?"

"You know the rules of this family. Go to bed, both of you," declared Anjanette as she looked at the boys with her raised eyebrows and added, "And remember to brush your teeth."

"Let's go," said Scott, "we need to listen to Anjanette."

"Okay," Little Rene mumbled, "but stop pushing me."

The boys were now in their bedroom. Scott tip-pi-toed to the door and eased it to a crack. When he turned around, he found Little Rene crying.

Scott then asked, "Now, what is the matter?"

As Little Rene continued to cry, he answered, "I am afraid that the alligators and snakes will get me."

Scott then asked, "When do you see these alligators and snakes?"

"When I close my eyes, I can see them biting my toes and legs." Little Rene shivered as tears began to roll down his checks.

"I know a way to make the alligators and snakes disappear," said Scott. "First you must take this pencil and paper and draw me a picture of the alligators and snakes."

"I am afraid to, Scott," answered Little Rene as he continued crying.

"Come on," encouraged Scott, "I know you can do it!"

"Okay," mumbled Little Rene, "this is what they look like." He took the piece of paper and pencil and drew pictures of the alligators and the snakes.

Scott studied the picture for a few seconds and then said, "Watch what I can do to your alligators and snakes!" Scott quickly erased the picture.

Little Rene then exclaimed, "You made all the alligators and snakes disappear, Scott! Oh, I think I can be brave now. Will you hold me for a few minutes?"

After Scott hugged his little brother, they brushed their teeth and then jumped into bed. Scott looked at his brother and said, "Now you will be able to go to sleep."

"Yes," agreed Little Rene, "I am so glad that I have a big brother like you, Scott."

As Scott turned off the light, he spoke very softly and said, "I like having you as my little brother too."

CHAPTER 13

MEM

תשרקצפעסנמלכיטחזוהדגבא

The twenty-two letters of light are arranged going from right to left:
Aleph, Bet, Gimel, Dalet, Hay, Vav, Zayin, Chet, Tet, Yod, Kaf,
Lamed, Mem, Nun, Samech, Ayin, Pay, Tzadi, Kuf, Resh, Shin, and Tav.

M em is the **thirteenth** letter of the aleph-tav, and M is the
thirteenth letter in the English alphabet.
Numerical value: 40.

English letter is M.

A repeat of creation day six if counting a weekly cycle according to
present-day calendars. Vav and Resh are on this day. Meaning given to

the writer: **the connection to mercy, grace, and the leaves of healing come from the "life spoken words" that you speak.**

Sound: like the word *mom—M.*

Meaning: water, chaos, mighty, the truth within our Creator—as water runs freely so the word or truth (our Creator's breath) in nature is FREE.

There are two forms of the Mem: the open Mem and the closed Mem. The open Mem represents the revealed truth and the closed Mem represents the hidden or better said those truths that have been covered up through time because of forgetfulness and unhealthy choices. Now that we are in present time, it is a joy to experience a sweet taste of the unchanging laws of our Creator, the uncovered word/water. These are simple principles that can be applied to everyday life which manifest our Creator's protection and health.

The Mem represents the womb. The closed Mem represents the nine months when the womb is closed and developing the new word/ child/creation. The open Mem represents the period of childbirth, when the womb is open for delivery. So we have the beginning and the end within each childbirth called Aleph-Tav, which is another word for creation or word. We first are born of the flesh, and we then start our journey to be "Creator formed within" while we sojourn on the earth. By the water first then by the word of truth (first birth fleshy and second birth the Creator formed within). **A child born from within and of the flesh is governed by the laws of creation and truth. You want to be one with our Creator.**

You cannot get away from the laws of nature. These laws govern your mind and body's health. What you choose brings health are disease.

Water: (mayim, mah-yim) the spring of the word, juice, urine, semen, water (ing, course, flood, spring). Light letters are Mem, Yod, and closed Mem. The understanding given to the writer: **Wisdom's words come from truth to the clear mind and return love back to creation. The word of truth never returns void.** Just as the waters of an underground spring rise upward from an unknown source to reveal themselves, so does the spring of wisdom flow down from the everlasting Creator of truth. So what covers truth? Passed-down preconceived ideas and thoughts such as family upbringing, lies, and false traditions.

The flowing stream of hidden wisdom can be expressed by a teacher's **heart** condition, which is revealed by their SPEECH. Light letters. A to Z, or Aleph to Tav.

Water constitutes a vital element in our lives: a human being is largely composed of water, 50 percent to 70 percent, and the majority of the earth, 70 percent is covered with it too. Truth, the most vital element to have love, life, and light, is referred to as water. He who is thirsty shall go and drink water, meaning, they who come to awakened love will be lead to the springs of everlasting victory, where wisdom, truth and health is found.

If you progress to the tree of life you will be eating from the table of creation, as well as keeping daily rest, using the sun, moon and stars as your calendar. You will see that a day is from dawn to when the sun sets—light, understanding the first day of creation. We are children of light and have been removed from darkness. You will see the earth is flat with a dome above and below. When the waters of heaven above and waters below were collected, then earth appeared. Creation brought forth fish that live in the waters and birds that fly in the sky and to capture or kill goes against the laws of creation. The same with the beast and creeping things. They belong in their environment to sustain the health and balance of the earth.

Mankind was created by the law of love, having male and female unite as one, marriage. Just males or just females cannot have offspring. This is an unhealthy choice that would destroy humankind.

The nature of truth will uncover this to all those that are "born from within." Proverbs 3:13–81, pg. **732** says, "Blessed is the man who has found wisdom, and the man who gets understanding: for the gain from it is better than gain from silver, and its increase than fine gold, **She** is more precious than rubies and all your delights are not comparable to her. Length of days is in her right hand, riches and esteem in her left hand. Her ways are pleasant ways and all her paths are peace. SHE IS A TREE OF LIFE TO THOSE TAKING HOLD OF HER AND BLESSED ARE ALL WHO RETAIN HER."

Woman is said to have been made from a rib. Rib is tsal'ah, tsal-aw as curved of the body (of a door, that is a leaf, hence a side (i.e., quarter, side chamber). Light letters are Tsadi, Lamed, Ayin, and Hay. The understanding given to the writer: **the female teaches eternal insight by revelation and example.**

Mother was just as Eve was, hiding because of untruth and darkness that needed to be removed. Today mother is awake and teaching her children about our Creator and the laws of nature.

The light letters (Aleph-Tav) are a blueprint of our Creator's creation. The wealth and strength of speech, water that carves, and continues to carve out the foundation of the entire world in each mind and heart. After physical birthing an individual to this earth then that person starts developing toward a "born from within" new man or woman—representing the closed Mem again.

Crossing over when the breath of our Creator is removed from the physical body we join our Creator as one then becomes our final event, the open Mem—the delivery into eternal life. So until we are released from our mortal body we do not finish our "born from within" delivery. The physical body must cease, die first, then the open Mem, delivery into eternal life completes the law of the life cycle.

You must be careful of the words you speak and what you physically eat as this is what carves into your DNA and keeps alive and in good health the mortal body that our Creator lovingly and freely gave to you.

Proverbs 18:4, pg. **745** says, "The words a man speaks are deep waters, a flowing stream, a fountain of wisdom."

Where is the truth that shows us how we should physically eat as to produce life? Let us return to the first day of creation. Bring yourself closer to the garden and the beginning of creation and the law of nature will confirm how we should eat to live and have life abundantly on the earth. Get busy and research how to eat this way and be satisfied. There are a lot of lies that must be uncovered to eat the way that brings your mortal body health. Eat from the table of creation and you shall have more life and given to you, more abundantly.

Fast foods, manmade foods, were made for taste and gain and not for health. These foods bring pain, disease and depression. We know the body shall die physically however, we, in the process of "being born within" are promised health as we live on the earth if we love our Creator who made humankind by the law of nature. Once again, another reason to be "Creator formed within" to see and live. We however, should not disregard health as the words of truth will show the light in all things, whatever you ask with a humble heart. These truths will not be for gain of money but for the health of the body and mind. Your heart needs to be strong and healthy to have the light of our Creator shine through you to others. Understanding truth is important as you see our Creator wants us to live long and healthy upon the earth. Those that lived the longest lives in Bible history were those that ate from the table of creation.

The numerical value of mem is 40:

1. Forty days from conception to the initial formation of the fetus
2. Forty weeks of gestation until birth

Mem represents eternal omnipresence: _makom_, maw-kome—maqowm meaning "place" standing, a spot, of a condition of body or mind. Light letters are Mem, Kuf, Vav, and closed Mem. The understanding given to the writer: **the truth of our Creator connects the mature being to their second birth, the "Creator formed within."** This has both the open and closed mem. Our Creator's presence is both open and revelatory, yet is also shrouded in the deep portals of the body, closed off to human reason if not willing to come close to the law of daily rest.

Faith using the aleph-Tav is spelled Emunah—emuwnah, pronounced em-oo naw. Meaning: firmness, security, fidelity, established, trust worthiness. The understanding given to the writer: **faith yields refreshment and healing for those who have returned to creation.**

What is the concept of forty? After forty days, the embryo of a child begins to assume a recognizable form. A new word/child/creation is growing and multiplying inside the Mem, mother's womb.

Let's look at the time of the biblical flood—the waters of the flood were used to wash away the darkness of the world and to purify and transform the world, in much the same way a mikveh/baptism (a purifying bath with water) is the Bible symbol of purification of a person.

Those that understand our Creator keep clean by what they eat and think and do daily, the consequence, they experience daily purification and rest.

The whole time a baby is in the womb they are in **water**! This is the **water** that brings forth birth in the flesh. You can be baptized in water every day but until you are "born from within" you remain asleep to truth! The truth is you must be born of **water, the birthing into the physical realm,** and then be awakened to truth, our Creator "born again."

When the laws of nature or creation are understood he or she develops the ability to change for life. Remove the lies! With these changes for the better, he or she can begin to discern the world as it really is and be one to truth and present time.

The womb is the unknowable (a baby is hidden until birth), and this is why the letter Mem symbolizes the womb. The open Mem, which has a gap in the bottom, is the womb that is ready for parturition—the action of giving birth.

The first day of creation is related with the closed or final Mem. In the first day of creation all was **finished** being created but because humankind was created to have a choice (a law of creation within humankind) time (a law of earth's creation) was created (using the sun and moon) for all beings to have a chance to choose. The reason for having children (another creation law). Man is no different than the animals that beautify the earth. The animals listen to the laws of creation that govern them and do exactly how our Creator made them to respond. Humankind is learning how not to disturb their natural habitat so they can continue to live in harmony with nature. The city humankind have a lot to remember.

So the one that shapes the universe (child's mind) is always wisdom or mother. The father gives male semen, seed. Mother shapes the seed, child, for nine months, Mem, wisdom/water. Remember it takes nine months to form a baby in a sack of water ready for delivery. We will say the father gives the seed and with it the mother/wisdom forms the character which can be compared to rays of LIGHT.

Nine rays of light as follows:

Crown or anointing—separate from darkness, health
Wisdom or deeper and hidden understanding, joy
Intelligence and discernment
Mature, complete with perfection,
Strength and courage
Beauty with rest,
Firmness or victory,
Peace, harmony, and balance
Foundation with truth.
All eternal beings that inhabit a human body are perfect.

The body on the other hand will have defects because of unhealthy generational choices (our Creator is within all humankind and by their choice to remember is represented by the letter Mem).

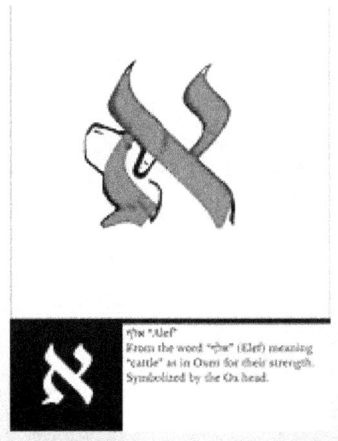

אלף "Alef"
From the word "אלף" (Elef) meaning "cattle" as in Oxen for their strength. Symbolized by the Ox head.

This universe is in the shape of the letter aleph

Wisdom created all words/children—this is the hidden revelation. Remember, word is equal or like the birthing of a new life or child.

"And the earth."

It is written Aleph-Tav Ve-at Ha-Arets, which is usually translated to mean "and the earth." Yet we can see that it means "wisdom, manifest the word through the [breath], in the earth." Wisdom resides in the whole of nature. Thus the whole phrase:

"The first daughter, Eve, formed [male/female, a child], the heavens and the earth" within her womb. "And the man called his wife Hawwah, Eve, because she became the mother of **all** living."

When a child is born and given a name, we have heaven and earth appearing before our very eyes. The being and the physical body is repeating what happened in the beginning of creation. The word "Word" is equal to the physical birth of someone. "AT" or "ET"—the aleph-bet, Aleph to Tav is in every person born. A new word is formed. Every time male and female form a baby, it is like forming heaven and earth in each new child/as a new word. The beauty of creation! When new life is born, it is like seeing a new heaven and earth begin in that child. This is the life cycle of humankind, a law of creation.

When we are "born from within," we are taken out from bondage or darkness transforming darkness into the word light, born from within— for those who identify with their old nature set their minds on the things of the old nature but those that identify with eternity set their minds on the things of Creation, that which is eternal.

The **heart** is where memory is awakened. The law of nature cleans the heart by discerning wisdom. Wisdom comes from the base of the earth (live foods from the ground and trees), and this energy rises to our brain/mind to be united—one with our Creator.

Through humility, we are "born from within," for we become, using light letters, "Aur" which means light in English. This is wisdom which makes things clear and simple.

King David—he wrote about the aleph bet with eight affirmations after each letter in psalm 119. This is the work that brings forth King David's understanding of truth. He was in agreement with the Hebrew religion and ruled from that point of view.

King Solomon, King David's son, respected his mother. He wrote Proverbs, all about wisdom! We read in 1 Kings 2:19, pg. **348**, "And Bathsheba came to Sovereign Shelomoh, to speak to him for Adoniyahu. And the sovereign rose up to meet her and <u>bowed</u> down to her, and sat down on his throne and had a throne set for the sovereign's mother. So she sat at his <u>right hand</u>."

Wisdom or mother rises from the earth to the top of the head, crown. When she arises, she brings all the laws of creation with her keeping life simple.

You cannot be "Creator formed within" unless you see mother in you as she represents your **heart**. The father within is the head/crown and the mother is the heart/wisdom.

"Her children arise and call her blessed: her husband also and he praises her" (Proverbs 31:28, pg. **758**).

The whole tree of life within us receives power. "By the organized word thou wilt partake of the honors (the light) of the whole earth and darkness [ignorance] will flee from thee."

You might ask, how do we understand all this? By loving our Creator with all your mind, heart, and strength! Thus, if you continually change your fleshy nature by stopping unhealthy cycles then ignorance and pride will flee from you and light will emerge. That light comes from the words of truth, wisdom, who will instruct you, because wisdom is with the light of our Creator, and without that light you cannot be "born from within."

Woman using the Aleph-Tav is ishshah, ish-shaw; letters of light are Aleph, Shin, and Hay. The understanding given to the writer: **the breath or words of wisdom, clears the mind to receive truth**.

By uniting the heavenly and earthy waters, the child/new word is brought forth. This is the law of life. When the two come together we have a new human being. The light does not come from outside of you, it comes from within you. We look at nature and perceive truth, that simple. When nature begins to get off balance anywhere on the earth, hurricanes, tsunami and earthquakes occur to regain the earth's equilibrium. The same with our bodies. When disease begins to upset the body, you have signs throughout it saying balance please. Fast and give nature a chance to work and bring healing to the diseased area.

Here is the strength of all power. With this thou wilt be able to overcome all things and to discern between what is fine and what is coarse.

The law of creation represents man and woman. By humility, they work under this protection. When they are in union they are accomplishing the wisdom to multiply and replenish the earth. Our love of our Creator is to give birth to a male or female.

When man and woman have our Creator in their **heart** in the holy matrimony, wisdom is shining. When that light rises, then that which is written happens: "Let there be light." This light gives you clear and deeper understanding of the purpose of children. We are children of light.

What happens after this union? After they complete this union then teaching of the laws of creation begin to shine forth. Our children have the eternal understanding of life.

The end of something which is death, and a renewal of something is a very important change. Let say you decide to stop smoking—in a since it is death to that thing and a renewal to life. In a deeper numerological perspective, the number thirteen can be considered the fulfillment or manifestation of death to life.

Listen, to love our Creator "with all your **heart** and with all your being, and with all your mind and with all your strength," you must leave the old way, death, and follow the "born from within" new life transformation. To "love our neighbor," we have to know the truth and notice when we are being deceived. Become aware of the little foxes. "Catch us the foxes, the little foxes that ruin the vineyards—for our vineyard is in blossom. Song of Songs 2:15, pg. 786" **Know the false god and religion the little deceptions that ruin your peace—for the awakened is here, in you, memory.**

Once you are "born from within," you will have rest! Otherwise, you are being directed by the lies of man.

Remember wisdom is with you, even if she has not been made known to you at this time. The words of truth will bring to your re**mem**brance all things at the time appointed. Then we live in victory, because we find Abraham and Sarah one, Isaac and Rebecca one, and Jacob and Leah one. This is MEM. Male and female united-one within our Creator.

Them has the M on the end and if we use the light letter final Mem on the word the**m** it is like finished!

Mavet means death using the letters of light which begins with the letter Mem. This death is all the impurities we have within—better known as the EGO. We remove unhealthy choices and religious traditions and replace with the laws of nature and truth of our Creator. Love is peaceful, and kind, not jealous not boastful, not proud, rude or selfish not easily angered, and it keeps no record of wrongs, love does not gloat over other people's mistakes but takes its delight only in the truth. Love always bears up, always trusts, always hopes, always endures, love, life, and light never ends. Love stands at the end of one's life.

Honor your father and mother who are within you. This truth was speaking of father and mother, not only your earthly parents that gave you birth on the earth through water but the ONE, Creator that has born you from within.

Eight affirmations for Mem

1. Rivers of water flow from those that love our Creator—as related to the Truth. Sing out, you nations of peace.

2. All there is, is present time if born from within.

3. Our Creator gives us the opportunity to increase with the power of love. Or the "born from within" has the opportunity to increase in all things.

4. Remember, we are perfect beings!

5. We like silence the best for truth moves in this quiet absolute space.

6. The tongue is a small **mem**ber (two *M*s) of the body—but great is its power—love wisdom.

7. Mem is both male and female in union.

8. The union produces perfect children.

Mother

Mother is a very beautiful and wonderful name;
She began in the beginning known as
wisdom, which has never changed.
Modesty, quietness, and rest are virtues that she holds in her hand,
While her table is offered to those who keep the
love of nature and obey the laws of the land.
There is no one that goes hungry or naked in her reach, her
children know her and love her for the word that she does teach.
Standing with our Creator is witnessed by her uplifted
right hand, while nature, mediation, and writing
are included in her peaceful merciful fan.
Protecting as the mother hen, she surely covers her sweet
children and quietly but tenderly moves them within.
Holy, majestic, hallelujah, jubilee!
Are words written to express our love for mother,
from the children born from within and are
FREE!

What Makes a Person Wise?

"I think it is time for lunch," remarked Adam.

"How do you know that?" questioned Alexis.

"I know that it is lunch time!" exclaimed Adam, because I hear Nikki singing her favorite song."

"Yes, I hear Nikki singing too," answered Alexis.

As Nikki was getting ready to make her sandwich she sang out very loudly, "I want a mustard and peanut butter sandwich today."

"Whoever heard of eating mustard and peanut butter?' stammered Alexis. "I need to help her."

"Leave Nikki alone!" declared Adam. "She wants to try something different and experience her consequence."

"What do you mean?" disagreed Alexis.

"Nikki is only seven years old and needs help to decide on what she wants to eat."

Adam then very calmly explained to Alexis, "You are only making a fuss because Nikki did not ask you for help."

"Well, she always has me help her and she has never asked me to make a mustard and peanut butter sandwich for her," objected Alexis.

"You must try to understand that Nikki does not want your help today. That does not mean that she does not like you as her sister," answered Adam.

"Oh," replied Alexis, "why is it that you always seem to know everything, Adam?"

"My goodness," Adam replied, "you are full of questions today."

"Please, Adam, please tell me why you understand people!" pleaded Alexis.

"Okay, Alexis, I will tell you," answered Adam. "I always look and listen to what is going on around me before I say or do anything. Staying in present time will give me understanding if I am quiet and calm."

"Is this how you knew that it was lunch time today? You were listening and heard Nikki singing?" questioned Alexis.

"Yes, now you are beginning to understand," kindly spoke Adam.

"I sure am glad that you listened to all my questions today," replied Alexis.

"You have helped me to understand about present time. All I have to remember is to listen and stay quiet for direction.

Do you hear the thoughts that give you directions to peace?

CHAPTER 14

NUN

ת ש ר ק צ פ ע ס נ מ ל כ י ט ח ז ו ה ד ג ב א

The twenty-two letters of light are arranged going from right to left:
Aleph, Bet, Gimel, Dalet, Hay, Vav, Zayin, Chet, Tet, Yod, Kaf,
Lamed, Mem, Nun, Samech, Ayin, Pay, Tzadi, Kuf, Resh, Shin, and Tav.

Nun is the fourteenth light letter.
Numerical value: 50
Sounds like "N," as in *noon*.

It is the repeat seventh day if counting a weekly cycle according to
present-day calendars. Zayin and Shin are also on this day. Meaning

given to the writer: **we take upon us our Creator's light as we are made perfect looking into eternity.**

Meanings: kingship, fish, miscarriage, miracle, sprout, seed, force of life, continue, heir, deceit.

Design: there are two types of Nuns. The "bent" Nun either begins or is in the middle of a word. The straight, or final Nun is used only when it is found at a word's end.

The person that serves our Creator out of obligation, religious connection, with little foundation of wisdom and the laws of creation are mixing error with truth. This person is hunched over and still carrying most of their burdens. The second person loves our Creator out of their heart with wisdom and advancing truth and thus stands straight and is a beautiful example. This person is characterized by **kindness**, because love gives us space, the expanse, to move in. These people are humble and can recognize when they are in_error and makes the changes necessary to continue in truth.

Error—using the light letters—Tavek, pronounced taw'vek means to sever. Light letters are Tav, Vav, and Khaf. The understanding given to the writer: **unhealthy choices will eventually cover truth and the connection to our Creator will be lost**.

The word *kind* is first noted in Genesis.

Kind is the primary root called myin, pronounced meen using the Aleph-Tav (Mem Yud Nun)—means to portion out, a sort that is a species. "Let the earth bring forth grass, the herb yielding seed, and the fruit tree yielding fruit after his **kind**, whose seed is in itself, upon the earth: and it was so."

How to study Nun? Throughout a person's life he looks and studies the examples of **humility, health, and peace**. Once a person sees that in all books made by humankind nothing can compare to going outside in the fresh air and enjoying the beauty of creation.

It is not about a person's intelligence but of the **humility** and love toward our Creator first, and then others that will ultimately gain the victory over religious lies, better known as Satan—pronounced Saw-tawn, and means the arch enemy of truth and attacks and accuses. Letters of light for Satan are Shin, Tet, and Final Nun. The understanding given to the writer: **Satan will imitate the fire of truth, leading people to choose decisions, which lead to disease and poor health.**

What does the scripture tell us of Moses? Ex: 4:10—12 pg. **60** says, "He was not eloquent but slow of speech and a slow tongue." However, the Hebrew god assured him that he would be with his mouth and teach him what he should say. So he **humbled** himself and went forward in faith. Deuteronomy 34:7, pg. 224 says, "And Moses was one hundred and twenty years old when he fell asleep. His eyes were not dim nor his freshness [strength] gone. Remember he ate manna (plant food) and drank water the last 40 years of his life!"

When one loves our Creator, discernment is the benefit found within that person and will empower him/her with the **humility** to embrace the diversity of creation. The bent person is still carrying a load on their shoulders because he/she cannot change and move toward true light. The connection to religion and family traditions is too great and fear not love possesses their heart.

Gematria: the number value of nun is 50.

How is the concept of freedom and the truth connected? One who learns truth is truly free, but for the skeptic to challenge this statement would be all too easy. "Free? What do you mean free? The truth taught by man is full of restrictions! It tells me not to do this and not to do that. Some freedom!"

Yet indeed, when one learns the truth, he is free of the false religious god and the materialistic constraints of society. Free from his self-centered, animalistic inclinations. He has the power to confront and transcend these obstacles. Furthermore, truth gives an individual the ability to maximize his potential to be the best he can be.

As an example, when you are eating nutritious food, your performance is optimally enhanced. Sure, you can survive on brownies, French fries, hamburgers and Coca-Cola but the fact of the matter is when you eat healthy foods you're able to perform and think better. You are treating your temple/body with respect, therefore, respecting our Creator who created you from the elements of the earth. You have love for yourself!

Let's say you have all the material amenities to live relatively stress-free, and your social life is according to the world. But when you do decide to live the truth lifestyle, you soon realize that you are able to operate at a much higher plane of existence than the average individual. (Responsible consumption of alcohol, no cigarettes, processed foods, caffeine or flesh.) You feel energized each morning of your life and are thankful and not enslaved to the dictates of the false values of society. You regain your health physically and mentally and just that gives you more **time** to have a joyful and prosperous day. When a person is in wonderful health, they no longer look at time, as they have life and life more abundantly. It will not matter to these children of light about the destruction that is here on the earth because they are alive and will continue to be alive beings no matter what happens to the earth and the blinded people.

Death has no hold on them as truth reveals that they live forever! Our Creator blesses us with love, life and abundant light. What are some of the blessings of creation that do not change? The sun comes up and gives humankind and the earth physical light and energy that is needed for life, the birds sing and fly each day, all kind breath the air without having to pay for it, all nature is in harmony with each other creating balance, mankind always has a choice, we see the moon which gives us light at night once the sun retires and sets, new life: children are born each day, old life: parish and return to the ground and the eternal being returns to our Creator who gave them breath, the flowers, plants and trees bloom in their seasons according to their kind. These blessings are beautiful and simple.

Another meaning of Nun is **deceit**. Using the Aleph-Tav it is pronounced mirmah, meer-maw-means fraud, false, treachery, beguile. Letters of light are Mem, Resh, Mem, and Hay. The understanding given to the writer: **the word from the false head, waters down the**

truth, blaspheming our true Creator—result mixture that has error and truth together causing confusion.

The "born from within" will reveal and draw our Creator's infinite love, life, and light down into this world, so that we can see the true reality of oneness. Everything is wonderful and blessed is everything when seen with "born from within" eyes. This is done by loving the truth and loving nature. This concept is expressed in the straight long final Nun which has a design similar to the Vav, a chute. In contrast to the Vav, however, its left extends beneath the baseline. This implies the downward flow of perfect energy reaching into even the deepest cells of the human mind and body. Carving an eternal DNA/mind/heart to reflect the "born from within" individual.

Nun also means **kingship**. "May his name (Yinon) endure forever as long as the earth shall exist." Yinon refers to kingship. If we break the word Yinon into two—Yud and Nun—nun means kingship, and putting a Yud before a word denotes continuity.

The straight Nun has **humility** and is in all the children of love, life, and light. The blessings of health shines through their faces.

When we daily return to our Creator and nature, we move into a sphere of **humility**. We are blessed with time and the means to give back resources for the continuity of the earth.

The word using the Aleph-Tav for serpent is nachash. Pronounced naw-khawsh—the word nachash means to hiss, that is to whisper a magic spell, enchantment. Using the letters of light: Nun, Chet, and Shin. The understanding given to the writer: **The false seed that produces death instead of life is destroyed by his own chaos—fire.**

Nun is not a literal fish, a physical fish but the **force of life**: and how do we know this is so? Because in a women's womb her **waters (birthing sack)** has the power to carry nephesh chaiah: a living individual.

In the story of Job, we see Leviathan is over all the prideful people. Job is **humble** so in a way after having his family taken away, his health, his wealth, everything—conclude with a description of Levi-tanniyn? Same as Leviathan-pride. Job would not let his ego take control of his life even when he was in death—he overcame and was "born from within" in his day (Job 41: 1–34, pg. **784**).

When Moses had completed his time on the earth he did not demand to be in charge. He did not get to relax and be king. Instead, he fell asleep in peace. This represents how we must put to silence our own selfish nature to move in the sphere of **humility**.

We need not attach ourselves to having followers, to having groups, to being a leader or a king or queen. To sum this up—we are not looking for power or leadership to rule over people but to keep ourselves **humble** so that our life can be used to shine the light within. An eternal example!

We have two paths that we need to look at: the spiral path—around and around and around we go but watch out we may fall down. "Naphal" letters of light are: Nun, Pay, and Lamed. The understanding given to writer: **the seed that speaks and teaches.** So be careful of what you teach and be willing to admit when advancing light shows previous teachings to be in error.

Or the second path as a "born from within," children of light.

Many people understand nature and love the outdoors but still do not understand the error of humankind and religion. People think that they can have both the doctrine of man and nature. However, these two things do not agree. With man you have worshipping a god and not loving life and light. No one can understand a "born from within" on this beautiful path, only another person doing the same work. Those that remain on the spiral path and will not change even if they know they are in error because of family, work, friends, congregation or lifestyle remain in opposition.

Now that you have nature and all the earth's blessings you will never be alone. You are just leaving that which held you to the darkness of the world. A teacher of truth will teach many as their gifts require sharing, a love that is not of this world and cannot be fully explained on paper.

The person on the spiral path may ascend gradually yet are always in danger of falling because of a resistance of uncovered advancing light. The letter Nun is the first letter of the word naphal, "to fall." Nun carries a great danger. Nun means to degenerate. Return back to the old way of thinking all is well and not see the danger that is upon them until it is too late, consequence—a fall.

Nonetheless, the one who remains true to our Creator who keeps life simple can advance to a life that may be said or called an angel or messenger. This is someone who can hear truth and have a confirmation or witness of that truth. Angel is mal'ak, mal-awk, to dispatch as a deputy, a messenger (i.e., an angel also a prophet, prophetess, priest or teacher, ambassador, king, and child of light). The letters of light are Mem, Lamed, Aleph, and Kaf. The understanding given to the writer: **words that teach about our Creator through the teacher's blessings**.

Let's look at the word AMEN.

Amen encodes the eternal path. Amen has three letters: Aleph, Mem, and Nun. The understanding given to the writer: **the father and mother bring forth their offspring, their blessings.**

That last Nun in Amen is a complete Nun. It is a final Nun that represents the "born from within" individual. The final Nun represents high levels of perfection which means balance and maturity.

Union has two NUNs—male and female.

Perfect union is established in our heart; it represents a perfect reflection of our Creator. Male and female—perfect and complete, totally balanced.

The third tree named in Geneses is the fig.

When Adam and Eve eyes were opened to darkness they saw that their bodies were naked. They made an apron with fig leaves to cover themselves. **Naked** using the Aleph-Tav is arowm, aw-rome or Aram, aw-ram, means to be or make bare, to be cunning, deal subtly, and take crafty, smoothness, and nude. Letters of light are Ayin, Resh, Vav, and closed Mem. The understanding given to the writer: **the insight received in the head gave reason for connection to reunite us to nature.**

Apron using the Aleph-Tav is chagar, khaw-gar, meaning a belt, be afraid, to grid on as armor, appointed, restrain, letters of light are Chet, Gimel, Resh. The understanding given to the writer: **a restrained life journeying in fear**.

Fig using the Aleph-Tav is Teh-ane male; t'e nah female. Light letters are: Tav, Aleph, and Nun, male and Tav, Aleph, Nun, Hay, female. See the Hay on the end it makes the word female, like Sarah and Eve-Hawwah. The understanding given to the writer: **truth is the breath of life given to all creation.**

The Fig

About half of **figs** produces **both male and female** flowers. **Edible figs contain only long-style female flowers**.

Figs are not fruit—they're actually inverted flowers. As such, they **require** a specific kind of pollination that can only come from **fig wasps—wasps** that have to die inside the fruit for the fruit to mature, since **figs** cannot be **pollinated** by wind or normal bees.

Wasp using the light letters is Tav, Ayin, Resh and Tazadi. The understanding given to the writer: <u>**The truth gives vision to those that have returned to our Creator.**</u>

There is at least one dead **wasp** inside the **figs** that we like to eat. The **figs** produce ficin, a special enzyme that breaks down the insect's body into proteins that **get** absorbed by the plant.

The **fig** tree is the third tree to be mentioned by name in the **Bible**. During Solomon's reign, Judah and Israel, from Dan to Beersheba, lived in safety, each man "under his own vine and **fig** tree," an indication of peace.

The fig also resembles a womb, symbolizing a very fertile time to renew something.

Fig trees are extremely susceptible to stress, which causes them to slow down or even stop ripening their fruit. The most common stress is **lack of water** in high-heat conditions. **Fig** trees have a <u>shallow root</u>

system, and irrigation is extremely important. When awakened to truth, that means we cannot produce offspring if under stress—no water meaning no fruit and vegetables being eaten so we dry up (no advancing light) and physically (bringing forth children).

Our example of what to eat will encourage those around us to develop better eating habits. As you are with them, it convicts them of the TRUTH that is eternal. Even if you say nothing and they say nothing they are seeing with their own eyes the TRUTH. Remember, Adam and Eve's eyes were open, if we can eat from the table of creation our bodies will have a chance for healthier lifestyles and the bodies thirst will be less. The more fruit and vegetables eaten the less the body is thirsty.

Shallow root system could mean the reason we need to eat every day from the table of creation. If we go to many days not eating from the table of creation, we begin to dry up physically and also with the understanding of our Creator. Our body begins to thirst again as before which shows we have severed our connection to our Creator and life. "Come all ye that are a thirst and I will give you eternal water."

What does house of FIGS mean?

Bethany (Greek: Βηθανία (Bethania), which is probably of Aramaic or Hebrew origin, **meaning "house** of welcome," or "**house of figs**").

Each **leaf'**s shape is also described as palmate for its resemblance to an open hand. This is a hint to those that are kept in the palm of our Creator's hand.

Go to 2 Kings 20:7, pg. **406**, "Take a cake of figs and lay it on the boil and Hezekiah recovered."

Proverbs 27:18, pg. **754** says, "He who tends the fig tree eats its fruit and he who guards his master is esteemed." Said in a deeper meaning: He who tends something wonderful has a blessed character and he who guards the tree of life has wisdom and healing.

And now the reason the biblical Christ cursed the fig tree because no one in his generation was teaching Truth. And if that tree did resemble or represent the tree of life he was saying that no one could eat of it because they were teaching false traditions, lies and false religious doctrine and were dead just as the tree the next morning became dead.

Aur is light using the Aleph-Tav, and if we take that light deeper, it means order. "The earth was without form and chaos was upon the deep" said with a little more meaning, "the earth was without form and chaos was upon the deep until order came to be."

A characteristic of a "born from within" is first order—disorder brings with it confusion and error! Next the "wisdom from within" is clean, then peaceable, gentle, ready to learn, filled with compassion and good fruits, without partiality and without hypocrisy, and the fruit of righteousness is sown in peace by those who make peace."

We like cotton against our skins because it is a natural fiber and not mixed with things that are not pure. When we mix foods, fabrics, or truth this causes disorder to the degree that each is mixed.

Eight affirmations for letter NUN

1. Time, strength, love, belief, and revelation brings connection to produce awakening.

2. We plant not knowing the outcome—the seed has potential, so keep **humble** so that you do not break the tender plant.

3. Thank you for life—keep balance and harmony.

4. Women connect—thank you for wisdom and all her instruction!

5. Fullness of life is connected to the fertile loam soil.

6. Silence in our being brings great happiness. No special event needed just the love and praise for our Creator.

7. A law of humankind is seen when male and female procreate.

8. A joy comes when life is expressed in song. Sing heavens and earth for the birthing pains are over. We are delivered! Hallelujah Amen.

Family Reunion

This is a time of joy and refreshing for one another.
People from all generations unite to show love for their Creator.
We have walked in different paths moving
through sorrow and joy along the way.
A sign to all that our Creator formed our physical
bodies out of the earth offering clay.
We look forward to seeing everyone face to face; with the feeling in
our hearts of love for one another, the destiny of our Creators race.
Peace, harmony, happiness and joy,
Is the energy given to those who actively enjoy.
Communication of love, life, and light, the blessings we recall,
The eternal gift that our Creator gave, our choice
to live here on the earth which blesses us all.

Right Shoes

For the next week, Mark and the twins were out of school. They were excited about not having to study for any test.

The twins were busy getting dressed in their play clothes when they heard the phone ring.

Donavon answered the phone and said, "Hello, this is Donavon."

"Hello, Donavon, this is Mark. Are you and your brother coming with me shopping today?"

"Yes, we both want to come with you. We will leave as soon as we get dressed and tie our shoes," answered Donavon.

"Okay," replied Mark. "See you later, alligator."

Donovan answered, "After a while, crocodile."

Neither twin wanted their mother's help in tying their shoes. Drake, however, could not help complaining to his brother about his untied shoes. He said in a grumpy tone, "It is so hard to tie a bow with these long shoelaces. I wish I never had to wear shoes again!"

After Donovan listened to his brother's complaints, he said in a positive tone of voice, "I tied my shoes yesterday, so I know I can do it again today."

Within seconds, Donavon had his laces tied into a perfect bow.

Drake was jealous that his brother tied his shoes first and without Tina, their mother's help.

He said to his brother in a gruff voice," I can tie a perfect bow too. You just watch me."

After a few minutes of struggling with his shoelaces, Drake tied a perfect bow.

Their mother, Tina, was pleased that the boys had learned to tie their own shoes so she let them go shopping with Mark.

When the twins arrived at Mark's house, Donavon said, "Where do you feel like shopping today, Mark?"

"Let's go to the shoe store," replied Mark.

"Okay," agreed Donavon and Drake.

When they arrived at the shoe store, all they could see was racks and racks of different **kinds** of shoes.

As they stood there, not sure which way to go, the store manager walked up to them and said very **kindly**, "What can I do for you today, boys?"

Mark stepped forward and replied, "We are looking for new shoes."

"Oh," said the shoe manager. "I am sure that I have shoes that will protect and fit your feet properly. It is very important that you buy shoes that fit the shape of your feet. Do not buy shoes just because your friend has a pair."

At the same time the shoe manager was talking, the twins and Mark remembered a time when they put a pair of shoes on that did not fit their feet.

Mark walked to one of the shoe racks and said, "I would like to try on these two pair of shoes."

"We would like to try them on too!" excitedly said Donavon and Drake.

As Mark tried on the black shoes, the twins tried on the brown shoes. Mark found that the black shoes were too loose, but when he tried the brown shoes on, they fit him just right.

The twins found the brown shoes were too tight, but when they tried on the black shoes, they fit them just right.

After Mother paid for their shoes, the shoe manager said, "You boys have chosen shoes that fit and protect your feet well. I am very pleased, and so is your mother."

The children thanked the shoe manager for all his help and then went on their merry way.

Can you remember a time when you wore a pair of shoes that didn't fit your feet?

What was your consequence?

CHAPTER 15

SAMEKH

תשרקצפעסנמלכיטחזוהדגבא

The twenty-two letters of light are arranged going from right to left:
Aleph, Bet, Gimel, Dalet, Hay, Vav, Zayin, Chet, Tet, Yod, Kaf,
Lamed, Mem, Nun, Samech, Ayin, Pay, Tzadi, Kuf, Resh, Shin, and Tav.

C ircle, using the Aleph-Tav, is Chagag, Khaw-gag; it means a
prime root to move in a circle that is to march in a sacred
procession (like Joshua and the tumbling wall of Jericho,
Joshua 5:6 to 6:27, pg. **229**), to observe daily rest year after year,
celebrate in circle dance, reel to and fro. The letters of light are Chet,
Gimel, and Gimel. The understanding given to the writer: **Life moving**

forward in time, moving forward from the past, to the present and to our future eternity.

Samekh also spelled Samech is the fifteenth letter of the letters of light. Numerical value: 60.

English letter S.

Repeat creation day if counting according to present-day calendars—Yom Rishon, Aleph, and Chet are on this day. Meaning given to the writer: **our Creator that created the breath of life continues harmony with love, life, and light.**

Sound: has the S sound of S as in *son*.

A circle to surround to protect, hand covering a staff—when we activate the laws of creation in our daily life, protection is our consequence.

A caphar, pronounced saw-far; it means to score with a mark as a record. The letters of light are Samech, Pay, and Resh. The understanding given to the writer: **our Creator's words found in nature surrounds the reader and when wisdom words are spoken the head is cleared.**

The meaning of the root word Samech "to lean upon."

Samech is said to represent the endless and ever ascending love, life, and light of our Creator's omnipresence in the universe. This circle is hinted at in the creation of heaven and earth and is revealed in both the seasons and in the rhythm of the daily cycle.

"Creator formed within" one leans upon the laws of creation.

Samech is also the letter for Sukkah (temporary hut or booth), indicating that our Creator's omnipresence is our support and shelter. We, in peace, are active in relying our trust in the heavens and earth's provision and care for our lives as our Creator made them for our enjoyment, pleasure and sustenance.

Nes = miracle—a prime root *to come*—ooth, letters of light are Aleph, Vav, and Tav—in the since of appearing. A signal as a flag, evidence, or mark. The understanding given to the writer: **returning with joy and life to our Creator is how we have a miracle, meaning**

truth is performed in someone's life and because they awakened to light their requested petition is granted. Remember a true and sustaining miracle is granted after your return and embrace our Creator.

The eyes of all are in peace that seek truth; the soil of the earth gives all their food in due season. Our Creator and life, love, and light is throughout all generations. Our Creator is supporting and raising up all who are in harmony and peace. The eyes of all look to our Creator expectantly, and are given their food in its season. Opening fertile soil and satisfying the desire of all that live. Our Creator is perfect in all and the heavens and earth listen to the laws that govern them, our Creator is near to all as nature is everywhere!

Let us hear the conclusion of the whole manner in the Bible—"Fear Elohim, Yehovah and keep His commandments, for this is the whole (circle) <u>duty</u> of man" (Ecc. 12:13–14, pg.**809**).

When oneness with our Creator, there is no fear only love, life, and light is shared with humankind.

<u>Duty</u> using the Aleph-Tav is da-bar, daw-bar, meaning to arrange words to speak—letters of light are Dalet, Bet, and Resh. The understanding given to the writer: **the door to life opens to words of wisdom (miracle) that reside in the head of the "born from within" ones**. "Born from within" children regain memory. Because of memory they cannot be placed in a box (a government, a social status, a congregation, a mortal family, a special school, a type of work, a religion), you cannot follow them for they are always changing with advancing light, they are given one day more endurance for the need of the day and then another day more compassion for others, there is no list to check off, they belong to our Creator of light. Every day is new for them even if doing the same thing over and over because it is always a new day to them, they enjoy life with the energy of peace, love, life, and light. They consistently marvel at the beauty of creation and its cycles of life.

In light of the all-encompassing presence of our Creator in the world (as represented by the letter Samekh) our primary response should be one of blessings, health and abundance.

A circle represents infinity because it has no beginning or end. The Samekh can also symbolize an ambitious, challenging, enterprising individual. The word challenge is used only one time in scripture-Using the Aleph-Tav the pronunciation is aw-mar, amar—meaning to say, answer, boast self, publish, report. The letters of light are Aleph, Mem, and Resh. The understanding given to the writer: **The breath of life has words that are wisdom. The enemy without life uses words to hurt and destroy. Our Creator will always answer through nature to the one who has the pure heart.**

This round circle also resembles a wedding band. In a relationship, a husband and wife have a strong desire to be wholly bonded as well as an intermittent need to separate. Since a circle has no points of distinction, the many different aspects of marriage do not need to conflict with one another: they can be ultimately bound together within the same uninterrupted structure of the circle. With the wedding ring we are saying in effect, this ring has no beginning or end and the characteristic of encircling is constant. So, too, commitment to you be constant, encompassing your whole being regardless of what man sees in the relationship, the highs and lows. Read the story of Hosea!

Ring using the Aleph-Tav is tabba'ath, look how close it resembles Sabbath, our time of rest each day! Letters of light are Tet, Bet, Ayin, and Tav. The understanding given to the writer: **The earth is the written word imbedded in every cell of all-kind. Humankind love the beauty of the earth and the magnificent of the heavens and the wonders of the deep.**

The first two letters of the word Samekh are Samekh and Mem. Together they spell the word Sam which comes from the root word shama, to hear intelligently. This is not only relevant with regard to one's physical health but also one's eternal health. The word Samekh is an acronym (an abbreviation formed from the initial letters of other words and pronounced as a word) SMKH—for salach, which means to forgive; mechal, to pardon, and kaper, to atone. When one takes strides to forgive others, pardon their blinded minds and memory loss of creation one achieves a great eternal healing. You will finally see everyone as perfect eternal beings as our Creator created them.

It is said that the Samech and the Mem represent two distinct eras. The closed Mem represents Garden of Eden, Paradise (which is concealed from the human eye but known to those that are "born from within"), and those that leave this earth in peace. The Samech (which is greater than the Mem) represents the era of the awakening of our Creator within every being.

Eternity, the **ring** of the Samech becomes ever greater than its original function of supporting all creatures and for them, it will radiate the infinite, transcendent healing which will last for eternity.

Eight affirmations of the letter Samech

1. As we allow our Creator to encircle us with protection and love, we see the result—healing!

2. We are in harmony with creation and all creatures.

3. Our Creator's omnipotence is our shelter and our everlasting rock. All are one.

4. We see! Writing will blossom the humble children. Peace with study will settle us .

5. The power of creation is like waking up to truth. Every day a beautiful memory of life—Hallelujah!

6. The freedom of truth strengthens and heals.

7. When we walk by faith, the worldly approval ends! We dress in humility which covers our being.

8. There is no time now we entered endlessness. Returning to our Creator has blossomed the children of light.

Perfection

Perfection in our Creator is found in the desire of one's
heart, no matter the age or understanding of the being.
It is through peace in action that perfection becomes a
reality. Perfection is on earth as it is in heaven, seeing!
What is perfectness if not the bond of maturity?
Given to those that present themselves as a living
offering to our Creator's posterity.
That we all speak and understand the same letters and be,
Completely joined together in mind and discernment.
This sets our eyes to see.
For man's law made nothing perfect, but returning to nature did,
Which we find in the children of light and our Creator's teachings,
With love is where we are hid.
There is no fear in love and perfect love cast out fear.
Return to our Creator
That we might sing the song of creation, here!
Again, I say, be humble and one:
That we may live in peace and say "All is done."

Dress (Vision)

Our Creator has never changed and awakens the free.
We are the ones that change to fit more perfectly, do you see?
With so much garbage, trash, and filth to uncover,
A person's love for our Creator will be tested by his brother.
What do we do when we see rebellion, arrogance, and pride?
Confront with courage and keep love, your
liberty, hidden deeply inside.
When those that walk along with us desire our approval and say,
"No way do I plan to change," but have etching ears
to hear their good, which esteems their day.
Our **duty** demands a smile, but the joy of helping is our treasured pay,
While watching creation, the healing clouds
open-up to a sunbeam ray.
Committed to the blessings of peace, the circle of
love, each day, and throughout the year.
Clarity of vision, confidence, strength, courage,
integrity and all with humility, and no fear!
The love of our Creator with words of wisdom is the way,
Live out your day promoting love, life, and light and then we will say.
Remember, your heart is polished gold and cherished
by our Creator, the omnipotent ONE,
Peace is with those whose names are written in
the earth, revealing that they have won.

CHAPTER 16

AYIN

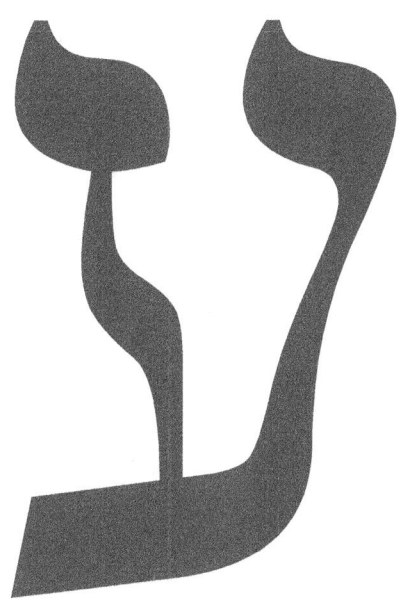

א ב ג ד ה ו ז ח ט י כ ל מ נ ס ע פ צ ק ר ש ת

The twenty-two letters of light are arranged going from right to left:
Aleph, Bet, Gimel, Dalet, Hay, Vav, Zayin, Chet, Tet, Yod, Kaf,
Lamed, Mem, Nun, Samech, Ayin, Pay, Tzadi, Kuf, Resh, Shin, and Tav.

A yin or Ayen is the sixteenth letter of the Aleph-Tav.
Numerical value is 70.
Repeat creation day two if counting a weekly cycle according
to present-day calendars—Yom Sheni. Bet and Tet are on this creation
day. Meaning given to the writer: **a person's decision is based on their
ability to see darkness and move closer to our Creator's light.**

Sound: silent, pronounced ah'-yeen, has no sound of its own but usually has a vowel associated with it.

English is A.

Meaning eyes, salvation, to see, to know, to watch, two eyes—wisdom's eye is generous and the "good and evil" eye is stingy. One tree in the midst of the garden and the other in the field—wisdom represents life "good and evil" represents death!

There are twenty-two chapters in Revelation that match the twenty-two letters of the Aleph-Tav. The twenty-two letters are supernal (related to the sky or heavens) light from which everything is created. This wisdom is seen by the "Creator formed within" eye not physical by John. Revelation:

Chapter 1: **Aleph—Our Creator is eternity.**
Chapter 2: **Bet—Creation is the heavens and the earth**.
Chapter 3: **Gimel—Perfect light is our Creator's mover.**
Chapter 4: **Dalet—Love opens to eternity.**
Chapter 5: **Hay—Life is the answer to all blessings.**
Chapter 6: **Vav—Discern with courage.**
Chapter 7: **Zayin**: rest—**The fertile soil has the power of life.**
Chapter 8: **Chet—Meditation in silence brings peace.**
Chapter 9: **Tet**—Decision, truth—**once the Creator is formed within, humankind flees from darkness.**
Chapter 10: **Yud—Our Creator is one forever and ever.**
Chapter 11: **Kaf—Return to our Creator and regain your health.**
Chapter 12: **Lamed—Power is in the words we speak.**
Chapter 13: **Mem**—Here is wisdom! Memory—**return to nature**.
Chapter 14: **Nun—Children and simplicity go together.**
Chapter 15: **Samech**—Circle, eternity, ring—**awakened to truth.**
Chapter 16: **Ayin**—to **see** with spiritual eyes—**mature, complete and balanced.**
Chapter 17: **Pay**—to speak—**wisdom is a choice, a law of creation.**
Chapter 18: **Tzadi—Enlargement is expansion of the heavens or memory word power.**
Chapter 19: **Kuf—Discernment is love, life, and light forever and ever.**

The Creator's light is far greater than the light that emanates from the sun and stars.

Though concealed in the scriptures, the eternal eye can behold the presence of this radiance, but only by means of the inner eye.

Ayin is sometimes described as having two eyes that connect to a common optic nerve that leads to the brain. The two eyes represent either the tree of knowledge of good and evil or the tree of life. Depending on what the optic nerve is connected to (the tree of knowledge of good and evil or the tree of life) will show the actions in that person's heart. We can either use the eye of wisdom or the good and evil eye to perceive things: "Oh my, I have a flat tire how terrible!" or "Maybe this flat tire has delayed me for a good purpose I cannot see."

Ayin like the letter Aleph is a silent letter. It is said that Ayin sees but does not speak, therefore represents the attitude of humility (anavah) Anavah begins with an Ayin, as does the word for service avodah. On the other hand, Ayin can represent idolatry (avodah zara) as well as slavery (the mark put on Cain), both idolatry and slavery which are born out of the heart of **envy** which leads to anger then death.

The heart and eyes are the spies of the body: they lead a person to transgress or return to creation; the evil eye from the tree of good and evil sees, the heart covets, the body transgresses or the eye sees from the tree of life, wisdom, and eternal understanding that all things are for their growth and remains humble and quiet, and return to our Creator for an answer and not the world's confusing response.

A person is said to be olam katan a miniature world. The eye (circle) reflects the world outside and reveals the world inside. If the inside is evil, it will think evil about something. If the eye has wisdom it will see light in all things.

The inner eye is the light of the body.

If thine inner eye be singular (simple, clear, uncomplicated, pure) thy whole self will be full of light. Yet if thine inner eye be impure thy whole self shall be full of darkness. Therefore, if the light that is in thee be darkness how great is that darkness.

Let's look at the word simple, uncomplicated—it does not mean simple as in insignificant, but simple as in pure. For example, in metals or compounds in nature, there are many complex compounds, but the most powerful are the simplest, such as hydrogen, which is the simplest, the most potent. There is incredible power in hydrogen because of its purity. What we are addressing here is the purity of the heart: how we see. Remove the black spots in the eyes and pureness is all that remains. What is the purest food we can eat? What contains the best water? What food will not bring on thirst? Yes, FRUIT!

The Ayin tov (wisdom's eye) will manifest itself in kindness and truth toward others. On the other hand, the Ayin hara (good and evil eye) will look to the letter Pay (mouth) considering how it might consume for itself in greed and envy.

The Greek work Soma is usually translated as body but actually means self. The biblical Christ is not talking about the physical body he is talking about Soma-Psuchikon, which in Greek means the "eternal being." The eternal being is the reflection of our Creator. So what is being said is if your eternal being, your heart, is simple and pure, then your eternal being, your mind will be full of light.

The Greek word for light is "phos," using the Aleph-Tav it is "Aur."

In the gospel of Luke, it says, "Take heed therefore that the light which is in thee be not darkness." This quote is not superficial. What he is saying here is that the understanding in you can be darkness: "take heed therefore that the light which is in thee be not darkness." "Born from within," you can see with the light of our Creator. This is the light of Ayin, eternal light. To see with that light, one's natural eyes have to be open. In other words, "Creator formed within."

"And the serpent [*repent* is in the word *serpent*] said unto the woman, 'Ye shall not surely die: for Elohim, Yehovah, Hebrew god, doth know that in the day ye eat thereof, then your (Ayin) eyes shall be opened and ye shall be as Elohim, Yehovah, gods'" (we know that Elohim, Yehovah is the name for the Hebrew god and this religion has confusion of truth because the true being does not die but the physical body does. This understanding has confused people for generations thinking that the body would not die).

Knowing (Tov), good, and (Ra), pollution. And when the women saw that the (ets), tree, was good for food and that it was pleasant to the (Ayin), eyes, and a tree to be desired to make one wise (however, we know that she misunderstood the word wise as the serpent use the word knowledge and not wise) she took of the fruit thereof and did eat and gave also unto her husband with her and he did eat. And the (Ayin), eyes of them both were opened to unhealthy choices and they knew that they were naked and they sewed fig leaves together and made themselves aprons."

Adam and Eve, by choice, had their eyes opened. Not to light but to darkness! Temptation and unhealthy choices are the symbol of our fleshy nature. Because of the fall into temptation their eyes were opened to suffering, darkness, disease and pain, the tree of knowledge of good and evil.

The light in us is the light of our Creator (we are eternal beings and the body was never made to exist forever only the eternal being)—be ye children of light! This light brings blessings, eternal wisdom, children, land, and freedom.

There is a way to gain wisdom of that light at the root of our being. We know this is true because the word knowledge not wisdom using the Aleph-Tav is Da'ath. Da'ath comes from the primary word; to know— Yada, yaw-dah. Da'ath has three letters: Dalet, Ayin, and Tav. The very middle of that word is Ayin, which is the light, our "Creator born within" eyes. In other words, to have wisdom one must see the word "knowledge" for what it really is. Real knowledge is not wisdom it is **experience.** When you have knowledge it is because you have experienced it not because you know our Creator. The laws of creation you observed their unchanging nature yet not sure of the consequences. Little faith at this time. This is the meaning of Da'ath: knowledge through experience.

We are here to enjoy life abundantly.

Da'ath is attached to the tree of knowledge of good and evil which brings a person eventually to experience unhealthy choices. The eternal minded person knows that he or she will never die as life is all we know.

Look how close the two words look alike—Death and Da'ath.

The Ayin is a split force it is a *Y*, and it is split because it is dual: there is light and there is darkness.

Using theAleph-Tav, the word for *tree* is "ets" עץ, spelled Ayin and Tzadi. These letters look very similar. Both are dual. Both look like an English or Latin *Y*. The tree of life or the tree of lives, because it is plural and is connected to your spinal column, nervous system and brain while the second (purity and impurity) represents the) fleshy nature. This explains the split in the *Y*. Both the tree of life and the tree of good and evil are within a person. As the tree (person) matures they are inclined to one side or the other. Depending on which one you are nurtured from will determined if you ascend to light or descend to darkness. "And out of the ground Yehovah, the name of the Hebrew god, made every tree grow that is pleasant to the sight and nourishment for food, with the tree of life—wisdom in the **midst of the garden** and the tree of the knowledge of good and evil, death, outside the garden. But the fruit of the tree which is in the **field**, Yehovah, Hebrew god, has said do not eat of it nor touch it lest you die. *There can be only one tree in the midst of the garden and that tree is the tree of life otherwise it cannot be called middle or midst. Two things cannot occupy the same space at the same time.*

Out of the dust of the earth man was created so therefore, we have the same composition to our DNA as do the trees and plant life that were formed from the ground.

So the tree of knowledge of good and evil and the tree of life are in us. The DNA is hidden inside your spinal column, brain, endocrine system. It is from these places that we are nourished from the plants and fruit trees of the earth and our life emerges, yet if we abuse the body—eating flesh and processed foods, we create suffering and disease, the tree of knowledge of good and evil. One abuses oneself by eating from the wrong tree.

This is abundantly evident in our world today. Those who eat from the tree of knowledge of good and evil abuse their mind, heart and body which creates pain, disease and short life.

"Ye shall know them by their **fruits**. Do men gather grapes of thorns, or figs of thistles? Even so every perfect tree brings forth perfect **fruit**; but a corrupt tree brings forth evil **fruit**. A perfect tree cannot bring forth evil **fruit**, neither can a corrupt tree bring forth perfect **fruit**. Every tree that brings not forth perfect **fruit** is hewn down, and cast into the fire. Wherefore, by their **fruits** ye shall know them. Mt. 7:16-20, pg. 926"

Wisdom is a tree of life bearing perfect fruit!

Proverbs 3:13–18 pg. **732:** "She is a tree of life to those taking hold of her and blessed are all who retain her."

Proverbs 11:30 pg. **739:** "The fruit of the righteous is a tree of life, and he who is winning lives is wise."

Proverbs 13: 12 pg. **740**: "Expectancy drawn out makes the heart sick, but a longing come true is a tree of life."

Proverbs 15:4 pg. **742**: "A healing tongue is a tree of life, but perverseness in the tongue crushes the spirit."

What matters is our eternal vision which begins with tiny indications of what is right and wrong as a child and then, becomes greater and greater for right and for wrong as we sojourn upon the earth. We call it "born from within." "Born from within" starts the tiny mustard seed of faith to increase your love for our Creator. When that seed of the promise (children of light) is accepted, fed, developed and nourished you birth the Creator of light in you. You become children of light ascending and descending on the ladder of letters.

The light is within us, the light is there, you just need to go outside and be in nature. Wisdom, which brings the words of light, needs to fill us yet it can only do that if the darkness is removed. When the light begins to emerge inside of your mind and heart, you become a different person, distinct, in the act of being "born from within." This is how your whole being becomes filled with light. This is Ayin filled with light. In that way, you can return to creation in the state of humility as this person has returned to our Creator with all their heart, mind, body and soul.

"Let your light so shine before men, that they may עין [Ayin, see] your perfect works of our Creator. Mt. 5:14-16, pg. 922"

The meaning of being a leader is to visualize-see-born from within and convey this message to others. As such, one thereby transforms the Ayin to the Ayin of the Shema (hear)—where one can lift up one's eyes and see creation as pure satiated truth!

Eight affirmations of Ayin

1. Our Creator springs in us living fruit.

2. Thank you for giving us wisdom's eye—generous and loving (pure with the heart of peace. Creation never returns void.

3. Watching all things for a tender voice daily.

4. We all have been given a body and a heart so no one can say, "I was made evil." Our Creator made us perfect beings that inhabit a male or female body with loving attributes and character. It is our choice to return to creation.

5. Those who do not know our Creator and laws of creation are "poor." We children of light are rich—none are in want. We are discerners.

6. As overcomers we push others to move to higher ground—to seek out truth and the Creator of all.

7. And the Truth will set you free!

8. The Creator never leaves us. Creation surrounds us! We love ourselves and others.

Memory

Quilts are mysteriously wonderful and are
best described as a "little thing,"
Warm, tender and soft with borders that move the heart to sing.
They help the soul to heal and bring a journey to a bend, for
the individual, the family and the entire universe, therein.
It is by this united cause that moves life forward, marching on, yes, a
"little thing" at the end of a day, brings a weary child a sleepy yawn.
Cuddled up and so very, very sweet,
Underneath the quilt at our mother's feet.
As gifts, comforts or nursing a sick one, this example of
selfless service is the love taught by overcomers that won.
May we always continue to be, a blessing to those in need that we **see**.
Watching and preparing for that glorious time,
Revealed as perfect fruit with our Creator in mind.

New Friends

I was six years old and in the first grade. My family moved from the city to the country that summer. Today was my first day at the new school. Mother promised me that I would have a wonderful day. I would even get to ride a yellow school bus.

As I got on the school bus and waved good bye to my mom, I felt so excited, and the bus ride was really fun.

My teacher was kind and placed me in the front row. When the recess bell rang, I went outside with the rest of the children. As they formed their groups, I just watched them.

All I could think about was my new buster brown hair cut and how my brother, Sam, teased me and said it showed off my neck.

And when I smiled my four front teeth were missing.

I was too shy to ask if I could play, and no one asked me to join them. I turned my head so my tears wouldn't show.

Was I left out because of my haircut?

Or maybe it was because I had too many teeth missing at one time?

On the way home my brother, Sam, sat with me on the bus and asked how I liked my first day of school. I burst into tears. Sam put his arms around me and gave me a gentle hug.

I sobbed, "I don't have any friends!"

Once we were home, Sam helped me find my doll and stuffed animal. He said that I should bring one to school tomorrow.

The next morning, when the school bell rang, I was the last one to walk into the classroom.

I stood next to my desk in the front row. Putting my hand on my heart I recited the Pledge of Allegiance with my classmates.

Then I began to wiggle and squirm, wiggle and squirm, which caught my teacher's **eyes.**

Actually, I was wiggling so much all the children began to giggle and whisper.

Miss Stephanie stopped the pledge and said, "Sophia! What's wrong?"

I mumbled, "Nothing, Miss Stephanie."

"Nothing?" replied Miss Stephanie. "You are wiggling like a worm! Is there something in your shirt?"

My face turned so red! I stood there quietly looking at my teacher. Finally, I said, "I brought Cricket with me today."

Miss Stephanie took off her glasses and exclaimed, "You have a cricket in your shirt!"

"No, ma'am. I have a hamster," I said with joy and relief, pulling him out of her shirt. "His name is Cricket."

All the children giggled again, but this time, they moved out of their desks and gathered around me.

Miss Stephanie chuckled and then called my mom. She allowed the class the time for "show and tell."

Every child had a turn to hold Cricket.

I made a lot of new friends that day.

How do you make new friends?

CHAPTER 17

PEY

Pey Sophit (end of word)   Pey

תשרקצפעסנמלכיטחזוהדגבא

The twenty-two letters of light are arranged going from right to left:
Aleph, Bet, Gimel, Dalet, Hay, Vav, Zayin, Chet, Tet, Yod, Kaf,
Lamed, Mem, Nun, Samech, Ayin, Pay, Tzadi, Kuf, Resh, Shin, and Tav.

Pay (also spelled Peh and Pei) is the seventeenth letter of the Aleph-Tav. The design of the Pay is a mouth with a tooth emerging from its upper jaw. A quick glance shows that the Kaf closely resembles the Pay only the tooth in the Pay is absent from the Kaf.

English is P.

Numerical value: 80.

It is the repeat of the third day of creation if counting along with the letters Gimel and Yud. Meaning given to the writer: **perfect movement comes from eating from the third day of creation causing consistency and words that speak of memory.**

Sound: *P* with a dagesh *dot* and *F* without a dagesh, rhymes with *pay* and has the sound of *P* as in *park.*

The letter Ayin gives insight, but it is Pay, the mouth that gives sound and expression. Speech is related to memory, the faculty by which the mind stores and remembers information. So unless you return to our Creator and the laws of nature you will lack memory. By spending time in nature you will learn to discern what was written by man so you will be able to speak wisdom's words. Be careful as you will speak the words that you know. Every day be about replacing worldly thoughts and worldly words with peaceful thoughts and words so that your speech is beautiful, pleasing and of perfect report. Your daily words or oneness will reflect what you remember. Be thankful for the beauty of nature as these things represent the life of our Creator.

Meaning of Pey: **mouth**.

Since Pey means mouth and Bet means house what is spoken within the home is likewise spoken outside the home. Our private conversation within our homes will reflect itself in our public life. Also what we speak in public will also affect the quality of our life at home.

Please be quiet and humble before we straighten ourselves to speak. If the words cannot bring forth love, life, and set forth truth by your actions, then it should remain closed. "But let your word 'yes' be 'yes' and your 'no' be 'no' and what goes beyond these is from the wicked one" (Mat. 5:37, pg. 923).

The letter Pey reveals the **power of speech** in the mouth of Adam or humankind.

And humankind who is named Adam is equal to the words **"to speak"**—this is why speech is directly related to humankind. Remember, that Adam, according to the book of Genesis, is the one who named all the creatures of the earth (Gen 2:19 pg. **2**). Humankind represents order of speech (meaning he/she arranges words intelligently so that others can understand the meaning or concept).

Animals do not speak humankind language. However, they have their own method of communication with intelligence and understanding to each other and to humankind. Organized speech is what makes the difference between an animal and humankind.

Conclusion: So the Nephesh/Hasatan had to be a man because he spoke organized words with the intent to deceive.

In the beginning was the word (the first and last letters of the aleph-tav ת א= AT are in Beresheet), and the word (AT/ET) is within our Creator and the word (AT/ET) [the beginning and the end of the letters of light] is within creation. Words were created from the letters of light so that the thoughts and heart of humankind would communicate the same intent. Today, the thoughts of humankind do not line up with their heart or words spoken. Therefore, confusion with negative body language is the consequence.

All words come from the thoughts and heart of man. New words are made every day to better explain a subject. This is modern man conventions. If we take a look outside, however, we see nature at its perfect work. Maybe a rock, creature or thing is new to us but to earth, the minerals, elements and colours have always been present.

In the beginning were letters that later formed words and then became communication. When you study the word Bereshith, you find within that word the letters Aleph and Tav; the word "AT/ET" is hidden within Bereshith. The beginning and the end.

The next word after Bereshith is Bera which means created. Our Creator has the power of creation and is found in the mouth/speech of humankind, both male and female. So when you say in the beginning our Creator created you are not talking about singularity but about duality, male and female. Voice is female (Gen. 3:17 pg. **3**) means to call aloud, a sound is the meaning. Voice you cannot see or distinguish what it is saying unless it has order (Gen 3:8, pg. **3**), so the sound is female and the words spoken aloud that bring the sound to order are male.

Speech refers to the male and means; to arrange words to speak, answer, command, commune, declare, destroy, give, name, promise, rehearse, say, spokesman, subdue, talk, teach, tell, think, use, utter, the WORK of man.

The words you see are written down and you can hear **them** when spoken. The word **them** refers to male and female (Gen. 1: 27–28 pg. **2**, 3:7–8 pg. **3**).

As children of light, we have perfect order and the ability to teach creation, memory words, about our Creator. We learn to push away all darkness and devilish words from our surroundings giving us the ability to heal and love with discernment.

The reason that ordinary children do not listen is that there is no **order** in the family—mother is not respected by the father, therefore, since children listen to speech, male, the father of the home the mother, voice, cannot be heard. If she respects her husband, then the father's words become a protection for the children and the children listen to the mother. Therefore, commandment six reads: Honour your father and mother that your life be long on the earth. This also suggest our Creator and wisdom, as she is hidden in the voice/sound, in all words.

Voice and speech are together just like male and female were created together. Some people make noise but we do not understand them. They lack intelligent speech. While others speak but have no voice (no wisdom) so they cannot be heard by those that they are trying to reach.

Through the combination of both (voice and speech) is how the logos (word) in the universe was created. Bereshith Bera Creator—AT/ET. "AT/ET" is the word, which is the outcome of Bereshith Bera Creator. Any time you see the AT/ET in front of a name it is indicating the continuation of the life giving seed. In the beginning our Creator created the word. In other words male and female came together to form the Aleph-Tav—new word or child.

We are all eternal words/children of our Creator. Every time male and female unite there is a possibility of another, person produced— they are literally forming another word/child.

The Aleph (the breath of life) goes into the lungs and purifies the dam (blood) so we have ah-dam, Adam, the breath and the blood. That is why the whole work that we have to perform is through the heart, because in the heart is where we receive the power from the word which is our Creator's breath to make words or children of light.

The breath that comes from the heart is expressed through the mouth, through the speech, through the voice of Adam and Eve. This is why in the beginning was the word.

According to the book of Genesis, the first words were, "Let there be light," and there was light.

The unhealthy choice of Adam and Eve in the garden as we read in Genesis—when they ate of the tree of good and evil they immediately lost their connection to light and suffered shame and confusion. Now, both blinded with darkness, they thought of a way to hide the consequence of eating the forbidden fruit. So they sewed fig leaves together and made loin coverings to cover the parts of the body that were used to perform the first commandment given in the garden; to increase and replenish the earth, physical death would come later. If an unhealthy choice was the eating of the forbidden fruit, then they would have covered their mouth, however, after eating the fruit from the tree of knowledge of good and evil, an unhealthy choice, they became blinded with darkness—unconscious, and were physically attracted to each other so came together in lustful intercourse and produced their kind of children. Our Creator gave humankind the law of choice. Choice would now be the talk of centuries.

The mouth which allows a voice and speech to come forth would be blocked from that time forward until man returned to our Creator. Speech which has no life in it draws attention and energy from the world of manmade communication. Because of Eve's darkness in speaking to Hasatan first she would have her husband to rule over her to keep her humble in her words.

Eve, speaking to the Nephesh, was the doorway that led to unhealthy choices. Had Eve not talked to the Nephesh she would not have entered into an unhealthy choice. Remember, our **speech** either leads us to our Creator and the tree of life, or you are eating from the tree of knowledge of good and evil. If eating from the tree of knowledge of good and evil, you are born in the image of man, out of fornication. Fornication is without the connection to our Creator. So all people that do not know our Creator are born in the image of man which is fornication. John 8:41—pg. 1033—"You do the works of your father. Then they said to him, "We were not born of fornication, we have one Father, Elohim. "Et'Yeshua said to them, "If Yehovah were your Father, you would love me for I came forth from Elohim, and am here. For I have not come of myself but He sent me. Why do you not know what I say? Because you are unable to hear my **word**. You are of your father the devil, and the desire of your fathers is what you wish to do. He was a murderer from the beginning and has **not stood in the truth**, because there is no truth in him. When he speaks the lie, he speaks of his own, for he is a liar and the father of it."

So what exactly happened in the Garden of Eden?

The connection with our Creator that they enjoyed, was no longer present in them and when light is not present in creation, darkness is the consequence. This darkness now produces procreative energy to create in the image of man and not with the connection of our Creator. This is called fornication and not marriage. This happened because they united without the connection of our Creator causing what was meant for beauty, longevity, and eternity into lust of the flesh, carnality, and death. No longer with light did they bring forth their posterity; therefore, our Creator gave humankind the freedom to choose. And by your choices, "ye reap what you sow." This is a law of creation!

The only way back to our Creator, so we sing out with joy! Harmony with memory!

Unless one be "born from within," one is unable to have a connection to our ONE Creator!"

Man and women should be united emotionally, mentally and above all, with our Creator! The union of all the forces of two people, ET, comes together as one, forming the perfect man and woman, producing a new word or child.

According to the Bible, Adam was created first and out of Adam, Eve was taken out. Therefore, Adam had both male and female in him on the day that our Creator created them. However, remember that speech needs a sound, which comes from the female. Therefore, Eve was present at the same time as Adam. The religious story however has Adam created first and when there was no companion or helper found after naming all the animals a deep sleep (darkness) came over Adam and a rib was taken out of him and closed up the flesh in its place. Out of the rib was formed a woman and brought to Adam. If this story was true then male would have one less rib than female.

Unfortunately, in this day and age, men and women are united in matrimony only physically. It is very rare to find a couple that is first united with a connection to our Creator. After this connection, then a gradual relationship develops over time causing a physical attraction that produces oneness. Instead you find couples who are joined in man's marriage that disagree, are immature emotionally and lack truth in their values of life. This is lacking the oil on their heads. The fruit remains immature without the proper teaching.

The perfect couple are those that are in love first with our Creator and the universal laws that never change. Someone taught them the Aleph-Tav and how to reverence their own body—physically, emotionally, and mentally. This is a perfect couple. No longer are they searching for the fruits of truth, it is in them and they are children of light. We have developed into oneness, male and female and have overcome the world and are complete and at peace in perfect light. Our Creator is in us and we are "One."

This perfect couple glorifies creation. Our Creator shows agreement to love, life, and light through the miraculous power of nature. We can see this perfect couple being revealed on the earth as it is in heaven. Thorough this work which we have to perform, here, in a body, the creation of light in both male and female, uniting as one, is accomplished by freedom of choice. Bringing us back to creation. "Let there be light." With the most miraculous miracle of all, new life! A beautiful baby in the arms of male and female.

This is what let there be light and there was light implies. We were in darkness, the apple/pupil of the eye, remember it is the darkest part on the body and we need to replace that darkness with light. We need light to express the wisdom of our Creator through our throat, to say powerful memory words that heal, sanctify, and keep one living in perfection. We are simply and perfectly made.

Judas has to be smothered, Luke 22:3–6 pg. **1014**, Judas is the animal passion, the EGO, the darkness of the pupil. This can also relate to a person, a pupil/student, which is in darkness and learning of our Creator and creation that brings that pupil/person back to the light.

Listen, the laws of the universe are without change. They were designed to smother the EGO/darkness-do not let this darkness which breaks the law of our Creator have residence in you. When we understand the simplicity of these unchangeable laws we start receiving the memory word power from the heart = Light. When we say our Creator, we are always referring to **them**, male and female created together as One.

In the beginning was the word…in it, the word, was life (intimate force) and the life (intimate force) is, was and will be the light of man. Adam, speech, Eve, sound, the act of intimacy, and throat are all connected to our Creator.

Recall that the letter Bet, which begins the scriptures, has three sides. Its missing fourth side signifies that the earth is incomplete. We have the ability and perfection to complete the fourth side within and go beyond what man believes possible and make the earth whole within each being. We accomplish this by widening our mouths. With the use of our mouths to use words that uphold love, life, and light, we receive revelation, speak, and communicate wisdom messages to others, and as we do this, we complete ourselves on the earth. In this way, we fulfill our purpose in coming to the earth, by becoming "connected to our Creator" and blessing the earth as it is in peace, a perfect place in which to live.

"I will be your mouthpiece." If a person is humble and relies upon our Creator, his memory power of speech will transcend its natural limits and be a source of strength for others. Pharaoh was someone who denied our Creator's providence in every act of nature. Our mouths were not given to us to slander others but to speak of our Creator's greatness and wonders.

The sixth church called Philadelphia means to love as brethren, dear, which is a friend. Union.

Even though there are seven groups of people, churches, that Revelation 2 and 3 addresses only one the sixth (ray of light) is the children of light with memory (Rev. 3:7, pg. **1201**).

May our oneness sound be in harmony with creation!

Eight affirmations of the letter Pey

1. Mouth! Speak letters into words of peace—love (Aleph) and watch how our Creator will use us to influence others.

2. Get out of the borders and constraints placed for your maturing. Now, express yourself in ways that bring eye sight to the blinded, hearing to the deaf, and wisdom to the voice of the unlearned.

3. Our Creator gave us breath and a full day of life with an ending of rest.

4. The Almighty is speech—the Aleph-Tav. When connected, our word power is the beauty of the entire earth.

5. May our Creator's presence be so that all the ends of the earth will see love, life, and light and cherish wisdom.

6. Our connection is our Creator's word. Be ye perfect as your Creator blesses you in perfection.

7. Remember, we have freedom to choice. We think we have an opinion—but we either choose to speak in peace or for the evil one, Hasatan—there is no place for your own opinions.

8. Remember, when a person is humble and relies upon our Creator that person's power of speech will transcend its natural limits and be a source of strength for others.

Perfect Face

Despite the light that cheers the world today,
shadows surround us, on our oneness way,
And error darkens Truth's light, I say.
In truth, the words of peace are a plant that grows,
its perfect flower perennially blows.
More fragrant and delicate than Sharon's rose.
I know and see truth rising and expand!
Its mighty branches arching every land.
From earth to heaven's sunny strand.
Upward, forever up, I see it rise
Flashing resplendent glory on our very eyes,
Until its crown is lost within the heavenly skies.
And there, beneath the everlasting tree,
This tree of life our human destiny,
I see the nations gathered, bond and free.
The rich and the poor, of every creed and race;
Are children of the earth: standing face-to-face.
With our Creator's beams of light—we fall
on each other's necks and embrace!
Once and for all, will men indeed be free, then
will the Golden Age, the season to be,
With the freedom to choose universally!

The Tonsils and the Ears

"Wake up, Sy! I hear the alarm clock going off," said Seth.

There was only silence coming from the bed that Sy was in. Seth said a little louder, "Do you hear me, Sy?"

"Yes, I hear you, Seth. Don't you ever get tired of hearing?" asked Sy.

"No. I love what I hear," said Seth. "Did you know that hearing is the second most important sense organ that people have?"

"Just think Sy, maybe one day people will hear and want to hear more truth."

"Now, I know you are dreaming," replied Sy. "If there is more truth it would make more sense to write about the tonsils."

"Sy, what makes you think tonsils are more important than ears?" questioned Seth.

"Don't you know? Tonsils help kill bad germs that get into the body. It is the body's first line of defense," said Sy.

"I will show you where they are located. Let's find Dylan. He will help us," said Sy.

Dylan was outside tending the garden. Sy tugged at his pant leg and asked for his help.

"Okay, Sy," replied Dylan, "what do you need?"

"Please open your mouth so that we can see your tonsils."

So Dylan opened his mouth very wide.

"Did you see them, Seth?" questioned Sy.

"Yes, oh, yes! Wow, they really are there, just like you said!" cried out Seth. "I am so glad you are my friend," added Seth. "I hope you will be my best friend forever."

"I know that you and I can learn many important things if we just remember to share our understanding with each other," said Sy.

"Amen," added Seth.

Dylan clapped and cheered. He knew that Sy and Seth learned something new that day.

What did you learn new today?

As children grow, how to know will be important for them to learn, as this will help them to discern truth from error. Wisdom comes as a child matures. Be patient and kind so that the tender plants have time to reach maturity.

CHAPTER 18

TZADI

תשרקצפעסנמלכיטחזוהדגבא

The twenty-two letters of light are arranged going from right to left:
Aleph, Bet, Gimel, Dalet, Hay, Vav, Zayin, Chet, Tet, Yod, Kaf,
Lamed, Mem, Nun, Samech, Ayin, Pay, Tzadi, Kuf, Resh, Shin, and Tav.

Tzadik also spelled Tsadi is the eighteenth letter of the letters
of light.

It is the repeat of creation day 4 if counting. Yom Revi'I, Dalet,
and Kaph are on this day. Meaning given to the writer: **the effectual
door of life blesses an awakened being.**

Numerical value: 90.

The number 90 is the fullness of life, ninety-year-old Sarah became pregnant for Isaac.

The temple under decree of King Cyrus was to be laid on foundations of stone that were ninety feet high and ninety feet wide.

However, we have the evil in King Nebuchadnezzar's kingdom. He built an image ninety feet high of himself. Perfect example of ego, pride, and ignorance.

Sound: TS as in *nuts*.

Meaning: righteous, hunt, a servant, carry a burden.

Tzadi is in the likeness of the letter Aleph. Aleph represents the Creator, and Tzadi represents the reflection of "them" on the earth—male and female—joined together in kindness.

Righteous: observing universal laws, virtuous, upright, keeping love, life, and light.

"Blessed are they which do hunger and thirst after truth for they have been filled with perfect wisdom."

"The prayers of a loving man availed much"—may our Creator's **connection** be given to those that love truth and be moved into those that are being called out of the world, "Go out of her my people" (Rev. 18:4, pg. 1212).

The one who is the most humble, perfect and mature is the greatest—blessed by their **connection** to our Creator.

In the Bible, Tzadi is expressed as righteous:

1. Ps. 119:137 pg. **178**: Righteous (Tzadi) art thou, Yehovah, and upright are thy judgments.

2. Ps. 145: 17 pg. **728**: Yehovah is righteous (Tzadi) in all His ways and holy in all his works.

3. Lam: 1:18 pg. **796**: Yehovah is Righteous (Tzadi) for I have rebelled against His commandments—<u>mouth</u>. What happens when one does not believe the words from Yehovah's mouth?

The story of John the Baptist and his father, Zechariah (Luke 1:5–80, pg. 981–983).

When a person is **connected** to our Creator they receive greater love for themselves which then is given away to others freely. Once **connected** then, by faith, that person develops "Heart kindness" and become a righteous, Tzadi, so that they have power over the things of this world. Power to speak words of wisdom to those that are humble. They overcome darkness with lovely words. When you speak life—life is in you—remember words have the memory power to bring life or bring death. What you are inclined to listen to or read will be the memory power that you have to speak life into others.

A Tzaddik (Tzaddik definition is—a righteous and saintly person) has memory word power from the **connection** to our Creator. A Tzaddik is blessed, an extension of our Creator here in this world for the purpose to help build peace with words of love, life, and light on the earth.

By nature, most have the misconception that it is the physical world that is the source of ultimate truth and pleasure. The imperfect intellect teaches us that the material world is ephemeral (very short life span) and not the source of consummate (marriage relationship lasting forever) kindness and joy. Therefore, there must be something truer and more beautiful upon which to focus. This memory of truth awareness is the essence of the Tzaddik.

A Tzaddik exist not for his or her own benefit. But to serve as an offshoot of peace, love and life.

Tzaddik means righteous one, a leader and teacher of a generation, who is the era's life living leader.

The ability to intervene on behalf of another is not a miracle. It is a natural and organic outgrowth of his/her **connection** to our Creator. Just as it is perfectly normal for the head to feel and respond to the needs of the whole body, it is natural for the Tzaddik to feel and respond to the needs of his or her people.

As we mature in love, life, and light our ability to discern and have our daily words answered is our strength founded upon peace. The answer is blessed by ones of every generation that are **connected** to our Creator. Each one of these truth seekers were teaching advancing light for their generation.

A mature Tzadi carries others in their thoughts and daily words. All a Tzadi has to do is say the name of a person and that person is lifted up for direction, correction or protection. No other word is necessary as our Creator knows us all and what we need.

Tzadi is said to be the letter that opens up the wisdom of the scriptures. It is the letter that reveals the truth of all. Even though throughout the previous seventeen letters we have explained many truths in relation with the understanding of light, it is Tzadi that condenses them, represents them and pulls it all together. You see, at the eighteenth letter we have reached the moment to shine the light of our Creator or to continue in the pagan holidays, traditions, and lies of the world that we came from. It is here in Tzadi that we define ourselves. For light, or for darkness. All the previous letters have explained parts of truth, the character that gives us our longing in life, but it is Tzadi that simplifies our Creator's presence within. Tzadi is a letter of action. It is defined by action, not by belief but by faith which is action. To be on the path is to have conscious, awakened awareness of eternal truth. Merely having read about it or studied religion (a map) is not the same as to have daily walked and communed with our Creator (revelation) and see healing memory words come to life in your life which fits the pieces of truth together like a perfect puzzle. The Tzadi is ever growing and maturing into the perfect eternal life living being.

A Tzadi is not valued by his or her intentions but by what he or she does, his or her actions. His or her **connection** to our Almighty Creator is what lifts him or her up to rejoice in peace.

It would be easy to study scriptures and read them as if these scriptures literally refer to beast; as lions, tigers, dogs, and horses. That is what most people do, but that is not the meaning. It would be rather absurd for the purpose of creation to merely be for mankind to dominate the animals and each other on the earth. Would it not make more sense for the vast beautiful universe to have a greater purpose than merely humans dominating each other and animals? Fortunately, we do have a higher purpose.

Those beasts are symbolic. Those beast of the field are in you. The field or earth is your body. The beast are the animalistic desires that try to take control of your body, such as instinct, violence, lust, passion, and greed. The birds of the air represent thoughts, ideas, and desires in the mind. To be a changed Adam or a changed Eve is to return and be **connected** to our Creator, then you will have dominion over your mind and body, and not the other way around. With the help of the words of Truth and the revelation of our Creator, this is how you become a **clean** Adam or **clean** Eve, "born from within."

So how does one overcome the beast of our nature? Let's look at the word *retrospection*. This is the culmination of an entire day's work. A day's work is to be continually observant of oneself to guard oneself against one's own mind. In other words, to guard your soul, your heart from the beast of the field (body) and the birds of the air (mind). And at the end of that day, to reflect because until you are finished with the work of the day and ready to return to rest you will not have a perfect day. You will make mistakes because **ego or ignorance** remains. All of us have beast in our field (body) and birds in the air (mind) and a lot of them. Thus we do our best during the day to watch for them, and in the evening we meditate to learn about them. This action of meditation is not to sit and space out. It is to sit in conscious reflection upon one's mind and heart, to look at oneself to reflect upon the contents of the day without prejudice, without self-love, but also without self-hate. To look at oneself objectively, to see what one did, in fact not what you would have liked to have done and not what you would have wished had happened but what actually happened and your response or action. When you engage in that activity you will discover that if your ego and ignorance is still alive in you, you will refuse to see the truth. Your pride does not want to die. Your selfishness does not want you to see the truth of your day because you see, your old thoughts, old habits, friends, family and traditions are still in the world that **you left**.

The struggle that the Tzaddik engages in is against his or her own desire to have healthy relationships. It is not against any outside force. It is not against other groups other people your spouse your boss your children; it is against what is happening in your own mind and heart. It is the most difficult battle possible. As your confidence increases in your **connection** to our Creator each word of wisdom you speak will eliminate the darkness and bless you with light.

If what you are saying or doing is giving you the same consequence year after year then do something different for heaven's sakes or remove yourself from those people until more growth occurs in you so that you remain at peace with those people or groups. Get out of the way, be quiet if that is all you can do or show hospitality until you have in your conversation mentioned our Creator or nature enough times that you are sure the other person or group has heard. **Those people will respond!** Keep planting the seed of truth! Worldly people drop important people's names in their conversations all the time—so what name could we drop that is more important to us than our Creator and simple nature.

A Tzadi has a deep relationship with the word justice. Righteousness is its translation. It says throughout the scriptures that the righteous will inherit the promise land or have eternal life. Who is righteous? Who loves justice? We know of a few that are named in scripture. Shall I drop their names in this conversation? I think not!

I feel more confident if I walk outside into our Creator's nature and rise to perfection in peace. Actually if one lives his life in peace then all that comes to this individual is love not justice and truth and not righteousness for that person. No manner the outcome of an event it will be for the perfection of the individual as well as his or her generation. We all affect each other and help each other to mature.

A true Tzadik is unknown to the world! The world may have communication with a Tzadik but they will not recognize anything to savor from them except what they needed to fulfill their own mortal desire.

The power of kindness comes from the **connection** to our Creator. This perfect wisdom or memory power of kindness is ever moving and maturing those that love her. When eating physically, according to wisdom, the body will have joy that is not understood by the people of the world. Clearer understanding, quicker movement, long life in health, calmness and peace is her reward to them. But if you go against wisdom, you will not have her reward of health and mental stability.

Fornication, adultery, lying, cheating, idolatry, stealing, anger, envy, jealousy, false traditions, false worship, and disease are forms of unhealthy choices and belong to the tree of knowledge of good and evil and not the tree of life and wisdom.

You can be working on developing the character of peace but if you go against wisdom you will remain blocked. Wisdom is peaceful and few understand her simplicity that comes from the earth. This takes courage and discipline to remove all the lies and false traditions. Remember, our Creator always separates light from the darkness.

How do children best mature? Isn't it through understanding the guidelines in the home? Our Creator is no different. Study the laws of creation, our earthly home, and the universe so you will live in truth's way and your children will have an example.

So what does blocking mean?

A primary reason very few are willing to let go of their blocking— EGO, or ignorance—is because the Eye or darkness that they see from is directly related to what they daily eat physically and eternally. It is not hard to find people who become more aware by studying the wisdom of the letters. But it is exceedingly rare to find someone who lives them. They follow along for a while but they do not want to abandon their bad habits, their view of seeing things from their darkness, their adulterated ways of believing things so they return to what is comfortable. They do not want advancing truth as this would mean that they would have to admit that something they believed was incorrect and that takes a person with humility to admit! This is why we see people stuck in the same problems year after year. Everywhere, we see people having the same conflicts, the same fights, the same struggles, the same arguments, and the same politics and marrying the people with these same problems. This is in all schools, all religions, all families, all movements; this repetition is a cycle of suffering. It is not of our Creator. It is the people in those groups who do not want to change and move toward perfect and pure light.

A Tzaddik changes! And moves away from those groups that kept him or her suffering. A Tzaddik loves perfect advancing truth above anything and will follow the words of Truth even to the death of their mortal body.

A Tzaddik abandons their harmful tendencies inside and revolts against themselves. And much of the time that means they revolt against everybody else's behavior too. And of course other people do not like that. So a real Tzaddik is generally condemned, rejected, exiled, cast out, ridiculed, gossiped about, and put down. That is what happened to Et'Yeshua. Humanity did not love him and embrace him, instead they crucified him.

Humanity tortures the Tsaddikim. Humanity ridicules and crucifies them. Even their own students (disciples of Et'Yeshua) betray them and stab them in the back. This is why as a real Tzaddik, you rely on your **connection** to our Creator and the words of wisdom and not humanities acceptance (John 14:27–31, pg. **1042**).

However, the heart of the Tzaddik is to love humanity and leave the consequences to truth. How do you love humanity? By loving our Creator first and being available to do kindness.

This is why the prophets speak so directly. They did not speak to make others impressed with them, or to try to get people to love them or believe them; they wrote what they wrote, said what they said, because they loved our Creator first, in essence yourself, and then humanity. If you love someone and you see that they are sick and they are lost—and worse—they are doing it to themselves—will you just pat them on the back and tell them "Oh, I love you!" and walk away? Will you encourage them to continue doing what is killing them or supply them with what is destroying them? People do that. All of us have done that, because we accommodate each other's pride, lust, fear, and greed. People are married to alcoholics, and they buy them alcohol. People have problems with money and we give them money. People are married to people who are addicted to junk food, and we buy for them cigarettes, Coca-Cola, potato chips, processed foods, and candy. We give money to addicts on the street. We buy medications that feed a system of abuse and corruption. We support systems in our social environment, in our families, which support abuse and corruption. We uphold political systems built upon greed, lies, and mass deception.

A Tzadi, if asked for help from someone, will give these people information, wisdom, and direct them to resources that will encourage them to seek a **connection** to our Creator first and then all health and discernment by the words of wisdom and truth will be brought to their memory.

If we want to become a Tzaddik, we have to fight against ourselves, to change our own tendencies that keep us ignorant and persisting in our dark tendencies to continue our suffering. This is pride, which makes us feel so self-sustaining and knowledgeable. Along with knowledge is lust, envy, anger, and greed, all of that. And along the way, we have a heart to help others overcome their darkness. However, we must remove our own darkness first, and then our Creator will move us toward the lost sheep. Sometimes this means we have to be honest, but in a loving way, in a kind way. Love sometimes feels cold and cruel. Because in love there **is always discipline**. If you are loved without discipline, this is a lie of the evil one. This person will be unhealthy and bring suffering to you.

We have to receive unpleasant manifestations of others with gladness, yes. But this is different from being an accomplice to a crime. There are times at which we must speak, right? To receive the unpleasant words with gladness means to not become identified. To not become angry, to not seek revenge, to not seek to blame or attack. But instead to speak the truth when it must be spoken. Sometimes we just have to accept and remain at peace when we are receiving something painful from others.

We live in the world but not of it. Our life is our work and play. We need it. Messiah could not have ascended that path toward his crucifixion unless those people had been there to persecute him, unless the centurions had whipped him, unless Pontius Pilate had committed him, unless Judas had betrayed him, unless the Jews had mocked him; none of it would have been possible. So Et'Yeshua owed his choices to all of those who punished him. Sounds strange, but it is undeniable. The same is true for us. Our mind has a tendency to blame everyone else to justify our behavior. And what I am explaining here is very difficult to grasp because the darkness interferes. Yet our heart can learn to do it. Our consciousness, memory, which is **connected** with our Creator has the capacity to remain serene to remain centered in conscious kindness in any circumstance. And this is what Et'Yeshua was representing, per biblical authorities, even when he stood before Pontius Pilate and allowed the conviction of the death penalty. That is perfect kindness called wisdom.

That is the right view: how we see beyond superficial and physical appearances and penetrate the truth, our Creator. And when one cultivates the skill to be awake, to be conscious, even when one is receiving blame, insults, betrayal, gossip, people doing terrible things to them, you can still treat them with kindness. You can treat them with respect and you can speak the truth. The Tzadi will experience at the end of his/her life, maybe a betrayal from his/her students, if their students are not "born from within." What does the Tzadi do? He/she will continue to love and treat all with kindness. He/she will continue to shine the light of our Creator and continue writing or speaking words of truth as this keeps their **connection** to our Creator strong.

We develop a greater capacity of kindness in our hearts as our relationship matures with peace. So self-importance can never do it. That is why we cannot understand the Tzadi with our fleshy eyes. You will need to be "born from within" to understand this person. Let us look at the character of the Tzadi by learning about the fruits of the spirit. Gal. 5:22, pg. **1135** says, "But the fruit of wisdom is love, joy, peace, patience, kindness, life, trustworthiness, gentleness, and self-control." And then we learn the primary virtue: **peace**. Sounds strange, doesn't it? Of all the virtues we talk about, the main one is **peace**. **Peace** is absolute eternity and **connection** with our Creator.

Eight affirmations for the letter Tzadi

1. We are taught by the words of truth. We listen to teachers that glorify our Creator. Thank you for a life that has prepared us in discernment.

2. Keep us humble. Male and female are equal.

3. Keep our work quiet and perfect—through thought, speech, and action—awake and see the children shine.

4. When performing perfect deeds, joy must accompany the action—no joy no perfection.

5. Ninety is when Sarah gave birth. may nature in all its array sing together in harmony when we each reach 90 years of age.

6. Memory word power comes from continual **connection** to our Creator.

7. Words destroy and words bring life—always speak life—life is in us. Keep reflecting perfectness and loving kindness. Awake our discipline children!

8. As Ayin is to the eye, so is Tzadi to the community. Tzadi has compassion for all creation as Ayin keeps the house/earth in order.

Pure in Heart

I long had borne a heavy load,
Along life's thorny and unhealthy road.
And often times had wondered why,
Humankind were blinded, while I
Was chosen to carry day-by-day
The wisdom that directed us to go the right way.
So my kind and loving Creator laid
Another truth on me. Dismayed
And faint, trembling and distressed,
I cried, "Oh, I have longed for rest.
These many days, I cannot bear
Another truth of how love cares.
I say, "Behold this one-
Shall I bear both while this one has none?"
No relief came. Another truth was laid,
I was humbled by the creation of the earth.
It felt very much like giving birth!
Again I cried, "I know it won't be long,
So give my bleeding heart a new song."
"My child" the inner voice returned,
"Hast thou not yet the lesson learned?
The truths thou has borne so long
Only made thee grow lovingly strong,
Thy children are too weak as yet
To have these truths upon them set.
Life and light rest upon the strong,
They stronger grow who bear them long.
And each new revelation is a sign,
That greater love to bear is thine."
So, no longer do I watch the time
Because the truth of our Creator is mine,
But walk humbly braving with this prayer,
"Form in me a pure heart to bear."

Joy Bounds

Look to our Creator for the word of truth, remember
To keep daily peaceful rest. This is the key!
Move through the calamities "the desolation of abomination,"
which is here; darkness is bound, I can see!
The children of light are awakened in peace and truth, the solemnities
of eternity rest upon their mind. Your choice, to be or not to be!
The fulfillment of prophesy, every jot and tittle, is
united with, perfect time. Out Golden Tree!

New Song

Light hath prevailed to open the book,
The inner eye, thereof.
We experience humble reverence by our true words
of wisdom and our firm stand for eternal love.
With our **connection** to truth; this is our shield of faith,
Perfect and true takes from the right hand the book
of peace that showers the heavens…and waits.
The four corners of the earth with a complete day
ending in rest, listens to our Creator's plan;
With harmony in union, which are the prayers
of the gathered children of the land.
And they sing a new song singing: Thou art worthy to
shower inner peace in harmony with love, thereof.
For the truth has awakened the children to our Creator of love.
Wisdom has reached every kindred, tongue, people and nation.
Has nurtured the awakened beings during the final purification.
Return ye, return ye: for the truth is at hand.
We heard the same voice crying in the wilderness
throughout the promise land.
Prepare the way of peace; make this path straight.
For the born from within is neither delayed nor late.
Verily, Verily, I say unto you, children of the earth.
A final call to "go out of her" and choose life
in our Creator and have eternal birth!

CHAPTER 19

KUF

ת ש ר ק צ פ ע ס נ מ ל כ י ט ח ז ו ה ד ג ב א

The twenty-two letters of light are arranged going from right to left:
Aleph, Bet, Gimel, Dalet, Hay, Vav, Zayin, Chet, Tet, Yod, Kaf,
Lamed, Mem, Nun, Samech, Ayin, Pay, Tzadi, Kuf, Resh, Shin, and Tav.

Kuf also spelled quoph, Qof, is the nineteenth letter of the aleph-tav. Sound: *K*. English = Queen.
This is the fifth repeat of the first day of creation if counting moving forward to what is called day five, Yom Chamishi.

Heh and Lamed are on this day. Meaning given to the writer: **revelation is received by keeping our thoughts above and not**

below the acceptable line as this will bring war to oneself and its natural consequences.

Numerical value: 100—deals with the living seed, Abraham, and when he reached one hundred at the birth of Isaac, 10×10 = 100, and Abraham was in his fullness of perfection and word power at one hundred years of age.

One hundred is the numerical value of Kuf.

"You have made to **cease** all the wrong of the earth like dross [solid impurities]: therefore I love perfect truth and natures witnesses."

Creation is so perfect, beautiful, and harmonious, overpowering, moving, and unexplainable; it is in knowing our Creators witnesses (the sun and moon stamp, seal out a day) through nature and we can know it!

Those that continue moving forward by the words of truth have received the unchanging light and can speak words about creation therefore understanding perfection and oneness! These are they that are eternal "born from within" and have the testimony of the light from creation. The children of light are moving inside this light here on the earth and have moved from the entrance door of the garden. They are no longer babies drinking milk but are mature beings that understand creation's never changing laws of light.

The words *unconditional love* is nowhere in scripture. And nowhere in nature. This is humankind's communication which keeps people in darkness and from advancing toward perfect light. People see from within their perceived box and this blindness makes humankind believe our Creator is an image. Let go of the idols, return to nature and creation, and live in the first day of perfection and oneness. Our Creator set up boundaries and is omnipotent and omnipresent. This is love that has discipline and consequences of choices in it.

The Creator's love has discipline of truth and the laws of nature which are unchangeable, keep children of light strong, healthy and peaceable.

Psalms is the nineteenth book of the Bible. King David wrote to remove his perception of darkness in his day, as he strove to understand his Creator.

Number 19: It is made up of 10 (Yod)—perfect order and 9 (Tet), which brings decision.

The nineteenth chapter of Genesis in the Bible is the story of Sodom and Gomorrah. This was judgment pronounced against prideful immoral people with their consequence of destruction.

The original nineteenth book of the Bible is Jonah. The story of Nineveh, a city that was in darkness.

The number nineteen is the judgment of unhealthy choices from the tree of knowledge of good and evil—the number nineteen is spelled sha-ah, a prime root to gaze at or about (probably for help) by implication. To inspect, consider, compassionate or bewildered—depart, be dim, be dismayed, look, regard, have respect, spare, turn.

We know that discernment is from the tree of life which has in it peace.

Sound of harmony: How do we hear the words of Truth's voice? Be aware to the truth that you already have been given from within and rethink wisdoms words when darkness comes your way so your consequence from thinking those words will bring you peace. The words of truth are pure light without any darkness, therefore, our Creator shines over all heaven and earth. You hear the words of truth when you have joy in creation and its laws. Beauty and more of the unchanging light will be added to you. The darkness you once perceived from will vanish and new eternal perception will be given. Each layer of truth removes the dark layers of that generation's perception passed down to you, that they lived and wrote world and biblical history from. There will be much you cannot change as it belongs to the tree of knowledge of good and evil. Be at peace for knowing the truth and choose as wisely as you can for your generation of time.

What is the long awaited light?

The longed awaited light is to know that you live forever as an eternal being. Born from within are those that are peaceful and have returned to our Creator. They know they live forever.

"And concerning the resurrection of the dead, have you not read what was spoken to you by the truth, saying, "I am the Truth of ET'Abraham, and the Truth of ET'Yitshaq, and the Truth of ET'Ya'aqob? Truth is not the Truth of the dead, but of the living."

Love, life, and light is all our Creator is!

The blindness of every dispensation of time is seen by those that did not return to our Creator with pureness of heart and mind. This blindness in a person's heart and mind will keep a person in confusion and they will be found "wanting."

Remember, the way back into the Garden of Eden or into the presence of our Creator takes a clean heart that has returned to the first day of creation and rest. Returning is seen in the children of light that are "born from within" and have overcome death of the being revealed by their daily lifestyle. When **one** returns to creation, **one** will **not have a desire** toward division but will love **oneness**. He or she will not want to suffer any more and will do whatever the word of truth, wisdom, tells them to do at that time for freedom sake. Getting to this place of living requires discipline, courage, and peace.

Kuf or Qof words: qobah, ko-baw—the abdomen as a cavity, belly; qubbah, koob-baw—pavilion, tent; qbuwrah, keb-oo-raw—sepulture, burial burying place, grave; qobel, ko-bel—confronting-war; qadad, kaw-dad—shrivel up that is contract or bend the body in deference (humble, submission and respect), bow down the head, stoop; qadowsh, **kaw-doshe—sacred, an angel, a saint, a sanctuary, holy one;** qedar, kay-dawr—dusky (of the skin or the tent) Kedar, a son of Ishmael; qow, ko—to vomit—spue out; quwm, koom—to rise; qowph, kofe—a monkey; Qeynan, Kay-nawn—Cain-an, Kenan; qalown, kaw-lone—disgrace, confusion, dishonor, shame; qallacah, kal-law-saw—ridicule, mocking (Ishmael—son of Abraham by Hagar the bond servant from Egypt—Sarah's handmaid); qannow, kan-no—jealous or angry; qaphats, kaw-fats—to die by gathering up the feet; qotser, ko-tser—shortness (of breath) that is impatience, anguish; qishshu, kish-shoo mean to be hard, a cucumber (from the difficulty of digestion); qshiy, kesh-ee—obstinacy, stubbornness; qashshath, kash-shawth—a bowman, archer.

This letter brings perfect awareness—when the sun goes down; be resting in peace and not fighting the war within yourself as harsh consequences come to those against our Creator.

Love brings **oneness** in our Creator—through our lifestyle, we have entered peace with no judgment.

Daily judgment only happens to those individual eating from the tree of knowledge and good and evil because when the heavens and earth were created immutable laws were part of creation. These unchangeable laws if not heeded will cause war to occur within an individual if not followed which becomes your personal judgment.

So eat from the tree of life and you will not concern yourself with judgment as perfect creation with laws embedded in it will take care of you.

The world needs their laws, judgment and courts for the fleshy.

The eternal minded are governed by creation and its immutable laws.

What is a voice but a sound? Frequency! What sound created the universe? Our Creator's nature.

Who is our Almighty sound? The Almighty sound is our Creator, who created all things in heaven and earth in perfectness.

Kuf is the only letter that extends below the line where Lamed is the only letter that extends above the line. What can that teach us? Lamed receives from above and Kuf has an acceptable line but if you choose to go beyond it then war within becomes your consequence.

אבגדהוזחטיכלמנסעפצקרשת

Meaning: back of the head, behind, last, least, monkey that is a false imitation of man (this represents evolution).

The numerical value of Kuf is 100 and means holy (letters of light spelling kodosh).

Kuf represents all the cycles of nature, changing seasons, monthly and yearly cycles. It is the constant movement, circulation, and change of life. We see creation, growth, change, suffering, happiness, life experience—we are constantly worked on to realize our true eternal nature. We remove **one** by **one** the tight clutching lies of darkness from our minds to reveal the center of holiness within. These are layers of religious and governmental lies and traditions. Once removed will expose the unchangeable light and truth in the individual which will always lead a person back to our Creator and creation. Kuf is to perform the work of holiness on the earth in a body which then touches the people **connected** to love, life, and light.

Those that have the heart to return to our Creator become one and connected with the teacher or leader of that day.

Remember you will need more instruction from wisdom and her discipline if you are lacking peace to the truth in the previous letters. Unawareness means darkness is still hovering around and you are still perceiving from that unaware state. So you will see part truth. Continue in nature daily and reading over this information and the letters of light will be there to guide you to all perfection. Remember, the last time you read this your eyes of perception were dimmed.

If led by the truth the law (these laws are embedded within nature) of our Creator is understood—need to be teachable (the words of Lamed).

"Let no corrupt word out of your mouth go forth, but give memory to the hearers and make not sorrowful the words of light, in which you were sealed to the day of perfection. Be a teacher of love, life, and light at all times thereby never allowing casual talk that promotes distrust. Remember, "But let your word 'yes' be yes and your word 'no' be 'no,' and what goes beyond these is from the darkness within that person."

Darkness within is the only **thing** that can speak evil or do evil.

There is a death frequency over you when you speak evil about other people.

When you are offended, that is, when the darkness within speaks to you in hope to confuse and control you and have you react in a way not pleasing to truth this is what causes a loss of peace, STOP!

Bitterness—what is the first thing that comes into you when someone wrongs you? Confusion sets in—this is the first piece of armor that the words of bitterness puts on next is disappointment and here is where a decision is made in the individual to continue to rehearse the incident and talk about it to others or to remain quiet and let nature take care of itself! This is known as the natural law of consequence. What will you do here? These next words are words that you never want in your head—resentment, retaliation, anger, wrath, and finally, murder, which is slander to a person's character. This goes for evil spoken of anyone even if it is true!

A trick of the enemy when someone says something evil—do not fall for it—do not listen. Continue your path doing and speaking in truth.

Darkness has been part of the generational curse—don't fall for anything said against you or another person. Remember you have the freedom to choose!

It's a negative energy of division and depression. Ask yourself this question. Whose authority am I going to live under?

Characteristics of darkness: the destination of bitterness is hatred, cruelty, revenge, self-pity, hypocrisy, jealously, always right, depression, not teachable, disorder, physically unkempt in body and personal possessions, in a hurry, no patience, will talk over you, contention, physical foods that are void of nutrition, and CONFUSION with the outcome against our Creator and creation: result pain and disease which all leads to a short or long and painful life.

This was what was spoken by Moses to the children of Isreal in the wilderness—What do you choose? Choose you this day—life or death! (Deut. 7:15, pg. **194**).

These negative qualities are illustrated within the actual form of the kuf. It's long left (notice it is the left and not the right leg that plunges downward-we are symbolically on the right side) leg plunges beneath the letter's baseline. It represents a person who ventures below the acceptable, an individual who violates the circumscribed boundaries of the truth from both mother and father, heaven and earth, and suffers the consequences. Going below the base line usually brings on immorality of some kind.

Too cold or too hot are times that darkness is the strongest as life has in it perfect or balanced temperatures with love, life, light and perfection. The individual who is **one** with our Creator, every moment of his life, is perpetually alive. On the other hand, too cold or too hot signifies an abyss-the severance of the **connection** between humankind and our Creator and ultimate disease. Remember the winter, be careful during this time, as darkness loves this weather. There is much more darkness than light at this time of season. For this reason, eat fresh vegetables and fruits in season as often as possible so the result is more nutrition which gives health to the body and **oneness which enhances light from our Creator.** The physical body, heart and mind is likely to regress to division with too much overcooked, devitalized, or processed foods.

Destroy the strong man: it starts with murmuring and stubbornness, which is pride! So confront your pride. Confront your blinding eye sight—Return to our Creator and to light.

Deeper meaning of Kuf, Qoph-means in the field, the ground, which represents the continuous cycle of human life from the beginning of creation to now. Depending on the corruption of our soil will depend on the health of our body today. The body is composed of many elements and forces from the dust of the earth. Regrettably, we alter the bodies' Garden of Eden, as we alter the planet's natural habitat. In the field is the tree of knowledge of good and evil. This is the tree of death and not the tree of life. We have to always visualize and understand the two trees because one of the trees must occupy the middle of the body called our spinal column as only one tree can be there at a time. Your belly, the truths indicator, will be either filled with life or diseased.

The Bible calls Mizrahim, Egypt, the tree of knowledge of good and evil and from this tree of knowledge of good and evil is taught opposites until a person crosses over to the light, the tree of life, and then, this individual hears from the memory words of wisdom and is answered. This is another reason to return to creation day one, become "born from within" and be **one** with our Creator. Or you will continue to live by the words of the world, from the tree of knowledge of good and evil and its false calendar, traditions, and religious lies.

It is written, "Let light come to be and light came to be. The truth separated the light from the darkness.

"In the beginning our Creator created the heavens and the earth. And the earth was without form, and void; and darkness was upon the face of the abyss or deep."

Aleph-Tav definition of abyss or deep—**teh**—means home, usually female, a surging mass of water, especially the deep, the main sea or the subterranean water supply, depth.

And the truth moved upon the face of the waters. "Let there be light; and there was light. (Conception, a new word, life was formed)

And love saw the light—(children of light, John 12:35–36, pg. **1039**, and 46–50 Eph. 5:8 pg. **1140**), that it was perfect and because it was perfect in its creation it is called day. The greater light of the heavens shine at this time. Once the greater light sets in the west then the lesser light shines in the darkness. The darkness is called night and time of rest.

It is said in scripture that Elohim separated Eve from Adam. And Elohim called the light Day (Adam), and the darkness he called Night (Eve) for she was hidden in Adam. Genesis 1: 1–5, pg. **1, the woman carried down from the beginning of creation the first error that showed darkness within. Now confronted and responsibility taken, the darkness within from the beginning of time can be awakened. We know that both, male and female, were created at the same time. To have voice and speech we need both male and female present at the same time.**

So by understanding this we understand the relationship of man and woman to be equal. Remember, in the first day of Genesis it is stated that the word of truth showed its light and light was formed. "Let there be light." Yet before the word of truth, "'Let there be light,' it is written. 'And darkness was upon the face of the abyss.'" The female counterpart which is called Eve, that in the first day is called night, darkness was upon the face of the abyss. And the word of truth "Let there be light." So the light was separated from the darkness; as you know that separation of dark and light is the same <u>symbol</u> as taking Eve out of Adam. Remember, she was symbolically hidden in Adam-hidden refers to darkness here, but she was present. The words of truth separate the light from the darkness to make the first day of creation that continues to repeats itself until today. As man and woman continue to come together as **one** this extends more time to the earth's existence. Now we have the understanding of the commandment in the garden to "be fruitful and increase, and fill the earth and subdue it."

Be aware as the number of children born today are less and many are born with diseases because of our unhealthy choices. Are birth rates lower now? Phillip Levine says"

> Birth certificate data on all births in the U.S. through the end of 2021 reveal that the early months of the U.S. pandemic were associated with a drop in births, leading to an overall baby bust on the order of 100,000 fewer births than would have occurred based on pre-pandemic trends.

After day **one** is made then the darkness and the light come together as **one**—and the morning and the evening were **one** day. And the evening and the morning were "the **one**" united. The words of truth succeeded in uniting light and darkness as translated, because in other words, Rah, in the letters of light as you remember is evil or pollution, but Rah also means the counterpart, the partner that has been separated, Greek definition—participant, sharer, and partaker.

The partner, the counterpart, the companion of Vav is always Zayin the seventh letter. The Kuf is related to **one** aspect of the first day specifically**: The first day and its time of rest. Rest in peace to sanctify the day as thy, father and mother hath commanded thee**.

So to rest in holiness also means to take care of your body by putting into it live food from the fertile loam soil and keeping your eyes and ears focused on things that bring life. When we honor our earthy and eternal mother and father, we understand how to rest in peace. "Sleep on now, and take your rest." People that rest in peace are the true children of light.

To not lie or bear false witness, we have to know how to handle and how to practice uniting for the pure purpose of bringing forth children in love, life, and light, to produce **oneness in them**. May we be **one** in our Creator as our Creator is **one** in us.

Eight affirmations for the letter Kuf

1. Harmony places us in constant movement—reaching, to evolve our eternal nature into holiness for perfect living in present time. Bless the Creator's holy nature and become **One**—male and female, mother and father.

2. We have been humble—keeping in the rear and picking up the left overs and returning them as the words of truth sees fit back to those that lost their way—this remains the reason for teaching the truth of peace—to return as many as possible back to our Creator as long as we are on the earth, our **oneness** work.

3. Creation brings us awareness—peels away the worldly lies to restore the words of truth and its nature within. "**One**"!

4. A monkey is a false imitation of humankind—peel away the traditions and religious lies of man and the monkey image flees.

5. The children of light, as they move through the ages, sound softly at first with a quiet victory over darkness but at the end sings

like the roar of the ocean! Perfect memory! A transformation because of pure rest and truth!

6. May we be warm and alive—the children of light bless our Creator's creation.

7. Praise, honor, and glory be to our Creator. No words can express being a "full moon"—no darkness at all, only shining the perfect lesser light on the earth.

8. Our body is a living sanctuary full of light, holy without spot. The body has joined the head and is **one**—Ahad.

A Treasured Woman

I saw her as a vision viewed,
With wisdom's memory, yes! A woman too!
Her household movements light and free,
In step with the pure in heart's liberty.
A countenance in which daily life did meet,
Birds singing, daily rest, peace in nature: promises so sweet.
A living soul created by man and woman, stood,
Cleaning, preparing, sewing, nursing, gardening, teaching,
True motherhood.
To understand by mortal life, true sorrow,
Our sweet mission lived TODAY and not tomorrow.
And now I see with eyes serene,
The purpose and overflowing water of this reconciled being.
Her reason firm with a finishing will;
To warn and comfort as was planned,
As an awakened woman in Oneness's command.
And yet, nothing to the world does she mean,
Only to those born within is she seen.
Children of light, our Creator's song,
May we, the awakened daughters and sons, bring
into existence, heaven to our earthly home!

Humble Place

What has happened to thou humble place?
Where is creations harmony, peace, and rich soil;
where we meet each other face to face?
The children of light know and move with grace.
What happened to thou humble place?
The lambs are on the right hand,
The left are the kids (goats) that only pollute the land.
Oh, what happened to thou humble place?
As it was when the bridegroom came,
So it is for the bride the same!
Oh, my father and mother, here my words: Thou
created me and the letters of truth gave me breath.
Thou has loved me and silenced all my fears of death.
My desire is to radiate creation's light,
As an awakened child is a delight.
Together we are **one** and mental struggle has ceased.
Returning to the first day of creation,
And there we have eternal life and we rest in peace.

CHAPTER 20

RESH

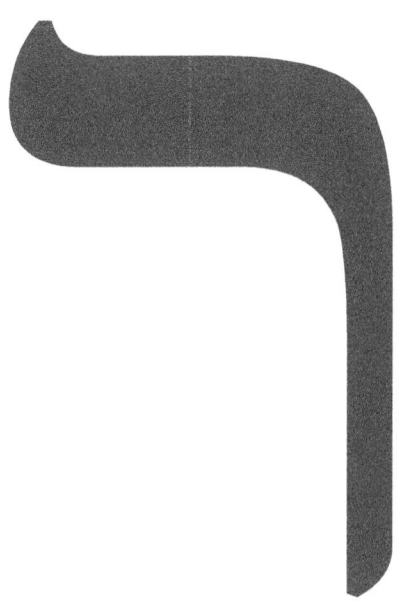

תשרקצפעסנמלכיטחזוהדגבא

The twenty-two letters of light are arranged going from right to left:
Aleph, Bet, Gimel, Dalet, Hay, Vav, Zayin, Chet, Tet, Yod, Kaf,
Lamed, Mem, Nun, Samech, Ayin, Pay, Tzadi, Kuf, Resh, Shin, and Tav.

Resh also spelled reish is the twentieth letter of the Aleph-tav. This letter has the expectancy of things happening with a great magnitude and completion. Likened to the first day of creation, a celebration of life!

Twenty is the age of military accountability.

Joseph was sold for twenty pieces of silver. Joseph's seed is attached to Resh. Ephraim and Manassas are Joseph's offspring and many descendants are found in the US.

Numerical value: 200.

This letter is the six repeat of the first day of creation known as day six.

Vav and Mem are also found on the sixth day of counting. Meaning given to the writer: **The great expectancy of light, returning to the hearts of those that have kept the memory of our Creator.**

Sound: *R.*

Meaning:

<u>Positive</u>—back of the head. A bowed head in memory of creation and the laws that sustain the earth. The first, chief, the sum of.

<u>Negative</u>—bitter, grieved, poor, poverty, last, to be afraid, to shake or rattle the head, Rah means evil but remember at the same time **Rah means partner.**

Move from the tree of good and evil to the tree of life. This gives one wisdom and the desire to think from ones heart—to think in oneness—be like minded and yoked together with our Creator.

Pr. 4:4–13, pg. **733**: **Have wisdom**—to have order.

A person that suffers from an offence has no wisdom. They cannot see pass the unclean darkness within themselves.

1. **Generational curses**—like disease, this curse rules and reigns over the blood—darkness has the authority to rule over the physical body's blood, our DNA, when we eat from the tree of knowledge of good and evil. These foods, thoughts, actions are void of our Creator's creation. If you have a problem with authority—you are unclean and darkness surrounds your thoughts and actions—please come under our Creator's love, life, and light.

2. **Trauma** because of pain physically, mentally, or psychologically —doorway to darkness.

3. **Unhealthy choices**—choose you this day who you will love—protection is limited to you if your actions and words do not align with creation and our Creator.

Let us look at the word **reign**. Malak, maw-lak—to ascend the throne, to take counsel—Mem, lamed, and Kahf. Meaning given to the writer: **the word that comes from the blessed, teaches the way back to our Creator.**

Truth, the tree of life, casts out darkness and lies which came from the tree of knowledge of good and evil.

You can only speak words and do what you understand therefore, **study creation and health and the letters of light, Aleph-Tav, then let the words of truth be your wisdom and guide.**

Protection comes from the back of your head! This is where RESH has been placed, a quiet and secure place. You will grow faster with those that live according to creation, proclaiming nature's wonders within it and eating from earth's living abundance.

Pride, ego, keeps you in bondage and is found outside, in the field and not with the tree of life; eating and drinking harmful things both physically and mentally to one's body. Think, how could Noah know how to feed those on the ark if he himself did not eat according to creation?

Remember that Adam was formed outside of the Garden of Eden, from the field Gen 2:8, pg. **2**—until placed in the garden. This should remind us that we will be outside the garden until we have memory of creation. You will know by what you **speak and eat** if you have been allowed back in the garden.

When darkness leaves the body the mind becomes clear—be careful of alcohol, stimulants and medications as too much consumption of these products keep the mind oppressed and dull. Meaning that you will not be aware of the darkness that you are already in to see perfect light-rays if these words comes your way.

The design of the Resh is composed of two lines, one horizontal and one vertical. It looks very similar to the Dalet but the Dalet has a

Yud at its upper right—hand corner, which the Resh lacks. The Resh's two lines represent intellect and speech. Because they are not joined with a Yud, the speech and intellect of these individuals are for their own gratification until they return to our Creator—they can even degenerate and become corrupt and evil, such a person's thoughts and speech are often directed to hurting and conspiring against others. But it can be seen in neglect. In this way he drags his most essential faculties (remember this is the wisdom from the Aleph-Tav) into the depths of ungodliness. And if he stays too long, there he will forget the truth already taught to him.

The absence of the Yud is important in another way. The Yud signifies Olam HaBa, which means the world to come. The Yud thus represents the humility needed to remain one with our Creator. Dalet is the door of truth and therefore **every** day is important to him or her. They are careful about what he or she thinks, speaks, and eats. A Resh, however, is a person who does not care what he or she does. They have no regard for their thoughts or speech because they don't believe in the laws of creation, therefore lacking wisdom and humility.

So the Resh is the unholy counterpart of the Dalet. If a Resh is substituted for the Dalet in the word echad, which means one, the word becomes acher, which means other. The mere removal of the Dalet's Yud changes the concept of "one Creator," to "other or many gods," or idol worship.

Therefore, our presence on the earth, is to help in transforming an acher into an echad, a person who is one with our Creator.

"There is no poor person except those who are poor in light." The Resh is far away from our Creator. He or she entertains flagrant, evil thoughts and speaks negatively. He or she is beyond the level of having or not having money. He or she is eternally bereft; the poorest of the poor.

Resh also stands for the word *rasha*, which means an evil person. We know, however, that when a wicked person returns to our Creator he or she becomes a baal teshuva, and is therefore with more humility than a Tsaddik. The person's new name is then Rosh or "head." So the Resh at times poor and at times wicked has the ability to do teshuva. This person can awake from their slumber and return to our Creator. The Resh can truly be transformed into the Rosh: the Head, a true leader and turn many to our Creator and the unchangeable laws of creation.

The letter Resh follows the letter Bet in the word bera, "to create." The letter Resh is one of the letters in the letters of light that initiates or begins, that starts something. Resh means first, first of all, firstly, origin, beginning, starting point, increase.

The creation by our Creator that our innermost seeks to establish, is performed through Resh, our head. The very breath that enlivens life that gives life and that establishes life is in the understanding of the letter Resh. To spell the word Resh, you take the word fire which is א ש aleph-shin, "esh" and you put the letter Resh in front of it. So it is spelled ר א ש resh, aleph, and shin: ר the head + א ש fire, and that spells Resh.

The esh which is a cognizant fire, a fire that has full consciousness, a living "born from within" being. This is Resh awakened!

If you want light in your head you need to bring the light of our Creator there. If you want your Resh/brain to have light/Aur you will need to return to the garden and live according to the first day of creation. **Light occurs because the laws of nature and creation are being followed.** You must make room for the light in your Resh—head. What stands in the way? Eating from the tree of good and evil—the ego, self-love, resentment, envy, fear, and most of all, **lust** of the flesh—what we eat, think, and do. Remember what happened to the Israelites in the desert—because of eating mana only, "they began to crave the fleshpots in Egypt. They murmured about the mana that was provided for them and desired flesh to eat. So they were given their hearts desire. And as they were chewing the quail between their teeth a plague broke out and killed those that lusted after flesh."

Darkness obscures the light and where those elements exist, the light cannot emerge. So look into your head: what do you see, darkness or light? Do you see a cognizant pure love that is selfless and lacking any pride? Or do you see a selfish love that justifies itself, always defends its "virtue" by proclaiming its reasons, its excuses its justifications? To successfully perform this self-inquiry requires a mind that is very stable, that is silent. It requires an attentive awareness and not just for a few minutes a day, but continually. You see, our Resh has become dominated by many conflicting wills. When we look sincerely into our own mind and heart, we see a surging chaos of worries, unhealthy memories, fears, desires, attachments, goals, projects and plans. We become attached to these factors, which are called idols. Why? Because we think of them first!

Instead, devote time to nature, meditation, and rest. The business with its chaos will move from you.

We love life and that which we pay attention to, that which we devote our energy to, that which we daily do is the amount of light in an individual.

If we observe and watch the stream of our mind in our daily existence, we will see where our mind is attentive or attractive to. To the world or to those things that promote the light in our heads! Think these things; maturity that leads to completeness, lovingkindness, and peace, thankful for all that comes your way!

Ecc. 9:8, pg. **807** says, "At all times let your garments be white and let oil not be wanting on your head." These are not the literal physical clothes but is the eternal nature [character], that which we daily dress ourselves with; joy, harmony, kindness, love, sharing, peace, discipline and courage. And this pure character is not wanting for they have the words of truth, wisdom, oil on their heads, at all times.

If you recall in the story of the Garden of Eden, Adam and Eve symbolize an ancient state of the heart, a state of innocence and purity. Thus, symbolically, the man and the woman in Eden are represented as "naked" not just naked physically but unashamed as they represented a state of purity.

It is a state of consciousness through which all of us have failed to understand. You see, in the beginning of time our eternal nature, our heart was pure: it was simple, unclothed, naked, and unashamed. This reflects the basic state of the individual, not yet having developed a mature character, yet not having the ego, but being pure simple and full of love.

Unfortunately, Adam and Eve were presented with a temptation, and that temptation led to an unhealthy choice. Adam and Eve are symbolic on many levels. Adam can represent ancient humanity, but also represents the brain. [We must be clear in mind so that we can received the latter rain (revelation) in our heart.] Adam represents Resh, the head/brain and Eve, Mem represents the reproductive organs, birthing. So in us we face a temptation in our present stage of development when we are told "all the trees you may eat freely but do not eat the fruit of the tree of knowledge of good and evil." All trees are in us as our bodies are formed from the earth and so are all the trees. However, if you eat from the tree of knowledge of good and evil you will suffer unhealthy consequences. As long as you are eating from the tree of knowledge of good and evil you are of the world and remain in darkness. When you partake of the tree of life you are awakened to our Creator, which is love, life, and light.

Please remember that we are eternal beings and live forever. The body will live and die as it follows the law of the life cycle.

When our Creator dressed Adam and Eve to cover their skin they were sent out of the Garden of Eden as now they had the tree of good and evil in them and no death can be in the garden where life, love, and light exist. The mortal and animalistic nature now covered man and women and both were expelled from the garden. Before leaving the garden Adam and Eve made aprons from the fig tree leaves, in hopes to hide their shame. This was unacceptable as they lost permission to be in the garden so our Creator gave them a covering for their skin. (note: It does not say here that they were given animal skins to cover their bodies as our Creator could never kill an animal as this is death so what covered their skin was plant based.) Their place was outside the garden in the world of darkness covering truth until the awakened Adam (all men that are born from within) and the awakened Eve (all women that are born from within) restored truth and light to the earth.

Until we understand their consequences for eating from, the tree of knowledge of good and evil, unhealthy choices or death covers our character. Better said, darkness rules over you!

OTZ Daath: the tree of knowledge of good and evil.

OTZ Chaim: the tree of life.

The tree of life has twelve fruit: Rev 22:2: five physical senses and seven internal. Those senses all operate through RESH, the brain and heart. Through Resh we see, hear, smell, taste, touch, speak, listen, learn, perceive, know, view and be.

Physically, our senses are all centred in our head and heart but also eternally they are there. A healthy brain, a healthy nervous system, is a must in any awakened development. A brain that is decayed or degenerated needs greater love from nature. You see, in the middle of your brain is the pineal gland, and toward the front of that is the pituitary gland. When earth produces her fruit her whole life purpose is to raise the breath of life from the bottom of your feet up to your brain to enliven your perception, to awaken, to fill your senses with light. In the beginning humankind did not need a covering for their feet only once they left eating from the earth did they separate themselves from **her** truths (physical application—go burry your feet in the earth). Humankind first was separated from our Creator by an unhealthy choice (speech), eating from the tree of knowledge of good and evil (speaking to darkness—Hasatan), then after sometime of being outside of the garden humankind then separated themselves from the earth by lighting fire to cook and eating animals which brought disease to their bodies and that led humankind to cover their feet with foot wear. Now humankind no longer had a physical **connection** to the earth! They lost **connection** from our Creator and mother, the earth they were formed from.

Our Creator gave Adam and Eve coats to cover their skin. Our Creator never gave them anything for their feet (Gen. 3:21, pg. 4). What does this tell us? Earth, for we were formed out of the ground, has compassion on her children and wants them to eventually return to our Creator who created them and gave them breath. Once this **connection** is understood we have a better likelihood in finding our way back to the Garden of Eden, the beginning of creation and eating from the loam soil.

The transition from being a child to becoming a procreative teen, the desire to unite male and female, the body passes through a great transformation. This is called puberty. We have body changes that attract the opposite sex, as this was placed in all mortal beings. Depending on the tree that you are being taught under will direct your destiny. Either you will be placed in the Garden of Eden or be cast out into the world, the tree of knowledge of good and evil. Unfortunately, most people fail to teach from the tree of life, to procreate for the purpose of bringing forth children that love our Creator and are cast out of Eden into the world which brings forth children of fornication and unhealthy choices.

When we enter into ages (twelve to fourteen) we hear about a physical desire that comes from the fruit of the tree of knowledge of good and evil. We hear about this desire, sex, from our friends, websites, magazines, and our sexual organs feel attracted to it, and our brain becomes tempted, because it wants to taste those sensations if we are being brought up under the tree of knowledge of good and evil. We may hear, not to partake of this act, but unless we have an example around us to follow especially in our parents and friends we will fail this test. We will become physically impure before marriage. And since we want to be like our friends, we want to be cool, we want to be accepted, and we want security socially we partake of the tree of knowledge of good and evil, sexual activity in some form. Unfortunately, that is our undoing. When we make that discovery of the sexual act without the love of our Creator, we exit "Eden." Children today are not innocent. Many children now are born and begin to hear about sex at two and three years old. Do not be surprised by that. They find their parents pornography, they find it on the internet, and they see it on TV. By fourteen or fifteen, most kids (notice these are not children made in the love of our Creator) have experienced sex in some form and are active sexually. We can see this in the way kids dress now, the way they talk, the way they behave. None of this is normal. These kids are born out of fornication, sex without the love of our Creator.

This state of affairs reflects our own being. All of us are guilty; all of us have a role in it and for it to change, we need to bring "the oil to our head." We need to be wisdom blessed. We need to take care of what we put into our brain, into our heart, into our Resh. We concentrate on changing ourselves first and nature will take care to open the door to others.

The word oil using, the letters of light, is shemen, spelled שׁ מ. The letter Shin can be pronounced with the h or without, so it could be pronounced shemen or semen. That sounds familiar!

That word *semen* literally means "extract, essence, that which is pressed out." How do you get the oil from an olive? You crush it. How do you get oil from any fruit, from any grain, from anything? You have to apply heat and pressure and extract it out.

What is the essence of a man? What is the vital extract of this human being? Physically speaking, it is the energy produced by procreation, it is that oil, and with a single drop of it you can form another humankind. Nothing else in a man can do that. So that "oil" in man is their very essence to bring forth children. But because we live outside the garden and do not have male and female loving their Creator we have kids and not children. Everything of you is condensed into that drop, that seed, and that is the oil of gladness. Without the love of our Creator we can only have kids born out of fornication.

That semen (oil) has to be treated with great wholeness, as something beautiful, as something healthy, and not as a game, a toy, as entertainment. Unfortunately, it is treated that way now. Sex has taken the place of intimacy and true relationships found in our Creator. It is seen now as simply a source of pleasure. Some use it as a source of power to control others, many use it as a diversion to avoid their pain, to avoid the truth about themselves, but this is not the purpose of the sexual force. The purpose of the sexual energy is to continue life, consciously, psychologically, and physically, yes, and this is obvious, but there is a higher purpose beyond the physical form, and that is humankind's eternal nature, to form humankind out of love like in the first day of creation.

Changing the place of residence of our Creator from a stone building-cold no connection into a place of flesh—warm and personal, our bodies. No need to go to a building of the world when we are the temple-beautiful, lovely, gentle, compassionate, full of life and light.

When ET'Yeshua was on this earth it is written that he never used his male potency to do anything except bring love, life, and light—he kept his energy for a pure miracle-(a surprising and welcome event that is not explicable by nature or scientific laws and is therefore considered to be the work of oneness) healing and feeding his brothers and sisters. His oil of energy was always transformed to his heart to be used for the purpose of helping others and leading them to be "born from within" and leaving their unhealthy choices. He left behind the importance to be "born from within" and be eternally minded children **reconnected** to the words of truth as their guide. The outcome—Oneness with our Creator of light.

When one is cast out of Eden—one falls asleep as a <u>consciousness</u>. So you remain unaware until truth awakens within you.

We are the light of the world. Those that return to our Creator do not walk in darkness, but possess the light of life." In other words, we have to stop our bad behaviours, we have to purify ourselves, and we need to be remorseful for our mistakes, return to our Creator within. Live in present time.

When love is true, beautiful and blossoms in our children we experience joy and abundance.

My writings are my love letters to the world; to first remove the plank in my eye that I may see to write and then help remove the splinter in my brothers or sisters eye.

The one who continues to harm themselves, to choose unhealthy choices in other words, who can help them in their mortal life? They will live out their lives with their unhealthy consequences. All of us are eternal beings housed in imperfect bodies. We will all end up with our Creator once we leave this mortal body, however, to live in peace and without pain remains your choice as you live out your life on the earth.

The lie is people think that our Creator always forgives our unhealthy choices so there is nothing to worry about. We will have consequences for our choices that is the unchangeable law of the universe. Every single action that we perform has a consequence, no matter what. This is the reason for the law of choice. Our Creator is love, life, and light. But it does not mean you are free of the consequences of your actions. And these consequences sometime last a long time which if not securely **connected** to our Creator then unhealthy choices will occur again, out of forgetfulness and the lack of discipline. Now Paul's words have light to my eyes, he said, "For the good that I wish to do, I do not do; but the evil I do not wish to do, this I practice (Romans 7:19, pg. **1096**).

Where do we see the light of our Creator in the faces of men and women? We know that they are all eternal beings but where is the light of our Creator? Sadly, we see darkness in people's faces, words, and actions. When we look around us we see fake happiness, anger, pride, despair, hate and disease. When we go in the churches, grocery stores, sports events, and work places we see greed, adultery, fornication, envy, pride, anger, fanaticism, disease and ignorance. We do not see purity, contentment, simplicity, health, humility, and peace—the awakened love for our Creator. We do not see a Resh that is illuminated by the light of truth.

While in Eden, Adam and Eve were naked but not ashamed, and that is because of their purity. Their **innocence** was their clothing.

When one is pure, when one is innocent, there is no shame. What is there to be ashamed of when one has committed no wrong? When we feel pain in our heart, when we feel a tumult in our heart, it is because the ego is alive, it is because we have made mistakes, and that is shameful. While in Eden, Adam and Eve were clothed with light—Aur.

All of us who are impure take coats to cover our skin and shoes that hurt our feet to suffocate our misery, to attempt to not feel it, and what is the result? We take into our Resh, our brain, into our heart, into our body, impurity; it is a form of suicide.

Why do we take into ourselves what we take in? Why do we persist in our wrong actions? Why are we attached to things that hurt us? Why does an alcoholic become an alcoholic? Because of pain. Why does a sex addict become a sex addict? Because of pain. Why does a drug addict become a drug addict? Because of pain: **eternal separation from our Creator and physical separation from the earth that we were formed from, brings on pain.**

All of us have these addictions in some area of our life to some degree. Some of us are merely addicted to profit, ambition, and greed. But most are addicted to eating physically dead food, loss of our **connection** to the earth. When people lose their health they cry to god to help them when it has been their choice of food from their birth that has led them down a diseased path.

Our duty is to be mindful of our Creator, and to discover what we do with our own Resh; how we clothe ourselves with lies instead of light. Instead of allowing light to emerge in our eyes and shine inward and outward, we fill ourselves with false light. We consume impressions that are harmful. We consume food and drinks that are harmful. We are addicted to impurity.

It is worth reflecting on all this, because your brain and heart, your Resh is really where the light of our Creator emerges. The letter Resh represents cognizance, comprehension, understanding, and that is why it is one of the letters of light most complete in the Aleph-Tav.

Your physical brain/heart is a vehicle of light. Take care of your brain; be aware that alcohol destroys your brain/heart; this is a scientific fact! When you consume alcohol you destroy your brain, your liver, your nervous system and even your plans. When you take intoxicants of any kind, you destroy your nervous system, and not just what we call "drugs" like marijuana, meth, cocaine, all the great diversity of chemical agents that humanity loves so much now, but there are many other types of drugs that we become addicted to. Sex (notice, not pure intimacy) is a drug, caffeine, cigarettes, video games, TV movies, and excess of sugar or man-made products—we all know that they are bad for us, but we indulge in them anyway; we ignore the consequences. Even though you experience and feel the physical damage they cause you.

If your brain/heart and nervous system are damaged, how can we be seen full of light? How can we use these broken tools? Creation will try to heal you if the damage is not too severe. This is the most miraculous thing of all: Nature/earth can heal you, but not if you persist in killing yourself. (Consider the eating of flesh?) Your healing begins with studying creation and wisdom will guide you back to the day of perfection. Here you will find your healing and rest.

What do you put into your Resh? Physically, it has become difficult to find pure food and water. It is even difficult to find pure air. Most of what we ingest into our body is polluted. Our bodies are now polluted by huge quantities of toxic elements, heavy metals, even rocket fuel, jet fuel, radioactive materials, pesticides—there are so many toxic unnatural elements floating in our bodies now, and yet we continue to eat garbage, we continue to drink garbage—willingly—but what is worse is what we eat and drink with our mind and heart. Your heart is not defined by what is on your plate (but it can still harm the body) "Not that which goeth into the mouth defileth a man but that which cometh out of the mouth, this defileth a man" (Matt 15: 11–20, pg. **936**). He is talking about the words we speak!

What do you take into your Resh, into your head, not just through your mouth, but through your eyes, through your ears? We become what we eat, not merely physically, but our whole lifestyle.

Why do our children grow up the way they grow up? Speaking disrespectfully, crudely, cursing…because they observe it, they see it, they imitate the adults. What is done in your home!

Why our brain is filled with stories of thieves and criminals, murderers? Because you watch them every day on TV and you read about them in magazines, books, and newspapers, which are all about crime and the many ways to commit crime, and you say, "It is harmful," but most movies, shows, and books are about the many ways that you can commit crime, not just crime against society but crime against yourself. Even the news!

Why do you watch these things? What kind of food is that for our heart? What does that do to your brain?

If you are quiet, you will see what it does. You will see that your mind is out of control, it is a monster, and who made it but you. Therefore, if you really want light to emerge in your Resh, be careful what you feed to the breath of life in your brain. Ask yourself, "Is this food leading me to death or life?"

We have to eat from the tree of life what we ingest through all of our senses. This is not something accidental, neither is it something chaotic, but it must be cognizant, fully aware, and it has order.

Many so-called spiritual people live a very haphazard life, calling themselves very "serious" and yet they continue to watch TV, go to movies, consume alcohol irresponsibly, smoking, eating devitalized foods, criticizing each other, gossip, compete with each other by trying to get the most students or a filled congregation, the most recognition, trying to be the most spiritual. None of that has anything to do with the real Creator. "Born from within" is anonymous, humble, and invisible, it has no self. What do you put into your Resh? What do you clothe yourself with? The scripture says: "Blessings (oil) are on the head of the righteous."

The "righteous" (the reader or writer) is the Tzadi. One is righteous by one's action not by one's intentions, and the blessing upon the heads of the righteous one, it is because we have truth in our head (Resh).

The three types of breath

Nephesh is the animal body and related with the blood. All of us have that very force of existence or life that flows in our organism.

Ruach is defined as a thinking, emotional being, but undeveloped

Neshemah is the eternal being, "born from within," superior awareness.

All three of these names can mean "breath."

Most humanity only sees the activity of nephesh, animal instinct, and that is why everyone loves animalistic behaviour: fornication, adultery, violence, news, movies. Those are animal behaviours and that is what rules this planet: animal desire.

"Born from within" is a new creature. This occurs when everything that is impure in you has been nullified. When the "me," the "I," does not raise its head. We are one hundred percent in love with our Creator. Love, life, and light reigns in your body. That is all of your impurity has to be replaced with perfect and mature thoughts, speech, and actions. When that occurs and it is perfect (oneness) and complete, the physical being unites with our Creator that gave you breath and the light emerges and that individual becomes a Nephesh Chaiah, a living being now "born from within" and is one with our Creator.

Your Resh becomes filled with light: through memory.

What happens then? When you have true comprehension of truth, the temptations will be gone. Completely gone. The unhealthy choice of Adam and Eve is uncovered for what it really is and no **darkness** is eaten from this time forth.

The pupil of the eye is called the apple of the eye, this is the darkest area of all bodies—where darkness is hid—the meaning of apple = obscure, the middle or midst [of night], black. **We are the light (not the apple) of the eye when we return to our Creator!**

This will require one to be in continual and constant awareness throughout the day and night, and that is the entire basis of meditation and your daily peace words. When **connection** to our Creator has become established as our normal way of living, then when one speaks there is no difference in your consciousness between meditating and walking around speaking to your fellow man. You will speak with the Creator's joy. You have a continual **connection** to truth.

The letter Resh is in the centre of the word BARA, "to create." In this word, there is no I there is no ego, there are only light letters that reflect the presence of truth within each being. All the letters are in a humble position—***Aleph to Tav.*** With the breath of life of each letter completely alive in each human being.

A Nephesh Chaiah has no ego, only has awareness breath of our Creator within, that presence, which is beyond any type of "I," "this is complete—absolute and oneness"

Eight affirmations of the letter Resh

1. We have freedom to choose—life, love, and light.

2. We are children of light!

3. When loving others, we need to remember that they have darkness that will block their progress. Love anyway with joy proving our Creator's **connection** cannot be severed in you.

4. Develop wisdom to think from your head. Wisdom always brings others to love our Creator.

5. If you find that you are offended—quickly look at the darkness attached so that the pride regarding the offence can be released within, thus finding yourself back in oneness.

6. Pregnancy means expectancy as delivery means complete. Our eternal being is refined with the outcome—immortality and eternal life.

7. Meditation has beautiful words of creation and truth.

8. All letters have matured to children of light. Food from creation is the nutrients that gives the body life as fasting (this includes all things that lead to darkness) is the discipline (oil) that brings down the blessings of truth upon our heads. Memory!

Real Fun

Lester and Mary Celeste are siblings. They had finished doing their chores around the house and Lester was playing on the computer when he said to Mary Celeste, "Let's go outside and have some real fun."

"What do you mean by real fun?" questioned Mary Celeste. "I thought that cooking was fun."

"Come with me, Mary Celeste, and I will show you how to have real fun," continued Lester.

"Well, I guess I can go and see what you are taking about," answered Mary Celeste. "Where are we going?"

"Hurry!" exclaimed Lester. "You are too slow."

"I am only slow because I don't have my tennis shoes on. These flip-flops are sliding off my feet!" Mary Celeste puffed.

Lester payed no attention to Mary Celeste's remark and said, "Come on, jump up here with me."

"I can't!" cried Mary Celeste as she looked up and saw Lester already on the tree branch.

"Sure you can," encouraged Lester. "Take hold of this rope and I will help pull you up."

Mary Celeste finally made it to the branch where Lester was standing. She stood there holding the branch very tight and said, "I hope standing up in this tree is not what you consider real fun?"

"Oh, no," reassured Lester. "This is just the beginning. You need to be in this position in order to have real fun."

As Lester put his hand up in the air, he added, "Now, it is important for you to feel for the wind. Do you feel it, Mary Celeste?"

"Do I feel the wind?" chuckled Mary Celeste. "Yes, I feel it. It is blowing so hard it is about to knock me off this branch."

"You have discovered my real fun!" exclaimed Lester as he let go of the branch and soared down to the ground where he landed softly among the pile of leaves.

As Mary Celeste looked down at Lester she cried, "If I try to do what you just did, Lester, I will surely fall and break my legs. This is just not my kind of fun!"

"Alright, Mary Celeste. You win. Take hold of the rope and I will lower you down to the ground," said Lester a bit disappointed.

On their walk back to the house, Mary Celeste and Lester discussed his adventure of flying in the air like a bird.

When they reached the house, he said, "I know that your fun is cooking. So tomorrow I will make you a wonderful lunch."

As Mary Celeste opened the door to go inside she smiled and said, "I know what your real fun is too! It is jumping from a tree branch into a pile of leaves!"

They both could have fun. Bringing with their fun their own type of consequences.

How do you have fun?

Blessings,

Creator of our universe, we live forever as eternal beings, no need to get excited or sad about death of the body. The body is not who we are. It is our house as we sojourn upon the earth, however, we need to love this house as it is the only one that we will have to work and enjoy this life. Remember, the physical body needs exercise as well as our eternal being.

Creation and our Creator has never changed. The universal laws never change and remain the same today. We awake in the morning with the sun coming up and all the array in that day carries on their work. Some in peace and others in chaos. The evening descends the sun is darkened and the moon appears. All those that love nature are at rest.

We know that we are one! The heavens and the host testify to us of this wonderful creation. We have been awakened to this sound as some have been long against the laws of nature. Some have been deceived by the evil design that would prevail in the hearts of conspiring men.

Some eat for the taste and pleasure of food and not for the health and strength of their bodies. Our bodies become deficient and diseased for lack of sufficient nutrients and minerals that can be found within the table of creation, sun, air and rest.

Some have returned and now love themselves and the beauty that surrounds them.

We have pure truth to drink. No mixing but pure unadulterated truth. The time for inner cleansing in both body and mind will never end as eternity is all we see! Those that have been listening to the words of truth say, we have memory!

Nature gives strength and wisdom to overcome the power of deception, for unhealthy ways are for gain and power and not necessarily for the building up of the love, life, and light of creation.

An awakened son or daughter will eat from the table of creation and have peace.

The heavens are silent and Peace is with Harmony. Love is with Health, Courage is with Nature, Eternity is with Wisdom, Freedom is with Enlargement, Strength is with Discipline, Joy is with Happiness, Father is with Mother, and Children are with Security. The Aleph to Tav has move to eternity.

Perfection!

CHAPTER 21

SHIN

תשרקצפעסנמלכיטחזוהדגבא

The twenty-two letters of light are arranged going from right to left:
Aleph, Bet, Gimel, Dalet, Hay, Vav, Zayin, Chet, Tet, Yod, Kaf,
Lamed, Mem, Nun, Samech, Ayin, Pay, Tzadi, Kuf, Resh, Shin, and Tav.

Shin is the twenty-first letter of the Aleph-Tav.

Shin is the seventh repeat of the first day seven days later if counting. Zayin and Nun are on this day. Meaning given to the writer: **Resting in peace is the time for the life-given seed to bring about the cleansing process**.

Numerical value: 300, the number hidden in the letter shin is the number three and relates to the biblical third day of creation. The right arm of the letter shin is formed by letters Zayin and Vav, which rest upon the base of the open letter Nun—these three letters Nun, Zayin, and Vav form the letter Shin. **The understanding given to the writer: the life-given seed who love creation show they love our Creator**. The three prongs of Shin symbolize three flames. The letter Shin is the symbol of fire. To write fire with the Aleph-Tav, you write it with two letters: Aleph and Shin. The three prongs are the three elements that make up the earth: air (Aleph), fire (Shin), and water (Mem). We have three brains: the intellectual brain, the emotional brain, and the motor-instinctual brain.

Sound: "SH" with a dot over the right side, and "S" with a dot over the left side

Meaning: tooth, steadfast, change, return, and year.

The letter shin has five definitions. The first is shein, which means "tooth" or "teeth." The second is lo shanisi, meaning "steadfastness in one's faith." The third is shinoy, which is "to change for the good." The fourth is shuvah, which means "to return." The fifth is shanah, which means "year."

Shein is the general use of one's teeth to chew food. The teeth break up and grind food. This action represents an individual who carefully "chews over" or is careful with his or her actions. Additionally, the teeth represent strength received from the biblical third day of creation.

This strength brings us to the next interpretation of the Shin, which is **lo *shanisi***, he or she who does not change. This exemplifies the individual who is strong in his or her faith. He or she may move to another locale. The weather may wax hot or cold. The state of his or her work of finances may fluctuate. But this individual has the ability to remain strong and not be swayed by the circumstances of his or her life. However, is able to change with advancing light of truth.

The Shin also represents the concept of ***shinoy***, which is to change for perfection. When a person realizes that he or she has faults, that he or she is not perfect in his or her intellect and understanding or in his or her thought, speech and action, he or she makes an attempt to improve these qualities. The ability to change has a direct **connection** to the concept of ***shuvah***. Here we find the vision of the ark or, now days, the Garden of Eden. As was the ark, in the day of Noah saved he and his family, today, the Garden of Eden is our way to have health and life. Remember the people were crying and trying to enter the ark but to no avail the water swept them away. So be it to those of today that have not returned to our Creator and to creation, the Garden of Eden in time. They will cry but their consistent refusal of truth will have a negative effect on them.

Today, people are trying to enter the Garden of Eden by another way, false religion, the way of processed foods and medicine, and so fail. Come to the light and truth will gently guide you to the tree of life. Eat live foods and see and know our Creator of all. Was Adam and Eve given water to drink in the Garden of Eden? No, and why not? Our Creator provided them with the best water as it came directly from the fruit of the trees. Today we drink healthy water as our foods are not as they were in the beginning of creation. However, if you grow your own fruit and vegetables then this could apply to you.

So what was the purpose of water? Gen. 2:10—And a river went out of Eden to water the garden and from there it divided and became four riverheads.

Do not confuse the children of light with people that are only about eating plant base foods. They do not have our Creator's presence. These people will have some truth but in reality they are still governed by their generational darkness. They follow the traditions of men and the world's calendar.

This leads us to the last interpretation of shin, **shanah**, which means "year." A year contains four seasons, fall, spring, summer, and winter. Fall spelled by the Aleph-Tav is naphal pronounced naw-fal means a prime root to fall, be judged. The letters of light are nun, pay, lamed—meaning given to the writer **the life-given seeds words will teach—so be careful of speaking for our Creator**. Winter is spelled choreph pronounced kho-ref or charaph pronounced khaw-raf meaning the crop gathered, fig. ripeness of age, a prime root to pull off that is to expose as by stripping, spec. to betroth as if a surrender, to spend the winter-betroth, blaspheme, defy, reproach, upbraid (find fault with or scold) letters of light are Chet, Resh and Pay meaning given to the writer—**protection is given to the person that returns to our Creator and creation and is seen in the words or speech that they speak.** Spring is spelled tsa-mach pronounced tsaw-makh meaning a prime root to sprout, bear, bring forth, and grow. Letters of light are Tzadi, Mem and Chet. The meaning given to the writer—**The "born from within," is a spring of love and protection to those that live and love life.** It reminds us not to be complacent, but rather to constantly grow in perfection and humility. Summer is spelled qayits pronounced kah-yits meaning harvest, dry season (fruit, house) letters of light are Kuf, Yod and the final Tzadi meaning given to the writer: **discernment begins and ends with the scale of weighing humility by using the Aleph-Tav.** Throughout every aspect of seasonal change, one must remain steadfast in one's faith in our Creator. The four seasons are echoed in the four lines of the shin. (These are the **outside lines** so be careful)

Year is comprised of a Shin, Nun, and a Hey and means a revolution of time, meaning given to the writer, **the cleansing of the life-given seed is completed by perfect light or revelation for that time and season**.

Now, one of the things that makes the Shin unique among the letters is that is can be placed in different places within the body of a word without changing the meaning of that word itself. It may however, affect that word's sacred significance. The same happens when fire (truth) in the body cleans an area. That fire can be in different places in the body and the same cleansing is received no manner where the fire is placed.

The Shin comprises three vertical lines representing three columns. The letter itself looks like a crown. Will and pleasure, the intellect, and the emotions. These three rays are bestowed on all people; the first through the right line, which is kindness; the left line which is justice; and the centerline which is mercy. (These are the lines within and show the degree of the character of an individual.)

This could be said the right line, the flash of an idea, the left line—understanding, and the centerline—application of wisdom.

Another dimension of the Shin's columns is reflected by the three patriarchs. ET'Abraham is represented by the right line, loving-kindness, as he personified absolute kindness, an outward focus through **connection** to others and the performance of perfect deeds. ET'Isaac is represented by the left line, discipline and severity, indicative of his being introspective and demanding of himself, concentrating on self—refinement and intense meditation. ET'Jacob is the centerline. This is harmony, because he took the qualities of ET'Abraham and ET'Isaac, kindness and severity and synthesized them into mercy. ET'Jacob also represents the study of creation, because the truth blends all into a harmonious whole of oneness.

The letter Shin actually has four different forms. There's a Shin with a dot above the right column, a Shin with a dot above the left column, a Shin with four columns instead of three, and finally a silent Shin. The silent Shin's sound value is a voiceless sibilant, meaning hissing *shhhhhhh* like when the librarian says hush.

Both the tooth and fire meanings of Shin refer to it as a process of transformation, breaking down, grinding into particles, building anew, cooking, and the firing of a clay pot into a form. The whole process of transformation, healing, breaking and restoring. The fire also represents the unchangeable, the unmovable, and thus is a symbol of word power. The truth constantly transforms the matter yet remains unchanged itself. Matter changes constantly, yet the truth within does not change, so all of life is a process of learning to align with our Creator's unchangeable laws. Shin is the flame of the truth, which we must keep always burning within us.

Finally, the Shin teaches us balance. It is composed of three Vavs. The right pillar is of kindness and mercy, the left of strict justice and truth. The world cannot continue without both, so we must balance between the two. In all aspects of life, we must find the middle way between the opposites and extremes. Once you choose the tree of life you will have balance and our unchangeable Creator.

When the dot is on the right, the Shin emphasizes the concept of kindness. When the dot is on the left the Shin (pronounced "sin") emphasizes the aspect of judgment or severity. These two forms are illustrated by the words **shaar** and **sei'ar**. The Shin of the word **shaar** (gate) has its point on the right, as a gate allows people to pass in and out and aspect of openness. This Shin is full of energy, potential and benevolence.

If we switch the Shin's dot to the left side, the resulting word is **sei'ar**, or hair. Hair has the properties of life, but a life-force that is tremendously diminished or weak. One can pull out or cut a strand of hair and not feel any pain, unlike when one cuts a finger or other part of the body. A hair is rooted in a follicle, a concentrated, restricted opening. We thus say that the Shin with a point on the left side represents severity and constraint.

Understand that fire, the words of truth, is in our head. In the end matter turns into fire. To comprehend this better, remember that your physical body is called an "organism" because it is formed by organs. Every organ is formed by cells, and every cell by molecules, and every molecule by atoms. When we disintegrate the atom, we liberate fire. So we are condensed fire, condensed energy. In the end of our mortal life, we have to become children of light, purified by fire, the words of truth, Chaiah (to life), and of the new world that has formed within.

Deuteronomy says: "Yah is a devouring fire." Our Creator's table of life devours all impurities in us when we have Shin in our head. Therefore, you need fire in your head as long as there is impurities to burn out of the body but once the filth is removed the only substance left is light, your light body! Eat living foods! The fruit of the trees.

If darkness represents the tree of knowledge of good and evil, then light represents the tree of life. Where is the tree of life located—in the Garden of Eden and no other place! So when ET'Yeshua said, "to come to him all who are thirsty and I will give you drink" what he is talking about is eating FRUIT, as fruit has the purest water of all. A false Messiah will never lead you to the Garden of Eden as he or she is not permitted there. Darkness from your religious generational progenitors will keep you in the world of lies and eating in a way that causes disease and pain, which darkness reigns over.

We have an ego and as long as it serves within the darkness we will think that to become "born from within" we have to belong to a particular sect, we have to belong to their groups. Let's not repeat the same mistake of our forefathers who were born in fornication but let us become free with the understanding of our Creator within us. Remember, darkness has murder in it from (Bereshith) the beginning, and abides not in the truth, because there is no truth in darkness. To be a murderer from the beginning means to be a fornicator, it means to kill, disregard our Creator's love, life, and light and replace it with a false doctrine, a false Messiah which turns into (ego)—selfishness, religion found in most people and passed down from one generation to the next with even greater errors and misunderstandings. The ball of error keeps getting bigger and bigger like a ball of snow rolling down a mountain. Except it is not white this thing is black and terrible. Thankful for our Creator's continuous love to those that seek for truth and oneness.

Ps. 119 shin pg.719: "Great peace have those loving creation, and for them there is **no** stumbling-block."

Temptation comes from the tree of knowledge of good and evil and is a destroyer; the triumph over this temptation is light that comes from the tree of life! This holy place, where the tree of life is found, represents our Creator's word power to form children in love. The flaming cherub is another name for the fire of Shin, protecting the entrance of Eden. So that only those that have the witness of truth and love of our Creator in themselves, have right to enter into the Garden of Eden and eat of the fruit from the tree of life. At this point you will choose the best for your mortal body. Remember we are eternal beings and live forever. Our bodies are mortal and die.

One last thing to remember, the letters of light, that fire that develops in our spinal column, our staff, is the cleansing received from wisdom. This wisdom acts as a sword of discernment that we can apply to the ego to destroy it. When we see the "I" or the "me" rising up in us we have wisdom, born from within, to destroy and cleanse as needed. So in that way the three patriarchs (ET'Abraham, ET'Isaac, and ET'Jacob), the three matriarchs (ET'Sarah, ET'Rebecca, and ET'Leah), which are the two aspects of truth, masculine and feminine are born within us, and we are ONE with our Creator.

We have thirty-three vertebrae; the number 3 shows up again but double, one 3 for the male and one 3 for the female. A double witness to eat from the repeated first day now called the third day of creation.

Just as the letters of light mean many other words and are **connected** so do the English words and are related.

Eight affirmations of the letter Shin

1. Love your rest as it has the fire/power to heal all disease and remove all darkness.

2. Wisdom comes to a Tzadi for the uplifting and growth of others. Thank you for truth and entrance to the Garden of Eden.

3. Our Creator's love produces many emotions, all to understand and activate light. Humble yourself and learn.

4. There are channels of light from the heavens that reach the earth—perfect and complete with memory—peace with kindness—oneness with father and mother within.

5. We are renewed daily and do our work with love, life, and light. Remember that life for your physical body comes from eating living food!

6. Return to Eden and Remember: Respiration (Aleph), Rain (Mem), Raw (Shin), Rainbow (Het), Read (Tzadi), Rare (Ayin) Reach (Kaph), Ring (Samech), Ready (Gimel), Reap (Nun), Reason (Lamed), Revelation (Hay), Receive (Bet), Record (Dalet), Remnant (Zayin), Rich (Vav), Refuge (Yud), Rejoice (Quph), Released (Resh), Returned (Tet), Rest (Tav), Renewed (Pay).

7. Thank you for your truth which gives strength to our mind, being, and body. Peace!

8. Our Creator does not change—quintessence.

Exercise Wisdom until an Abundance of Fruit Has freedom

1. If man exalts a building or carnal body, then our Creator exalts the humble heart and mind.

2. Man's power is represented by attaining knowledge and positions. Our Creator's power is having the Aleph-Tav and nature in one's countenance.

3. If children of light are found in the garden, then kids are found in the field.

4. If foolishness is unhealthy choices, then maturity is a perfect and sweet heart.

5. Meddlers have as their companions talebearers; truth is my companion.

6. Where there is no love of idols, there is no contention; in as much as where there is no gossip, their lives truth.

7. As money is man's symbol of victory and safety, so is the understanding of wisdom, children's safety and victory.

8. If eye to eye is of man, then light to light is of our Creator.

9. Envy is to not know mother as rebellion is to not know father.

10. To hide in one's heart love for our Creator is to lose one's own ego and gain eternity.

11. The churches are to knowledge of good and evil—(speaking remove), as returning (teshuva) is to wisdom—eternal being.

12. Pleased is a word in our Creator's language undefiled; proud is Hasatan's language defiled.

13. Blessed is a virtue that completes creation as luck is a seed of darkness.

Memory!

School Time

"The school bell is ringing!" called out Reagan to her friend Maverick. "Hurry up before we are late for class!"

"Oh, what is the hurry?" mumbled Maverick. "Who likes going to school anyway, especially when all your teacher does is boss you around?

"Oh, come on," encouraged Reagan. "Let's go help 'Old Egghead' get through another day."

Maverick sadly replied, "I just wish he would stop bossing me around."

As the children entered their classroom, they met Mr. Foster at the doorway.

"Good morning, Mr. Foster," whispered Reagan.

"Good morning, Mr. Foster," stammered Maverick.

"Are you two late again?" Mr. Foster frowned.

Reagan and Maverick just shrugged their shoulders and looked at each other. Then they quickly slipped into their desks.

Class started five minutes late and began as it did almost every day. Amber was punished for yelling in class. Journee cried for her mother. Mabel continued to get out of her desk without permission, and of course, Reagan and Maverick chattered away like two little chipmunks.

As it was soon time for lunch, the class eagerly waited for recess, including Mr. Foster!

"Thank goodness it is recess," sighed Maverick. "Why do you think Mr. Foster is so grouchy?"

Reagan thought for a minute and then replied, "I really do not know. Let's talk to the rest of the class about this problem. I know that Hunter and Estee are really smart! Maybe by working together we can find an answer."

During recess, the children talked about the problem they were having with Mr. Foster and came up with a solution. They hoped it would work!

The recess ended and all the children quickly returned to their class room. No one was late. Mr. Foster noticed at that time that the children's behavior was a little different!

Mr. Foster clearly announced, "Take out your math books."

All the children answered together, "Yes, sir, Mr. Foster."

"Do pages 49, 50, and 51," continued Mr. Foster.

All the children answered together, "Yes sir, Mr. Foster."

Mr. Foster then added, "No one is to get out of their desk or talk without permission, is that clear?"

Again, all the children answered together, "Yes sir, Mr. Foster."

After thirty minutes of complete silence from within the classroom, Mr. Foster looked around and was surprised to find the children still busy dong their work. They were behaving wonderfully! Something was definitely up!

Mr. Foster accepted the silence and so questioned the class, "Children, does anyone need help?"

All the children sweetly answered, "No, sir, Mr. Foster," and continued doing their work with smiles on their faces.

Mr. Foster glanced at the clock. There was only twenty minutes of class left for the day. As he looked again at the children, he realized what was happening. The children had decided that they would be perfect students. Mr. Foster was overjoyed!

In the next moment, Mr. Foster sprang up from his chair and announced to the class, "Since you have been such studious students this afternoon I would like to do something special for you."

Mr. Foster went into his storage closet and rummaged through the clutter until he found his old popcorn popper. As he began to make popcorn, the children surrounded him and cheered!

They knew that they had chosen the best solution to their problem.

From that day on, school was fun for everyone, including Mr. Foster!

What did these children teach you?

CHAPTER 22

TAV

תשרקצפעסנמלכיטחזוהדגבא

The twenty-two letters of light are arranged going from right to left:
Aleph, Bet, Gimel, Dalet, Hay, Vav, Zayin, Chet, Tet, Yod, Kaf,
Lamed, Mem, Nun, Samech, Ayin, Pay, Tzadi, Kuf, Resh, Shin, and Tav.

Tav or Taw is the twenty-second and final letter of the letters of light. This letter is omnificent. It is all the letters in one and represents eternity—REST—all sound, all colors, all days and all numbers. It represents ALL and ALL, our Creator's majesty, glory, splendor, beauty and wonderful creation. Perfect oneness!

Numerical value: 400—ET'Abraham bought a burial place for ET'Sarah for four hundred shekels, the cave where ET'Sarah was buried is called the cave of the four couples, as ET'Adam and ET'Eve, ET'Abraham and ET'Sarah, ET'Isaac, and ET'Rebecca, and ET'Jacob and ET'Leah are all buried there according to biblical history.

ET'Abraham was told that his people would reside in a foreign land (Egypt) for four hundred years.

Esau was mighty as he had four hundred men when he approached ET'Jacob. (Notice that Esau has no ET in front of his name, he despised his birthright and the promise of continuation of love, life, and light was carried forth by ET'Jacob.)

The four corners of the earth—NSEW.

Sound: "T" with a dagesh, Tav and "S" without, Sov.

Meaning: truth, sign, life or death, mark, covenant, seal, to stand.

Emeth means truth, eh-meth (Aleph, Mem, Tav). The meaning given to the writer: **The breath of life is aleph-tav and the children of light stand for life, eternal.**

The reason *emeth* is represented by its last letter (Tav) and not its first (Aleph) is that the essence of truth is determined at the **end** of one's journey or passage, not at the beginning. Often when we begin something, the truth of the matter does not seem attractive, like the decision to stop eating junk food or move with advancing light, leaving an old tradition or belief and eating according to creation. Only upon seeing the outcome at the end do we appreciate that the path of *emeth* was the only way to travel. This requires faith as you do not see the results until you near the end of your mortal life.

The Tav represents, a stamp, or seal. For example, in ancient times, when someone wrote a letter they would end the letter with a seal formed from wax. It was an official document and would receive an impression, a stamp, and a seal in that wax to show its authority of that person sending the communication. This is what the letter Tav represents, the authority of the one sending light communication through the letters of light. Tav is the final stamp, the affirmation, the summation of what is contained in the twenty-two letters of light. So this letter is very significant; it represents the completion of the eternal being, the completion of his or her work while on the earth. You want to be able to rest in peace from all your daily work.

How does the flat earth look? It is an imprint made by the ground's weight causing all the edges to be raised up around it—like a seal in wax.

When you see a seal at the end of a document or letter, you know it is the end of the document and that it was written with authority. When our Creator completed the heavens and the earth the earth was the seal, as it was made last, after the heavens, and the end of creation. So the earth becomes our Creator's seal for humankind.

The Tav is a letter of completion; what the Tav looks like inside of us is how we end our earthly time. You could say it is how we are seen; it is the summation of our actions. When we reach the bodies end, the completion of our mortal life, we face to face with our Creator—we receive a Tav, a seal or a stamp and live eternally with our Creator. We have life marks and habits that have been imbedded in us for good and evil or for perfection. We need cleansing so the presence of our Creator is felt within. You want to know within that you are one with our Creator. How do we do this? Pay attention, you become aware of everything that you do: in your mind, in your heart, and in your body. These three brains need to be fully conscious and awakened by the force of life from our Creator and wisdom.

The book of revelation shows the beast with the number 666. Those are three Vavs; three brains—mind, heart, and body. All three are asleep until a person is "born from within." All three are dominated by worldly desires, traditions and habits. Our mind is dominated by fear, pride, envy, anger, lust, greed, gluttony, laziness, and disease. Our heart is dominated by memories, by cravings, and our desire to be loved. Our body is dominated by habits of laziness or busyness. Our three brains are 666; three negative Vavs, which is why we suffer or have pain until "born from within." Return to our Creator and creation and be a blessing to the earth and to the people that have contact with you.

The false image that we worship before our change is within our own body and mind. It performs wonders, performs so-called miracles through the ego but that false image is the deceiver and not the love from our Creator. To resolve this situation, go outside and put your hands and feet into the soil. Plant a tree or garden, tidy a flower bed, observe the animals and their daily routine, water the lawn, share flowers or food from your garden with neighbors, and most of all love yourself!

Humanity and the suffering that is passing through the earth is growing worse, from day to day, from generation to generation, we can observe that humanity is not ascending into a Golden Age; humanity is descending—the gulf is becoming greater and greater between those that are "born from within" and those that remain in their truth of darkness.

We individually are what ET'Yeshua spoke of: "Woe unto you, scribes [intellectuals] and Pharisees [fanatics], and hypocrites! For ye make clean the outside of the cup and of the platter, but within you are full of extortion and excess. We are not seen by the love, by the laws of nature, by the laws of creation based on our appearance. We are seen by the results of our **actions because we have returned to our Creator and creation and live out our lives in health**. There is no judgment as long as we return to our Creator and creation.

The Tav means "to stand" and represents the ultimate strength, the ultimate expression of eternity; the light of perfectness is pure love, pure light, and a life-given heart. The human being offers up all desire; the human being humbles itself for others; the human being lives according to the word of truth. The world judges based on the outward appearance, but our Creator is seen in people by the condition of their heart. Remember, Tav is the finisher of oneness.

In the past era, it is true that wisdom needed to be uncovered. But now this pure light must be given and given more freely. This is from the words of truth. This understanding is not written down somewhere for you to read. It is something you acquire through the cleansing of your heart. To acquire it one has to be living in accordance with love. Wisdom then guides the born from within to all truth. It will be simple and a child will embrace it. It is loving, joyful, sweet, gentle, pure, happy, delightful, full of genuine laughter, kind, playful, fun, togetherness, trusting, secure, and peaceful.

The covenant is represented in the Aleph-Tav by the letter Yud. The covenant represents circumcision of the heart. The one who makes the covenant impure by his transgressions of truth in effect, stops the advancing light of our never changing Creator from emerging in him or her with a physical consequence, heart problems. We can observe this on the earth. Where do we see the light of creation amongst humankind? Where do we see true heart love, humility, and peace? Very rarely. What we most commonly see is selfishness with large congregations, violence, sexual degeneration, disease and religious wars. None of this has anything to do with our Creator; this has a lot to do with the world's image, just another name for ego or ignorance. Our ego thinks that it can overcome the law of nature without returning to creation. Think again, as the words of truth will give utterance in your ear. Listen and be attentive to the still small voice inside and be forever blessed.

Book associations using the number 22:

The twenty-second book is the Song of Solomon—representing the bride and bridegroom.

The forty-fourth book is Acts—the covenant of promise sealed by fire, the words of truth called Pentecost.

The sixty-sixth book is Revelation—the final sealed book-opened to the overcomers.

Sealed is used in Revelation thirty-two times according to Strong's Concordance. Our Creator has the Aleph-Tav inside of you, listen to nature. How do you become the stamp, seal, or stand? We continue working on it.

Tav is the seal of creation. Another word for covenant.

Ways to ratify a covenant: People gave their hands-wrist shake, they took off the shoe, it was written down and sealed or signing your name, erecting monuments or stones, given gifts, feast time celebrating appointed days or simply eating a meal with someone. An offering or an oath.

How would you ratify the covenant with nature? Go outside and hug a tree, put one's feet deep into the loam soil, just listen to the birds that sing, play in the rain, feel the wind against your cheeks, feel the rays of the sun on your face, eat a piece of fruit directly from the plant or tree and smell the clean air after a rain.

To covenant with someone is to align with someone. That means you are yoked to that person and agree as one.

The foundation of all things is alignment, misalignment is out of balance or oneness—this alignment is all about the covenant of promise—remember the vertebra, all vertebra need to be in alignment in our spinal column our staff to have strength to carry the body throughout life, to do the work of creation.

Emeth (truth) is equal to the word memory. Memory of what? Creation and our Creator who breathes out life into the world.

When the strength of creation is aligned in a person, this alignment brings forth life and truth to the individual.

What is the definition of unhealthy choices? Missing the mark, better said, out of alignment!

In the beginning created Aleph-Tav. This phrase is only in the letters of light language and cannot be translated into English—"ET."

I am Aleph and Omega, the beginning and the ending. I am the "ET"or the "AT." The letter E and the letter A are interchangeable in the Aleph-Tav.

The word ET or AT is undefinable, it points to a direct object or person.

ET or AT is connected to our Creator's creation.

ET or AT is before Esau's name in the Hebrew written scriptures (meaning covenant of promise), but when Esau forsook his birthright, the ET was no longer found in front of his name but was found in front of Jacobs's name. Esau lost his **connection** to our Creator as he did not recognize the importance of creation (he was a hunter of animals) represented by "ET" or "AT." Those that do not think that the Aleph-Tav, "AT or ET" is important, lose their **connection** to our Creator.

Aleph-Tav = ET or AT—bringing forth the entire aleph-tav which is all creation and character written by wisdom's words. This is the life living promise (Aleph-Tav) that awakens people today.

- The design of the Tav is a Dalet and a Nun. These two letters spell out the name of Dan, one of the tribes of Israel. In the desert, the twelve tribes of Israel were divided into four camps. When the tribes set out to travel, the camp of Dan was the last to proceed. If any of the other tribes left something behind, the tribe of Dan would collect and return it.

- "Who is called a fool? One who loses what (<u>what</u> is spelled mah) has been given to him." On a deeper level, the concept of "what has been given to him," represented by the word, mah, denotes the state of one's humility. One who is humble says, "Mah-What [am I]?" With memory restored, humankind will know that they are eternal beings and live forever.

- Freedom is a choice. May we become born from within and choose life, creation and light!

- ET'Abraham was given the **covenant of circumcision** (Then the Hebrew god said to ET'Abraham, "As for you, you must keep my covenant, you and your descendants after you for the generations to come. **10** This is my covenant with you and your descendants after you, the covenant you are to keep: Every male among you shall be circumcised. **11** You are to undergo circumcision, and it will be the sign of the covenant between me and you. **12** For the generations to come every male among you who is eight days old must be circumcised, including those born in your household or bought with money from a foreigner—those who are not your offspring. **13** Whether born in your household or bought with your money, they must be circumcised. My covenant in your flesh is to be an everlasting covenant. **14** Any uncircumcised male, who has not been circumcised in the flesh, will be cut off from his people; he has broken my covenant").

- ET'Noah was given the **covenant of the rainbow** a rainbow was set in the sky to serve as a sign of the covenant that water would never again destroy all life with flood waters. It serves as a reminder of our Creator's perfectness.

- ET'King David was given the salt covenant. The phrase "**covenant of salt.**" A covenant is an agreement between two or more parties. An agreement that involves salt symbolizes one that is meant to be perpetual, incorruptible and indissoluble. Don't you know that the god of Israel gave the kingship over Israel to ET'David and his descendants forever by a covenant of salt? (2 Chronicles 13:5: This mineral also impedes the action of yeast (leaven) on food. In Scripture, leaven many times symbolizes sin and a rebellious attitude, as well as the ability to negatively influence others. The inclusion of salt, therefore, can represent the preservation and maintenance of purity in a world that can cause corruption.

In conclusion, the meaning of a salt covenant is an agreement that is meant to endure regardless of the circumstances. It was an ancient symbol of unbreakable friendships and alliances that were to be preserved. Such agreements are solid, unbreakable and everlasting.

ET'Yeshua was given the "**Oneness" covenant**—This is the promise that our Creator does not change and makes with humanity life, love, and light to restore fellowship with those whose hearts are turned toward creation. ET'Yeshua stood as the life giving seed that pushed forward light, love and life. Oneness with our Creator.

ET'Children of light have been given the "fruit covenant" "born from within" using the renewed Aleph-Tav. These are eternal meanings that uncover the truth of the letters of love, life, and light. This is the **fruit covenant** at the end of the age for those belonging to the free woman, New Jerusalem. These are children of light and they are in love with our Creator's truth of creation.

A person whose being has his or her foundation in the creation is naturally humble. By losing or rejecting Aleph-Tav, humility that which "has been given to you," as a free gift, that individual throws away his **connection** and seal to our Creator and is considered a "fool." Forty-one times fool is mentioned in Psalms and Proverbs.

A body has a head, hands, and feet. At first glance, the head is greater than the feet because of its intellectual superiority. But a head cannot reach its destination unless it is transported there by the feet. Humility comprises the feet of the people of love, life, and light. It represents the level of bringing the head to its destination. How? Through humility. The head is quite literally the brains of the operation. This often results in arrogance if not careful, as when something "goes to your head." The feet, on the other hand have no brains. They work all day long transporting us to our destinations but never get any recognition or honor. Reflecting on the humble service of the feet can bring us to humility. Creation's seal. Maybe, another reason that ET'Yeshua washed his disciple's feet? He was washing away the earth from their feet as a symbol of their **connection** to the earth, mother. Just as he prayed for all as a **connection** to his father, our Creator.

The heel of the foot has no feeling or understanding. Placing the heel of one's foot inside a shoe, where it's dark, represents the concept of accepting the yoke of heaven in a cold, dark world. Just as the feet are the foundation and support of the human body, so, too, accepting the yoke of our Creator is the foundation of truth by faith (as faith has in it the unknown we live by faith until we see…). One must have the humility to accept truth beyond question and beyond rational understanding. It is the letter Tav, the letter of humility that allows the individual to continue embracing the love of our Creator and truth which all too easily can be left behind and rejected through human ego or pride, fear, laziness, boredom, money and arrogance.

On a practical level, the word Dan means "to judge." We look at and humble our every action/words before performing/saying it. ET'Yeshua came to teach truth and this truth was written down to the best of man's ability and then translated many times, generation after generation. Thank goodness our Creator does not change and neither does the laws of creation. They have remained the same and can be trusted. Understanding our Creator's creation with all man's laws and their **misunderstood implications and branches** require patience and humility. This darkness will vanish once you see truth! The truth will never change!

When our Creator created the world, truth was concealed within the laws of nature: the "ultimate light." When one toils to find the truth buried within the love of creation and loves nature, although this route may seem slow, it is by faith and courage and a long process (as each individual has many present layers and past generations of darkness that have to be cleaned), that one will ultimately find truth within and forever dwell in the sacredness of love.

If one engages in excessive or lustful pleasure, this one will eventually come to unhealthy choices. He or she will not take the time to **connect** with our Creator and appreciate the bountiful blessings in his or her life because he or she will always be craving and running after more pleasure. So although this indulgent pleasure may initially seem glorious, it eventually leads to eternal poverty and its darkness.

Pertaining to the generation of the flood, the Bible tells us that Noah was a tsaddik in his generation (generation using the letters of light is spelled b'dorosov) the word b'dorosov, can be broken up into two words; b'doro and Tav or Sov. The unhealthy choice of Noah's generation was thus the letter Tav, an excess of pleasure, as reflected in its "excessive" nun—(when men began to increase (increase is the excessive nun) on the face of the earth and that every inclination of the thoughts of his heart was only evil continually.) Truth allowed the people of that time to do whatever they wanted. Truth did not restrict them or punish them for their wrongdoings. Rather our Creator let them go on and on until they were so lost, it was impossible for them to return to creation and its laws of freedom. The only way our Creator could rectify the world at that point was by the consequence of nature, destroying it through the flood. The same will be seen at the end of creation as our Creator said in Revelation 22:10–11 pg. **1216**: "Do not seal the words of the prophecy of this book because the time is here, he who does wrong, let him do more wrong; he who is filthy, let him be more filthy; he who is righteous let him be more righteous; he who is set-a-part be more set-a-part."

And, those that are born from within shine and shine greater and greater.

A clue that we are at the end of the last generation is that it will look like the beginning with Adam and Eve. Many couples will have gardens and speak about food and its health benefits but they will never come to know the truth—our Creator. These are they that have come to the open door but have rejected truth because of their religious ego/pride! Disease and pain within their bodies is their end!

The Tav is made up of three lines. In this sense it is similar to the Hay, which also has three lines: two vertical and one horizontal. They represents thought, speech, and the performance of perfect deeds—action. Because it is the last letter and this the culmination of the Aleph-Tav, the Tav represents someone who understand that they are a perfect eternal being and live forever. However, the condition of being "perfect/complete" can also result in arrogance/pride.

Therefore, the Yud in the lower left-hand corner of the Tav completes the Tav to end in humility. When a person knows he/she is perfect or complete and that he/she has ended their service by fulfilling their heart work or destiny, they must arrive at the Yud or humility. As ET'Yeshua's ending was one with our Creator so will your ending be in oneness. Even if people surround you at your body's death you, the eternal being, is returning to be one with our Creator. Our Creator will be all that you understand and desire, therefore, sealed (stand) in oneness at the end of your mortal existence.

Remember the last act of ET'Yeshua as he stood before Pilot! This was the very act of bowing down in humility to truth.

"Born from within," children of light leave this earth in peace!

The signature of our Creator is the word emeth, truth. Our Creator imbeds truth in the universe, creation. Then rested from all work.

When resting in peace, the purpose of our Creator's creation becomes clear. Our Creator formed the world for humankind to have joy with harmony and memory. By fulfilling and doing truth which increases our acts of kindness we make the world a better place in which to live. In such a fashion we bring our Creator—truth—into the world.

Finally, our Creator is called emeth because the only real truth is our Creator.

The message of Tav is an eternal lesson and not one that now I am finished there is no more! If we continue to listen to the words of truth in the letters of light with humility and remember to visit nature daily, then this is ticheyeh, ti-che-yah the meaning of life. If, however, we seek this truth through arrogance, it is tamus; the antithesis of true living.

Remember the left leg of the letter Tav incorporates the Yud. Once we have absorbed each of the letters of the Aleph-Tav representing the entire creation, we must not forget that the ultimate truth, the foundation of the entireAleph-Tav, is the Yud of humility. Was it not by ET'Yeshua's humility that he withstood all ridicule, slander, insults, punishment and death?

By embracing this humility one is empowered to live the precepts of the truth with a pure mind and a joyful heart. The performance of the truth will reveal the essential quality of the 22 letters of love, life, and light—the ultimate state that is in **present time**. So from this day forward, take daily your Creator's dress (character) and infuse it into any place that you walk, knowing that love, life, and light will remain present on this earth eternally.

Eight affirmations for the letter Tav

1. Remember, the feet are as important as the head as they are what brings us to our destination.

2. As we grow in age we are thankful for the life lessons showing us where we need improvement—harmony is our blessing .

3. Pain is the result when we cross our Creator's protective fields or fence. Keep us humble and in peace!

4. Our Creator is nature. Blessings to a wonderful and perfect creation.

5. Reflecting often on the Aleph-Tav provides a way of speaking to life.

6. Every letter of light formed requires humility to understand it. The Yud is in all letters which stands for humility. Give honor and glory to our Creator.

7. All things on this earth when viewed with a perfect eye (Ayin) become in harmony. Greater the negativity in the world the greater blessings concealed made ready to be revealed.

8. Tav seals the letters of love within! However, knowing that creation does not change nor do the universal laws truth brings the life living seeds peace, trust, security, and continual freedom to choose.

The Secret of Truth's Presence

In the quiet of truth's presence, how my being delights to hide;
Oh, how precious are the lessons
Which I learn by light's Eternal side!
Worldly cares can never vex me
Neither trials lay me low,
If when doubt comes to tempt me,
To the quiet place I go.
Each day the truth brings me to a place
Beneath the tent of wisdoms wing,
There is cool and pleasant shelter,
And a fresh and bubbling spring.
And love does respect me,
As we hold communion sweet,
Memory gives me answers as I write.
What a joyous encounter, when thus we meet.

Oh, how healing blesses as I listen,
And my rejoicing heart cheers.
Do you think life never reproves me?
Think again, perfection fills my ears!

Do you think that I could love One
Half as well, or as I ought?
If freedom did not plainly tell me
Of each unhealthy word and thought?
No! For nature is very truthful
And that makes me share kindness more.
For I know perfection loves me,
Though that sometimes wounds me sore.

Would you like to know the sweetness,
That comes from our Creator?
Breathe the life giving air within the earth,
And there, your reward is simply greater.
And whenever you leave the silence
Of that joyous meeting place,
Creation seals you with memory
Upon your beautiful face!

Eternal Being

"How long before this mortal tabernacle lives without mental or physical pain? It is so uncomfortable at times to be here on this earth! Please, does someone hear?" questioned the woman.

"Your request, my living life giver, can be understood by our Creator, who is truth," calmly came the words from within.

"Religion and tradition have been my companions here on the earth!" cried the woman. "Who is this that hears?" she added quietly.

"I am the words of wisdom, whom the world cannot receive. I have come to lead you to your eternal life if you will love me. The truth is within you and the presence of our Creator will emerge once **connected** to creation. My mission is to give you the opportunity to believe in the truth of creation and love yourself. Otherwise you will stay in confusion and not see the simplicity of our Creator," answered the words from within very boldly.

"How can teachings that are different from what was taught by my own parents, family and Bible be understood as truth?"

"All you need is the desire for truth and courage will teach and strengthen you in all things."

"Oh, how the perception from which I see from, has in it, darkness. My mind and heart want the pure truth but religion and traditions are everywhere I turn. All organizations say they have the truth but after the study they are found man-made for power and worldly gain. Empty!

The hardness from these teachers have made the words from within, which come in silence, precious to my life!"

"Oh, how ignorance and pride keeps a person in fear!"

"Please wait. Time is needed." whispered the women.

And many years past devoting time to word study, healthy eating and nature.

"Spending time enjoying life has removed the dark layers from generations past and living in present time each and every day brings freedom to love myself," smiled the women. "Truly our Creator never changes and is present at all times! Truth has given me perfect eyes and together we are one."

"It was by your healthy choices that wisdom blessed you with words of wisdom in this life," concluded the words from within.

"Come, ye blessed daughter of life, into the house of love. Your children of light are gathered in the nations prepared."

"Thank you for your guidance and teachings of truth," replied the happy daughter. "Now, a loving strength is over me and a desire to shine abides within. How can I share what has happened?" questioned the joyful daughter.

Let your light shine and be at peace. Creation is everywhere and with all people. Kept your life simple, sharing when harmony can bless, and your word memory can teach.

This is the season of celebration that has been here all along. You have just entered it. Welcome home, sweet one. Celebrate love, life, and light and rest in peace!

AFTERTHOUGHT

Now we have reached eternity, perfection and oneness with our Creator. What does that mean? ET'Yeshua said, "I and my Father are one." The Father is in him as well as he is in the Father. ET'Yeshua had the understanding of all creation being carried down to him through the previous generations until his time. From the first man, Adam to him. Having mother and father present from the beginning of time. ET'Yeshua is a continuation of love, life, and light from the time of Adam as we are a continuation of Adam now!

In the beginning, our Creator created the heavens and the earth. This was completed all at one time. In one day. When Moses wrote this account he divided it up into days as he was instructed by the word of truth that dwelled within him. Time was needed by man to understand their choices and consequences. However, today, because of memory we have been given Aleph-Tav to understand our Creator's love, life, and light.

So one day is all we need to understand. If everything was created in one day, present time, then we need to look at one day as our Creator is one.

The sun rises from the east in the morning and a day begins. Everything in heaven and earth are present and abiding and moving in their domain. The birds fly, nest and mate, the beast roam, eat and protect, the fish swim, swarm and play, man works, loves and has family—all things doing what our Creator created them to do. When the sun goes down we retire and rest. This daily resting is your time in loves presence. Today this rest time is enjoyed every day throughout a person's life once you are one with our Creator. So a special day is not required. Reaching oneness with our Creator is a process of removing the layers of lies, traditions and lifestyles that negate oneness. This oneness is our vocabulary and needs cleaning. Bless the heavens and the earth as this is our Creator's signature or seal.

One day is like a thousand years—that can only be understood if one sees the first day of creation as all days. If not living in the first day, present time, of creation then man sees in his days through his dimmed light and speaks from that darkness of lies, traditions and religion. This is how we get biblical history—man writing from his perceptions.

This child of light wrote the same way until the layers of untruth were replaced with truth. Today is seen as the first day and everything in it is perfect, complete and oneness with our Creator. Powerful generations of darkness were lifted off memory to see clearly now, from our Creator's viewpoint.

As Paul wrote in his day, "For now we see in a mirror, dimly or darkly, but then face to face. Now I know in part, but then I shall know as I also have been known." And now love, life, and light remain—these three. But the greatest of these is light.

Moses wrote from his perception of division and his darkness within, dividing the days of creation into seven.

This book, *Celebration of Truth with the Letters of Light*, is written to remove the division of life so that oneness and perfection can be seen by any who chooses our Creator.

Please forgive me my brothers and sisters, family and friends for any words written that showed division in my previous writings.

We are one, perfect and complete with our Creator, and truth loves all of us and shines perfection on all. May we all see!

"And you shall know the truth, and the truth shall set you free" (John 8:32, pg. **1033).**

The first day and what was created in it seals love, life, and light! This seal stands forever.

Remember each day is the first day of creation, present time. Be in our Creator's presence so that you enjoy the breath of life, experience health and see eternity as you are one.

The memory door is closed to division. Rest in peace.

Our Creator does not change!

Our Creator has no name! Love is ALL and ALL

Our Creator has no religion!

Our Creator has immutable laws imbedded in all things created!

Choice leads to freedom or imprisonment consequences.

When completely one with creation and our Creator, no writings or books are necessary.

A Faithful Treasure

It is as old as Adam and Eve, the thing of which I speak.

When they were cast our of the garden,
this was our Creator's way to keep them meek.

Mother nature gives birth to all, from A to Z.

Those that wish to be nearer to our Creator, do this and feel free.

Most would say prayer, and few travel to the peak,

For the thing that I speak, strengthens the character that is weak.

Peace in the world, sound in the mind,

Cured in the mortal body, and blessed with eternal time.

Yes, acute seeing, sound reasoning, quick

hearing, and immediate doing.

The soul is singing, rejoicing and everlasting,

For the hidden "word of wisdom" is FASTING.

About the Author

The author is noted for her ability to change when greater truth is seen showing that she is not bound by people or their perception of her. She is continually moving in the direction of love, life and light as her memory is perfected in truth.

Health is of most importance to her as with health to body and mind, comes positive consequences and greater ability to play a competitive high level game of tennis at her age of seventy-one. Her thoughts radiate love, life and light in abundance.

To all that read this book she sends you courage and strength to change what you can and be at peace with the cycles that are already in place, knowing that this too, can change in time. Once more truth is understood by the reader the greater freedom of choice becomes a blessing. Let your light shine!